Portrait of
NORTHUMBERLAND

NANCY RIDLEY

ILLUSTRATED
AND WITH MAP

ROBERT HALE · LONDON

First edition July 1965
Reprinted October 1965
Reprinted January 1966
Second edition October 1968
Reprinted March 1969
Third edition July 1970

Robert Hale & Company
63 Old Brompton Road
London, S.W.7

ISBN 0 7091 1719 1

PRINTED IN GREAT BRITAIN
BY LOWE AND BRYDONE (PRINTERS) LTD., LONDON

Dedicated to the memory of my parents
Robert and *Ann Ridley*

CONTENTS

ILLUSTRATIONS

ACKNOWLEDGEMENTS

The photographs reproduced in this book were supplied by the following: Mr. Frank H. Meads, no. 1; Mr. J. Allan Cash, 2; the late Mr. W. F. T. Pinkney, 3, 4, 10, 11, 12, 14, 15, 16, 17, 18, 19, 20, 21 and 23; Mr. J. E. Hedley, 5; The Mustograph Society, 6; Mr. H. O. Thompson, 8; the late Mr. T. Russell Goddard, 9; Mr. G. Douglas Bolton, 13 and 22; and Mr. D. H. A. Sleightholme, 24 and 25.

AUTHOR'S NOTE

This book is not in any sense a comprehensive history of Northumberland, nor is it a guide book.

It is an attempt to express in words the great love which I have for my county, its scenery, its history and its people.

I should like to convey my most grateful thanks to the many people who have given me help and information, and who have encouraged me in my efforts to write this story of a county, which is in character neither England nor Scotland, but is its own incomparable self—Northumberland.

Nancy Ridley

FOREWORD

This book is a happy combination of historical fact and legend. Each will have its own peculiar fascination for the reader and each has its own value.

The facts will stimulate some to further research and fresh interpretations of the bringing of Christianity to the North; of the Roman Occupation; of the Danish Invasions, and of the long Middle Ages so rich in feudal, military and ecclesiastical history, as also of contemporary times.

The legends, which contain much valuable history as well as romance and poetry, are a part of the lore of our county. Many have survived for centuries, sometimes changing a little in the telling. Each generation adds a few new legends, just as each makes new history, and we are fortunate that Miss Ridley has combined both for us in this new volume at a time when increased leisure and ease of transport are bringing new visitors to the romantic Northumbrian countryside and to our historic places.

Northumberland

July 1964
Alnwick Castle
Northumberland

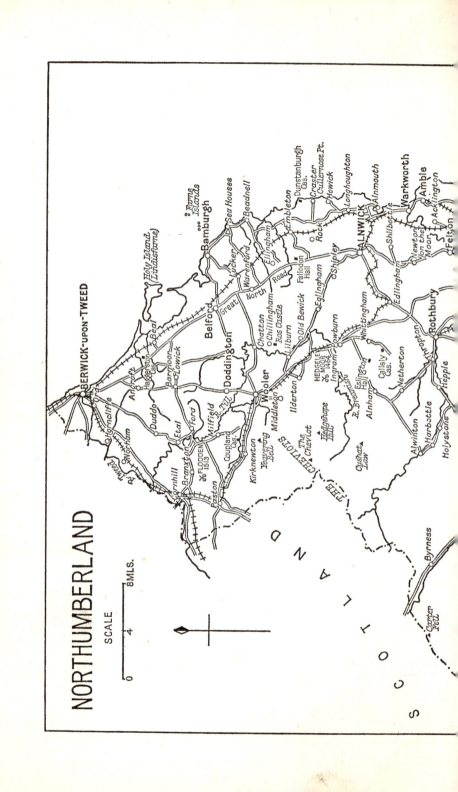

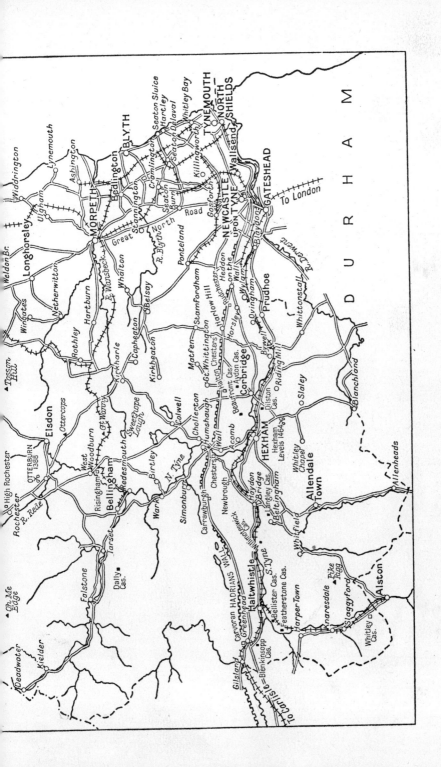

INTRODUCTION

Northumberland, the most northerly county in England, and the fifth largest in size, is one of the least known of all the English counties. It is a county which travellers from the south pass through on their way to Scotland, either by way of the Great North Road or by train from King's Cross. Under the erroneous impression that Northumberland is one vast coalfield, these travellers, by passing through the county, miss some of the most glorious and varied scenery in the British Isles. A coalfield there certainly is, and, in the past, the mines have produced some millions of tons of coal which have contributed to the prosperity not only of Northumberland but of the whole country.

Unlike other counties which have vast mineral wealth, the industrial area of Northumberland is concentrated into one part, the south-east corner. Stretching from the little port of Amble, twenty-five miles north of the mouth of the Tyne, to a short distance west of the city of Newcastle, the Northumberland coalfield is contained within a triangle. This area includes the thickly populated district, famous the world over as Tyneside. Here on the north bank of the river are the great shipyards where ships as famous as the old *Mauretania* and *King George V* were built. In spite of the depression in the shipping industry, the yards of Tyneside are busy today.

The Tyne still maintains its reputation as the greatest ship repairing river in the world. Gone are the days of the great slump, when grass grew in the yards, and tons of shipping were laid up in the river. Although many of the mines are becoming redundant, work is being found for the majority of men who have been "laid idle" to use a Northumbrian expression, and plans are on foot to attract new industries to the area, where already "new" towns are being built within the industrial triangle. Nine-tenths of the population of Northumberland live in this south-east corner, while the rest of the county is one of the most sparsely populated areas in England.

Triangular in shape, Northumberland is bounded on the north by the River Tweed and Berwickshire, on the west by the Cheviot Hills and Cumberland, on the south by the Tyne and the county of Durham, and on the east by the North Sea. Covering an area of 2,016 square miles, of which only about one tenth is coalfield, the county is mainly agricultural. With a coast line stretching from north of Berwick upon Tweed to the mouth of the Tyne, forty miles of which has been designated as scenery of outstanding natural beauty, Northumberland also has a National Park, its boundaries marked by stones, emblazoned with the picture of a curlew.

With an area of 575 square miles, the National Park also includes the great Border Forest, which has transformed the scenery in this part of the county. From the Cheviot Hills southwards to the Roman Wall stretches this park, the purpose of which is to preserve the exceptional beauty of this unspoilt country, and not as some people imagine, to allow visitors to do as they please within its boundaries.

Northumberland is rich in scenic beauty; the hill country of the Cheviots, where Cheviot itself rises to a height of 2,676 feet, is the watershed of the many fast-flowing rivers which run their courses from the hills, through well-wooded valleys on their way to the sea. All Northumberland's many rivers but one, the South Tyne, have their source within the county. Most famous of the fishing rivers is the Coquet, which enters the sea at Warkworth. The only river which is industrialized is the Tyne, and then only for the last few miles of its long journey from the Border to Tynemouth.

Uplands and lowlands, rich river valleys, a coastline with miles of sandy beaches, and vast acres of moorland, such as the wild country known as the Ottercops, make this county one of infinite variety; where the scenery is always changing, and where from the many vantage points of the hills and crags are panoramic views which extend towards the Pennine Range and the Scottish Hills.

Once the city and county of Newcastle is left behind, there is no industry of any appreciable size to mar the beauty of this most unspoilt of English counties. Northumberland's towns are market towns, the capitals of their river valleys and the centres of prosperous farming areas. Alnwick, Hexham, Rothbury, Wooler, Bellingham and Halt-whistle all have populations of under 12,000. At Alnwick and Berwick trading estates are being developed principally for agricultural machinery.

Alnwick, the ducal and county town situated thirty miles north of Newcastle on the Great North Road, is not only of historic interest, as the home of the Dukes of Northumberland, but is an ideal centre for exploring this very lovely part of the county. Alnwick has excellent hotels, is less than ten miles from the coast, and the fishing tackle made by the firm of Hardy is exported to many parts of the world. There is also an old established brewery.

The last town in Northumberland on the Great North Road is Berwick upon Tweed. Berwick also largely depends upon farming for its prosperity. Here on the great arable farms of Tweedside is grown some of the barley which is sold to the Scottish distillers. The name of Berwick is inseparable from that of salmon; on the lower reaches of the river the salmon are netted, while further up are the fabulously expensive private stretches of water which command such high rents.

Every Northumbrian country town has a live-stock mart for the sale not only of home bred but also Irish cattle, of which between 70,000 and 80,000 are brought over each year to be fattened on the rich grazing land of which there are 483,000 acres.

The other market town of importance on the Great North Road, and only fifteen miles north of Newcastle, is Morpeth. More urbanized than Alnwick and with several new housing estates Morpeth is a borough, an excellent shopping centre, and its charm has in no way been spoilt by its close proximity to the coalfield. In the thirty-one miles between Morpeth and Wooler there are no towns at all on the road which leaves A.1 just north of Morpeth and crosses the Border at Coldstream.

This road runs through some of the most dramatic scenery; over moors ablaze with gorse, as at Longhorsley, and over the wild uplands, before dropping down into the Vale of Whittingham at Bridge of Aln, and eventually to Wooler. Wooler is the gateway to some of the grandest of the Cheviot Hill country.

Like Alnwick, Wooler has some good hotels, but it is as well for those who are visiting the county for the first time to realize that there are long distances between Northumberland's hotels. On the New-castle–Jedburgh Road (known in the county as The New Line to distinguish it from the old road which went by Cambo to Otterburn) there is a distance of twenty miles between the Highlander Inn near Belsay and the Percy Arms at Otterburn!

Pleasant little Otterburn, thirty-two miles north-west of New-castle, has a woollen mill which is world famous. At this family-owned mill are manufactured the tweeds and woollens which have made the trade mark "Otterburn" the standard of the highest quality.

North of Otterburn, the road to the Carter Bar is joined by the Roman Dere Street, which enters Northumberland from the south on the Durham Border. This road causes a great deal of confusion, as the Northumbrians insist that it is Watling Street. Even the maps are not consistent, some referring to it as Dere Street, others as Watling Street; the writer, being Northumbrian, has decided to refer to it as Watling Street throughout.

To reach the town of Hexham in Tynedale, the traveller from Otter-burn can go by way of Watling Street to the Five Lane Ends, near Chollerton. Whether reached by way of Chollerton, or the more direct road from Newcastle, from which it is twenty miles distant, Hexham is worth the journey. It is famous for its ancient abbey, its race meetings, and, as in the case of all Northumbrian towns, it is the centre of a thriving farming area. Hexham is also one of the best centres for visiting the Roman Wall country. With good hotel accommodation, pleasantly laid out parks, and within easy reach of unspoilt scenery. Hexham is very popular with visitors. The

Visitors' Book at the abbey contains names from many parts of the world.

Although the supermarkets have made their appearance, many of the shops have been in the hands of the same families for generations.

Not far from Hexham at Warden is the only paper mill in the county, and at Frankham are quarries, owned by Mr. W. A. Benson, two of the few marks of industry in South Tynedale.

Some sixteen miles west of Hexham in South Tynedale in the little town of Haltwhistle is a thriving paint manufacturing firm, with the appropriate name of Hadrian Paints. Haltwhistle has suffered more from unemployment than the other towns of the county. At one time the people relied for employment on the two collieries, which are now worked out. Quarries near to and in some cases on, the Roman Wall, are sources of employment today, together with a firm known as "Kilfrost".

Bellingham, in North Tynedale, specializes in lamb sales, and in this valley whinstone is quarried for road-making.

Last, but by no means least of the Northumbrian towns is Rothbury, the capital of Coquetdale. Thirty miles from Newcastle, the road to this pleasant town, which lies under the shadow of the Simonside Range of hills, leaves the Wooler Road at "The Anglers Arms" at Weldon Bridge. For the visitor the chief attraction of Rothbury is the grounds of Lord Armstrong's home, Cragside. These grounds are open to the public from Easter to September, and are famous for the display of rhododendrons, the rock gardens and artificial lakes.

These prosperous little towns have their cottage hospitals, local newspapers, flourishing Rotary and Young Farmers Clubs and many other organizations which help to make them self-supporting communities. Many people are employed in the sale and maintenance of agricultural machinery and in all the towns are corn and seed merchants.

The Women's Institutes in Northumberland number more than 170. Some of the more remote W.I.s, as they are called, meet according to the light of the moon, though the movement also appeals to the more urbanized areas of the new estates. For those who prefer the sea, the coast has much to offer. There are miles of golden sands, sailing at Beadnell, wild fowling on Fenham Flats, bird watching on the Farnes, golf at Alnmouth which has two courses, and ideal places for family holidays. Bamburgh, with its mighty castle; Seahouses, with its harbour, where trips to the Farne Islands can be made in fishing cobles; Dunstanburgh, Embleton and Warkworth—all have their own charm. There are several golf courses, and for those who care for them numerous caravan sites.

But above all Northumberland is a farming county. Since the raiding days ended, and peace came to this county, which in the old days was a buffer state between two countries, farming has been, and is the principal industry. Times have changed since the days when Northumberland was described as "a waste", with no mention in Domesday Book, though some writers insist that the omission is because the Northumbrians were never subdued! The county has one of the greatest populations of sheep in the country; approximately one and a half million, largely the indigenous Cheviots and Blackfaces, graze on Northumberland's uplands.

Cattle too are an important part of Northumbrian farming. It has never been a great milk producing county; it is in the fattening of his cattle that the Northumbrian farmer excels. Pedigree cattle are also bred with great success and the bulls exported to many parts of the world. The Aberdeen-Angus herd of Viscount Allendale at Bywell on the River Tyne, and the celebrated Friesian herd, the "Hunday" strain of Messrs. Moffitt at nearby Peepy Farm, are two of the most famous in the country. Northumberland also possesses a herd of wild white cattle at Chillingham.

It is interesting to record that when the Royal Agricultural Society of England held their show at Newcastle on the wide expanse of the Town Moor, there was always a record "gate". The County Show at Alnwick, the Tyneside at Corbridge, the North Tyne at Bellingham, and the Shepherds' Show at Alwinton in Coquetdale are only a few of the many held in Northumberland.

Eleven packs of foxhounds hunt the county, some of which hold a point-to-point meeting annually. The Newcastle and District Beagles are a well patronized pack for those who like running across country, and although association football has a strong hold in the industrial area, rugby is also well supported.

The history of Northumberland as befits a Border County is a wild one. At times the county has been described as a battlefield, and certainly two most famous and bloody battles were fought on Northumbrian soil, Flodden, in the north of the county, and Otterburn in Ridsdale, where the county's hero, Harry Hotspur, fought.

With more castles than any other county in the British Isles, Northumberland is a historian's paradise. Alnwick, Bamburgh, Ford, Haughton, Chipchase, Dunstanburgh, Warkworth, Langley, Bellister, Thirlwall, Norham, Featherstone, are some of the strongholds which have contributed to the history of the county.

Scattered over wide areas of Northumberland are the Pele towers; some are now in ruins, others have been incorporated into dwelling houses, as in the former vicarage at Elsdon. These Pele towers were fortified dwellings, where the cattle could be driven into the ground floor rooms, to protect them from the Reivers and Moss Troopers, who from October until the spring "Rode the Foray". This rough way of life appears to have appealed to the Border men, both Northumbrians and Scots, as they were "lifting" (stealing) sheep and cattle long after the Union of the Crowns.

The greatest historical monument in Northumberland which attracts visitors from all over the world is the Roman Wall. Built by the Emperor Hadrian it was until recently accepted by the most eminent historians as being a line of defence. Now there has arisen a school of thought which has decided that the wall was built as a garrison, but the writer has no intention of becoming involved in the controversy. From Wallsend on the Tyne, runs the great line of the Wall, mile-castles, forts and camps, to Burgh by Sands on the Solway. The road, known as The Military, follows the Wall in its course through Northumberland.

To appreciate the Wall, the visitor must walk. Hexham on the Tyne and the George Hotel on the North Tyne at Chollerford are both excellent centres, and armed with Dr. Collingwood Bruce's *Handbook to The Roman Wall* (revised edition), warm clothing and strong shoes, many happy hours can be spent studying "the glory that was Rome". There is a plan on foot to restore part of the Wall as it was when Hadrian built it.

Long after the Roman legions left, Northumbria became the Cradle of Christianity. To a little island off the Northumberland coast, now called Lindisfarne, or Holy Island, came St. Aidan from Iona, who preached the Gospel to the heathens of Northumbria. He was succeeded by Northumberland's own saint, Cuthbert, who carried on the teachings of St. Aidan. Many Northumbrians were converted. Paulinus also carried on the good work, though it is doubtful if so many Northumbrians were baptized by Paulinus as is claimed. In those far off days, with such a small population, the numbers appear to have been exaggerated with the course of time.

Contrary to the popular belief that Northumberland's villages are grim and grey, the county can boast of so many lovely spots that it is hard to decide which are the most attractive, but any visitor coming to Northumberland for the first time must in the course of his wanderings visit Blanchland in the extreme south of the county. Here is one of the oldest and most attractive inns "The Lord Crewe Arms". This village was chosen by *Town and Country Planning* as one of the perfect villages of England.

In the south-west, capital of the district which bears its name, is Allendale, which always describes itself as a town, but takes first prize for the best kept village! Now a land of hill farming, Allendale was once the great lead-mining area of the county. The lead industry was started by the Beaumont family, of which the present head is Viscount

Allendale. The tall chimneys are still to be seen, as are the paths by which the ponies brought the lead to be transported.

This is one of the most popular holiday districts of Northumberland, where the same people go year after year. There are many good boarding houses in Allendale town, and the river and hill scenery are enchanting, especially at Staward, which is a deep gorge through which the river Allen flows on its way to join the South Tyne.

Of the fishing villages Craster is one of the pleasantest. Craster Tower, where the ancient Craster family has lived since 1290, is soon to change hands; but there will still be Crasters at Craster Tower because the present owner, Sir John, the well-known naturalist, is selling it to two of his cousins.

In its long history, there have been many famous Northumbrians, as different in character and in their manner of achieving immortality as the varied scenery of their county.

Saints and Border raiders have their names woven in the tapestry of Northumbrian history. Politicians and sailors, martyrs and heroines, and the great pioneers of industry who made Tyneside famous.

Northumberland has produced one prime minister, Grey of the Reform Bill, and another member of this well-known family was foreign secretary when the 1914–18 war broke out. Nicholas Ridley, the Marian Martyr, was born in the South Tyne valley; Collingwood of Trafalgar fame was born where a block of offices in Newcastle stands today, Milburn House on The Side; and Josephine Butler, the reformer, is buried in the little churchyard of Kirknewton under the shadow of the Cheviot Hills.

The Armstrongs of Cragside and Bamburgh were the founders of what is now the Vickers Armstrong Group, and the Joicey family of Etal were some of the largest colliery owners until nationalization took over the mines. Bewick, the engraver, and Stephenson the inventor of the locomotive were Tynesiders.

Northumbrian families have deep roots; to read the list of the sheriffs of the county since it was first compiled in 1154 is a reminder of how strong are these roots. Many of the families who held high positions in the county so long ago have descendants who are carrying on their responsibilities today. Percy and Fenwick, Grey and Widdrington, Charlton and Ridley are still familiar names in the present-day life of Northumberland.

Proud though Northumbrians are of their past, they live very much in the present. Independent, outspoken, sometimes to the embarrassment of the southerner, with a strong sense of family pride, the Northumbrian is the product of his past, when his county was fought over by the English and Scots kings, and his land laid waste. Life in Northumberland has been a struggle which has made its contribution in forming the Northumbrian character.

Not long ago the writer was told a perfectly true story of a farmer from one of the river valleys who went to London; when the time came to declare his nationality in the hotel register, he simply wrote "Northumbrian". Such is the pride the Northumbrian has in his county.

I

ROMAN WALL COUNTRY

For Hadrian's pride shall open lie
To bittern's boom and curlew's call;
From Solway sands to mouth of Tyne
Vale is whispered on the Wall.
                    Howard Pease, THE LAMENT OF COMES BRITANNIAE

Straight across the county it runs, from east to west, the Great Wall of
Hadrian, from Wallsend on the Tyne, the Sedgedunum of the Romans,
crossing the border into Cumberland at Gilsland, to end its journey on
the shores of the Solway Firth. The first wall built by the Romans, the
vallum, which runs south of the stone Wall, built as it was of earth,
had failed in its purpose to keep out the Picts and Scots who attacked it
from the north, and the Northumbrians from the south! The fosse or
ditch on the north side was an additional protection. There are seventy-
three miles of fortifications, camps and milecastles, in its course, set
in some of the wildest scenery in the country.

For three centuries the Romans occupied the line of Hadrian's Wall,
which is simply known in Northumberland as "The Wall". When the
mighty Roman Empire fell, and the conquerors departed, they left
behind them in Northumberland the finest Roman remains in the
British Isles.

In the centuries after the Romans left, when the Wall fell into decay,
incongruous uses were made of the stone the Romans had quarried to
build their mighty Wall, which in its glory was second only to the
Great Wall of China.

In many places the Wall and milecastles were torn down, and the
stones used to build houses, and even some churches in the Roman
Wall country were partly built with the stone the Romans had so
laboriously quarried! Most incongruous of all, the crypt the Saxons
built beneath the great Christian Abbey of St. Andrew at Hexham, is
of stone from the Roman town of Corstopitum at Corbridge.

The Military Road, which runs from Heddon on the Wall to Green-
head—the road associated with General Wade—is in many parts of its
course actually on the Wall. It was after the Jacobite Rebellion of 1745
when owing to the state of the roads between Newcastle and Carlisle
troop movements were impossible, that the road was made; this road

that goes up and down like a switchback. Even when the Wall begins to climb the heights of the Great Whin-Sill, the road is always within sight. There is a local legend that Wade sheltered under a tree near Walwick.

Between Wallsend and the city boundary of Newcastle at Denton Burn, little is left of the great military line of the Wall; in the name of progress it has disappeared, and it is due to the historians of the past that it is possible to get a picture of it before the vandalism began. Camden in 1587 included a description of the Wall in his *Britannia*, and Horsley's *Britannia Romana*, published in 1732, contains much valuable information. Dr. Collingwood Bruce's *Handbook to the Roman Wall*, revised edition, should be read by all those who wish to make a scholarly study of Hadrian's Wall.

It is largely due to archaeologists such as Algernon, fourth Duke of Northumberland, and John Clayton of Chesters, near Chollerford, that so much has been preserved, so much excavation done and so many treasures discovered. At Alnwick Castle is the famous Corbridge Lanx; a silver sacrificial dish, which was discovered near Corbridge Bridge in 1735. The Lanx is one of the most valuable Roman relics in existence and is sometimes on loan to the British Museum.

Now the Wall is safe, an ancient monument cared for by the Ministry of Works, for much of its length within the National Park of Northumberland. The twentieth century unfortunately is all too obvious west of the Limestone Bank a few miles beyond Chollerford where the huge pylons of the Electricity Board detract from the otherwise unspoilt beauty of the scenery.

Where the county sign of Northumberland appears, the city is left behind and the road goes on to the appropriately named Heddon on the Wall, where a large part of the Wall has been preserved. Heddon, once a quiet little village, is growing rapidly as a result of housing estates and has lost its village character, but the church perched on the hill is delightful, looking down as it does on the War Memorial Cross, which in spring and summer is surrounded by flowers.

At Heddon, "The Military", as it is always known in Northumberland, starts its long straight journey to the west; straight as an arrow it goes, past the Roman Vindobala, the modern Rudchester, one of the many chesters on the line of the Wall—Whitchester, Halton Chesters or Hunnum—until it reaches the most famous of them all, the Chesters of John Clayton.

Treeless though the country is, it has a fascination of its own; the little village of Harlow Hill looks down on the reservoirs of Whittle Dene which bring water from the Border to the thickly populated districts of Tyneside; industrial Tyneside which seems so far away from this road of the Romans.

The fosse appears in places and the earthen work of the vallum can be traced; at Wallhouses, a farm built of Roman stones, there are trees and flowering shrubs growing in the fosse. A little way beyond Wallhouses, where the road to Matfen goes north, are two stone pillars, known as Matfen Piers. A short way along this road is the picturesque village of Matfen, where a stream runs through the middle of the village, and Matfen Hall, a little to the south, looks over its parklands, watered by the River Pont.

Matfen Hall is the property of the Blackett family, a family prominent in the county for generations, and whose baronetcy dates from 1673. The Hall has recently become a "Cheshire" home, and was let to the association by Sir Douglas Blackett at a peppercorn rental of 10s. a year.

South-west of Matfen is the little hamlet of Great Whittington, where in the village inn are murals of Dick Whittington and his cat. Surely Whittington never came so far from London to turn again! Tradition has it that Queen Margaret on her way to fight the Battle of Hexham, crossed The Military Road near Great Whittington. From Matfen Piers the road runs by Down Hills to Stagshaw Bank, where the Roman Dere Street (much to everyone's confusion also called Watling Street), crosses "The Military" on its way to Scotland. At Stagshaw Bank is the "Errington Arms", the only public house in the county to commemorate (by its name) this family once famous in the county, whose name may have originated from the little Erring Burn not far away.

Long ago a fair was held at Stagshaw Bank, and even today when the house or farmyard is untidy, the true Northumbrian will say it is like Stagshaw Bank Fair. Like many old customs and traditions the fair is no more, but the memory lives on.

Beyond Stagshaw Bank, Northumberland rolls out like a map, high above sea level. The views are magnificent. South-westwards, beyond the valley of the South Tyne, the Pennines can be seen; Cross Fell near the South Tyne's source, and in the foreground Tynedale Fell beyond Haltwhistle. Due south the land is climbing towards the Durham Border, and in the north-west North Tynedale dominates the scene, while northwards, like a great bastion, the Muckle Cheviot divides England from Scotland. East and south of this the unmistakable ridge of the Simonside Hills near Rothbury make their contribution to this glorious vista of Northumberland. Here on the roof of the county, before the steep descent to the North Tyne, at the top of Brunton Bank, stands a wooden cross commemorating the site of the Battle of Heavenfield, where in the year 635 a Christian king of Northumbria, afterwards canonized as St. Oswald, defeated the heathen forces of Cadwalla. The cross is said to mark the place where Oswald prayed before the battle. It would be interesting to know who places a wreath of Flanders poppies at the foot of the cross every November. Our first historian, the Venerable Bede, gives a graphic description of the battle which, he says, raged as far afield as Hallington. (Bede can be claimed as a Northumbrian as when he lived the county was a kingdom which stretched from the Humber to the Forth, and it was Edwin, King of Northumbria who gave his name to Edinburgh.)

The defeated Cadwalla fled from the field of battle, and was later captured and killed near the lovely Rowley Burn in Hexhamshire. In the field north of the cross stands the little church dedicated to St. Oswald. South of the Roman road rises Fallowfield Fell, which is a mass of gold when the gorse is in bloom, and, according to the old rhyme, that should be always as

> When gorse is out of bloom,
> Kissing's out of tune!

At the foot of Brunton Bank is Chollerford. The river here is wide, flowing under the arches of the modern bridge—modern by Northumbrian standards anyway; the old bridge was washed away in the great floods of 1771, when the only bridge to remain standing over the Tyne was at Corbridge. It was here that in the sixteenth century the notorious Mosstrooper, Jock o' the Side, an Armstrong from Liddesdale, having escaped from gaol in Newcastle, swam the North Tyne when it was in spate and reached the sanctuary of his own country. According to the old ballad:

> But when they came to Chollerford,
> There they met with an auld man.
> Say, honest man, will the water ride?
> Tell us in haste, if that you can—
>
> I wat weel no, quo' the guid auld man,
> I hae lived here thretty years and three,
> And I ne'er yet saw the Tyne sae big,
> Nor running anes sae like the sea.

A little way down stream, close to where Jock o' the Side swam the river, can be seen the foundations of the Roman bridge. Beside this most beautiful stretch of the North Tyne the Romans built their important station of Cilurnum.

> O proud Cilurnum, city of the past!
> Where are thy legions in their fierce array?
> No more, no more the martial trumpet blast
> May summon thy plumed cohorts to the fray.

So wrote a Northumbrian poet, and even for those who have no interest in history, Roman or otherwise, the setting of Cilurnum is so beautiful that even the most prosaic must be stirred.

Here on the tree-lined banks of the North Tyne, where in the background stands the mansion house of Chesters, once the home of John Clayton, the archaeologist and antiquary, whose memorial is Cilurnum. This is an archaeologist's paradise, where practically the whole plan of the camp can be traced. Marks made by the chariot wheels are still discernible; chariots which would drive out to visit other stations on the Wall; to Corstopitum at Corbridge, which was more of a town than a garrison; to Watling Street and The Maiden Way, and along the Stanegate which runs from Corbridge, through Newbrough to Vindolanda at Chesterholm and ends at Carlisle. How civilized the Romans were in comparison with the Northumbrians who appear to have taken little advantage, if any, from the culture of their conquerors. Here are the bathrooms, used nearly two thousands years ago. Hundreds of years would pass before there would be bathrooms, even in the great houses of Northumberland. There is evidence of a central heating system, store houses for the grain and the inevitable temples for the worship of their heathen gods.

The museum at the entrance to the camp is a treasure house; jewellery which has been recovered from the well dedicated to the goddesses; coins whose dates corroborate the period of the occupation; mill stones, and above all the altars to the gods. Altars to the river-gods whom, no doubt, the Romans wished to propitiate more than any other, as the North Tyne rises rapidly and could have flooded the foundations of the camp.

It is all so peaceful now, but long ago when the legionaries in their hundreds were stationed there all would be bustle and activity; they would be constantly on the watch for enemies, especially here where the valley is so wide. Many a young centurion must have felt homesick for his native land, and there would be no friendly inn as "The George" is today, where he could fraternize with the local people. But soldiers are the same in every age, and perhaps when a posting came to return to their sunny homeland, some may have been sorry to say farewell to the North Tyne girls.

Not far from Cilurnum, at the village of Chollerton, north of the bridge and on the east bank of the river, the war memorial bears an inscription, so pathetic and appropriate:

> Ye that live on in English pastures green,
> Remember us and think what might have been.

A fitting farewell to Cilurnum and the men who long ago lived and died for the "grandeur that was Rome".

The tree-lined banks of the North Tyne are left behind, and the steep climb begins, up Walwick Bank to the Tower Tye, a house built of stones from the Wall. At Tower Tye a road goes north to Simonburn past a farm with the curious name of Cockplay—a main may have been held here in the days when cockfighting was a popular pastime (surely it couldn't be called sport).

Southwards the road runs down to the valley of the South Tyne, passing the farm of Parkshields. It was on a site west of this farm that the first Boy Scout camp in England was held in 1908. A cairn has been erected on the top of a hill, a hill from where one can see for miles up the fertile valley of South Tynedale. The cairn bears the inscription:

> This cairn marks the site of the first Boy Scout Camp,
> held in 1908 by B.P. later Lord Baden Powell.
> The Chief Scout Lord Rowallan relit the camp fire,
> 9th June, 1957.

Every inch of this part of Northumberland is history; south of Parkshields on the top of Warden Hill are the extensive remains of an early British encampment. Long before the Romans came, prehistoric man would look down from his strategic position, on to the country that is now known as Tynedale. Where the two Tynes meet at Warden Rocks would be scrub and forest land; centuries would pass before cattle would graze in the rich pastures, or a church such as St. Michael's at Warden be built—part of it with Roman stones.

The road from Warden church to Walwick Grange, the peaceful little Homer's Lane, was in 1826 the scene of a particularly brutal murder. The cottage where the victim, Joseph Hedley, lived has now disappeared, as did the murderer long ago, as the crime was never solved. As the old man was receiving Parish Relief, the murder could not have been committed for gain. Joseph Hedley was an expert in the craft of quilting; he was always known as Joe the Quilter, and although it is more than a hundred years since Joseph Hedley was killed in his humble little home by the banks of the North Tyne, some of his exquisite work is still in use. A quilt believed to be Joe's handiwork has been on exhibition at the Bowes Museum, near Barnard Castle, and more recently at Eslington Park, the home of Lord Ravensworth, and the pear tree which Joe may have planted still flourishes. In 1831 a book was published; on the outer cover appeared the following inscription:

The Hermit
of
Warden
or
The Tragedy of Holmer's Lane
(Holmer's Lonnin)

Containing
Some Anecdotes of the Life and Character
of
Joseph Hedley
Commonly Called
Joe the Quilter
and a particular account of his
Most Horrible Murder
Committed Tuesday January 3rd 1826

New Edition, with additions
Hexham
Printed and sold by M. Armstrong
1831.

Joe's skill inspired a local poet to write the following verses:

> His cot secure, his garden neat,
> He loved the lone and still retreat
> Glad were his neighbours all to meet
> With honest Joe the Quilter.
>
> Of each he had some good to say
> Some friendly token to display,
> And few could cheer the winter's day
> Like canny Joe the Quilter.
>
> By efforts of superior skill
> He paid these tokens of goodwill
> Humble but independent still
> Was grateful Joe the Quilter.
>
> His quilts with country fame were crowned
> So neatly stitched and all the ground
> Adorn'd with flowers or figured round
> Oh! Clever Joe the Quilter.

West of Blackcarts Farm and north of The Military, there are the remains of a milecastle. These quarters for the garrison were built at regular intervals of every Roman mile of seven furlongs. Rowan trees have their roots in the masonry, and sheep graze where once the sentries kept watch against the Picts and Scots.

The land is now rising steeply towards the summit of the Limestone Bank, and the Great Whin-Sill is appearing, the whin-sill to which the wall clings on its course through the most spectacular scenery of all, running like great waves towards its highest point on Winshields Crags. On the windswept heights of the Limestone Bank, where the ground drops steeply several hundred feet to the north, the Haydon Hunt until a few years ago held their point-to-point—weather permitting! The weather so rarely permitted, that the meeting there has been abandoned. Where long ago many a cold and miserable Roman soldier will have done his sentry duty, the spectators shivered in the biting wind that blows over Northumberland in March. To endure, much less enjoy the Haydon, the spectators and the riders had to be as sound in wind and limb as the horses! A Northumberland point-to-point, whether it be on the Limestone Bank or any other part of the county is no place for those who are used to the glamorous and fashionable meetings of the Shires and the South Country. On the Roman Wall "spectator" sports clothes were no protection against the biting wind. Surely the Romans were issued with protective clothing; laurel leaves and togas would be of very little use on the Limestone Bank. It was dangerous to attempt to find shelter by scrambling down the precipice—and precipice it is—to cower behind one of the dry stone walls of Northumberland, as, at any moment one might land in the slack below; slack—a word beloved by Northumbrians, and so much more expressive than hollow. When the last race, the "Farmers", was over, and advice and encouragement had been yelled and shouted in every possible Northumbrian accent, the silence returned to this wild and lonely stretch of Hadrian's Wall. Now only the ghosts are left, Roman ghosts, ghosts of the Border Raiders and perhaps ghosts of horses who ran in a long ago Haydon. Popalong, Knocknagreena and Yellow Peril may jump their last fence again.

From the nearby Fort of Procolitia, where units of Batavi Infantry were stationed in A.D. 122, ghosts may come to watch their old enemies, whom they may be forgiven for thinking haven't changed very much as far as endurance is concerned in nearly two thousand years!

Close to Procolitia, on Carrowburgh Farm, a temple dedicated to Mithras, god of the morning, was discovered as recently as 1950. Who knows what other treasures may still lie hidden in this wild and barren land with its indescribable fascination. The well of Coventina, from which so much of the jewellery now in Chesters Museum was found, is close to this beautiful and in some ways pathetic temple to Mithras.

The Wall is now at its most impressive as it climbs Sewingshields Crags, where to the north lies the little lake of Halley Pike. Sewingshields is the theme of countless legends connected with King Arthur and his knights. In an old book published in 1876, describing itself as *Historical notes on Haydon Bridge and District* there are detailed and rather

The Duke of Northumberland

verbose accounts of the many strange legends in which that most chivalrous of kings is the chief character. The author of this most entertaining book was a postman whose daily round was "out-bye", and now, nearly a hundred years after, the postmen who serve the Roman Wall country often have to abandon their modern form of transport and tramp the rounds as William Lee, the writer of *Haydon Bridge and District*, did long ago. According to William Lee there was in the last century an old shepherd living at Sewingshields, who spent a great deal of time, when he wasn't "seeing" the sheep, sitting on the crags enjoying his favourite pastime of knitting. One day when he was so employed, his ball of wool, or "clue" as he would call it, rolled away down the crags. The old man set off in pursuit and followed the trail until he came to the entrance to a cave, in which, true to tradition, an eerie light was glimmering. The old man followed the light until he came to a great hall where he was confronted with the astonishing sight of King Arthur, his queen, knights and a pack of hounds. It has never been explained how the old man recognized the illustrious gathering, or how he knew what to do when he saw a table, on which was a garter, a sword and a bugle; one can only assume that he had second sight! He drew the sword and cut the garter and then his intuition must have failed him as he forgot to blow the bugle. King Arthur himself, aroused from his long sleep, addressed the unexpected visitor in what appears to have been a well rehearsed verse:

O, Woe betide the evil day,
Upon the witless wight was born,
Who drew the sword, the garter cut,
But never blew the bugle horn.

Having delivered himself of this poetical effort, King Arthur, his queen, knights and hounds fell asleep again. The old shepherd ran as fast as he could into the house at Sewingshields to inform his family of the exalted neighbours he had discovered. In spite of much searching the cave was never found and there to this day sleep King Arthur and the Knights of the Round Table. Surely had there been a cave someone would have found it. Many a hunted fox has taken shelter in Sewingshields Crags, and King Arthur, had he been on the alert, could easily have mistaken the sound of a hunting horn for a bugle.

Another of the Arthurian legends connected with Sewingshields is very much out of character with one alleged to have been as chivalrous as he. Two rocks, each weighing about twenty tons are known as the King's and the Queen's. The King's rock bears markings which, the story says, were made by the queen's golden comb. The king and queen were arguing heatedly while she was combing her hair (no doubt

3

Whin-Sill and Roman Wall

golden, like the comb). Arthur, in a most unknightly manner threw his twenty-ton rock at his lady, which she warded off with her comb. What they were arguing about, or why they were at Sewingshields at all, we have never been told.

Whether the Sewingshields legends be true or not, the Wall goes on; from here to the Nine Nicks of Thirlwall, it is in a wonderful state of preservation. In parts it is six feet high and with some breaks where roads have cut through the gaps it is possible to walk on the Wall itself to the Cumberland Border. One of these gaps was appropriately named "Busy" Gap because of the raiding days when stolen cattle from both sides of the Border were driven through the gap in the Wall defences. On towards the large and wonderfully preserved camp of Borcovicium, or Housesteads, climbs the Wall. Built on the southern slopes of the Whin-Sill, and commanding glorious views of the South Tyne valley, Housesteads is one of the most frequently visited stations on the Wall— a long "step" from The Military Road—and there is now a special car park. Housesteads is dramatic, with its milecastle and museum and its strategic position on the heights.

Not far away on The Military Road is the quaintly named Twice Brewed Inn which succeeded a much older house of call, now East Twice Brewed Farm. This old inn was frequented by the carriers who travelled between Newcastle and Carlisle.

In this wild country, where the sheep greatly outnumber the human population, a Farmers' and Shepherds' Show is held annually. The Northumbrian shepherd is allowed by his master to keep so many sheep of his own and these are known as "pack lambs", some of which are exhibited at the Roman Wall Show. The shepherds either ride on horseback or travel the lonely hill country by Land-Rover to tend their flocks. A shepherd commands a high wage and, in lambing time, his hours of work are long and arduous. It is becoming increasingly difficult to attract young men to this exacting life, where the cottages are isolated and the children present a problem when they reach school age. Although, if their home is a certain distance from a school, free transport is provided by the Education Authorities, they often have to walk a considerable distance to the collecting point. The school for this part of the Wall country was at Grindon until its closure about six years ago. Today a shepherd is indistinguishable from any other countryman in his manner of dress but, not so long ago, every shepherd wore the distinctive black and white plaid of his county. The beautifully hand-dressed crooks and walking sticks with horn handles, often in the form of a blackfaced sheep's head, are on exhibition at the local shows. Television has brought the outside world to the isolated homes of the shepherds but life remains, fundamentally, what it has been for generations, a life devoted, whatever the elements, to the livestock in the shepherd's care in the windswept country where every gap on the line of the Wall and every crag has a name. Through the Busy Gap runs the Black Dyke of Northumberland (the earthen entrenchment whose purpose has never been discovered). The Dyke runs from the north of the county and forms a barrier between east and west, through the Muckle Moss to the South Tyne at Water House. Cuddy's Crag, the Northumbrian abbreviation of Cuthbert, and Rapishaw Gap near Hotbank Crags, are some of the appealing names so frequently heard in this district.

North of the Wall lie the little Northumbrian lakes: Broomlee, Greenlee and Crag. The latter, the most attractive of all, lies at the foot of the sheer basalt crags where a small plantation breaks the starkness of the scenery. Broomlee and Greenlee are spread out, but have their own peculiar attraction. In Broomlee there is not only buried treasure, but Sir Lancelot's sword Excalibur! To retrieve the treasure one must have the conventional outfit: white oxen, the seventh son to forge the chains, and all the usual paraphernalia of legend. In these days it would be extremely difficult to collect all the necessary equipment, so Broomlee must keep its treasure for all time. Beside Greenlee is a house with the delightful name of Bonnyrigg, once the property of the Blackett family, and now the headquarters of the West Northumberland Sailing Club, whose members sail their craft on the lough. Quiet and peaceful now, it was once the haunt of Border raiders. Near Bonnyrigg in the bad old days, a member of the South Tyne family of Ridley escaped from his pursuers and, in true dramatic fashion, fled from his native land playing the Northumbrian pipes!

In this wild land north of the Wall are farms with the most romantic names, "Hope Alone", "Saughey Rigg", "The Longsyke", and loveliest of all, "Farglow" on the Tipalt Burn. Cat Stairs, so well and truly named, and Steelrig Gap lead on to the summit of Winshields Crag 1,230 feet above sea level. On a clear day from the Winshields it is possible to see the Solway and away in Dumfriesshire the towering mass of Criffel, while looking south there is Barcombe Range overlooking the Roman road of Stanegate.

The Romans quarried stone from the heights of Barcombe to build the Wall, the Barcombe of the Long Stone, a landmark that stands out for miles; and when seen too clearly it is a sign of bad weather, say the country people. The stone itself has no connection with the Romans; it may have been part of an Early British circle. Down in the valley beside the chattering Chainley Burn is the camp of Vindolanda and the Roman milestone.

Wander as one will from the Wall, its fascination draws one back. The Wall that is nearing the end of its march through Northumberland. By Shield on the Wall and the Caw Gap, where the quarries are and the little Caw Burn that changes its name to that of Haltwhistle where it runs into the South Tyne.

On the slope south of the Wall is the farmhouse of "The Walltown", overlooking the Moss of the same name. Lonely and unpretentious, yet its name is engraved in history.

In 1555, Nicholas Ridley, who was to die a martyr's death at Oxford, wrote his last letter to his "Dear Cousin, John Ridley of The Walltown". It would be long after Nicholas Ridley died at the stake that the letter would reach his "Dear Cousin". The descendants of that John Ridley were still living at "The Walltown" until a few years ago.

Beyond "The Walltown" is Bloody Gap, another appropriate name for this lawless land. The last great station in Northumberland is at Great Chesters, the Roman Aesica; the Wall then traverses the serrated ridges of the Nine Nicks of Thirlwall, before it follows the Tipalt Burn to Thirlwall Castle, once a great stronghold, now in ruins, which looks as though at any moment it will fall into the burn below. The name Thirlwall is from the thirling or piercing of the Wall by the Scots; Thirlwall was built entirely of stones from the Wall.

The Wall goes on towards the Cumberland Border and leaves Northumberland behind. Roman Northumberland, Roman Wall Country, where men have fought and died, built their Pele towers, pillaged and raided their neighbours' lands, and where, near the Walltown, St. Paulinus baptized some of the heathen Northumbrians and it is hoped made them good Christians! A wild land and a lovely land, a land of black faced sheep and outliers, as the hardy cattle are called, which stay out all through the bitter northern winters; where the curlew's call is heard or the call of the wild geese. The legions have gone, the fighting is over, but the glory remains—not only the glory but little homely anecdotes which make one realize so vividly that the men who manned the Wall so long ago were flesh and blood, not just carvings on a stone. Near "The Walltown" chives grow in profusion, brought it is said by the Romans long ago.

Sir Walter Scott picked purple pansies on the Wall and gave them to his wife, the wife to whom he proposed at the Popping Stone at Gilsland.

> Take these flowers which purple waving,
> On the ruined ramparts grew,
> Where, the sons of freedom braving,
> Rome's imperial Standards flew.
> Warriors from the breach of danger
> Pluck no longer laurels there.
> They but yield the passing stranger
> Wild-flower wreaths for beauty's hair.

wrote Sir Walter.

The sun is setting in the west over the Solway. Centuries ago the sun set on the mighty Empire of Rome, never to rise again; but here in

Northumberland the glory of Rome lives on in the Great Wall of Hadrian, and when the sun has gone down and the lights shine out from little farms like "Seldom Seen" on The Stanegate, vale is whispered on the Wall.

II

HEXHAM AND THE SHIRE

Hey for the buff and the blue,
Hey for the cap and the feather,
Hey for the bonnie lass true,
That lives in Hexhamshire.
The Hexhamshire Lass (TRAD.)

In the year 674 Queen Ethelreda of Northumbria gave to her favourite,
Wilfrid, land in Tynedale on which to build an abbey. Now, more
than a thousand years afterwards, the great church which Wilfrid
dedicated to St. Andrew still dominates the ancient market town of
Hexham. The town was known in the past as Halgutstad, Hangustald
Hexildesham, Hextoldesham and now finally Hexham. Not only did
Ethelreda give her favourite the land on which to build the abbey, she
also gave him that vast tract of beautiful and unspoilt country known
today as "The Shire". Originally this district was a palatine or liberty,
and formed part of the Northumbrian queen's marriage dowry
when she became the wife of King Egfrith. At one time the
parishes of Allendale and St. John Lee formed part of The Shire, but
today it is the country south-west of the town to which the name is
applied.

Wilfrid, who was at that time Archbishop of York and who was later
canonized, appears to have acted in an oddly unbishoplike manner as he
eventually persuaded Ethelreda to leave her husband and take the veil.
Not surprisingly the king resented Wilfrid's influence over his wife and
later, when Egfrith remarried, he and his new queen were bitterly
antagonistic towards the man who had now become bishop of Hexham and they contrived to bring about his downfall.

There can be very few churches in the British Isles more loved by its
members and townspeople than the abbey of Hexham. This has been
amply proved within the last few years by the generous response to the
Restoration Fund, to which people of every creed have subscribed.
Donations to help in the work of restoring the fabric have come from
the old enemies who in the past did their best to destroy it. The Scotsmen who on so many occasions crossed the Border to sack and burn
Tynedale, and the Norsemen who ravaged the town and the shire, are

38

atoning now by their generous gifts for the deeds of their warlike ancestors.

In the Abbey Church today there hangs a blue and gold standard bearing the date 1514, a lasting reminder that the old enemies are now friends. In the bad old days when the Borderers spent their time raiding one another's territory, the Hexham men made their way by the valley of the North Tyne into Scotland and sacked the town of Hawick, a town defended by youths or Callants, most of the older men having lost their lives at Flodden the year before. Carrying their gold and blue standard, the Hexham men lay down by the Teviot to rest before setting out on the long journey home and, as they slept, those Callants who had survived the raid stole upon their enemies and captured the flag, inflicting heavy losses on the Hexham men. Within recent years the people of Hawick presented the town of Hexham with a replica of the flag which caused so much trouble long ago. The original can be seen in Hawick Museum.

When St. Andrew's Abbey was built it was said to be the finest north of the Alps. Its history can be read in detail in the Venerable Bede's *Ecclesiastical History of England*, a work of immense value and published today by Everyman's Library. There is also a short but fascinating little guide written by Mr. W. T. Taylor who, until some years ago, was clerk and verger and whose knowledge of the abbey is unrivalled.

To attend Evensong in Hexham Abbey is to step back into the Middle Ages. The choir in their red cassocks descend the Night Stair, the steps worn by the feet of countless monks, past the memorial to the young Roman Centurion, and from there to the chancel. Perhaps, though, the most impressive service of all in this heart of a great agricultural area is the Harvest Festival, when the sheaves of golden corn, the flowers and the fruits shine in all their colourful glory against the grey stone walls. Then one is not only thankful that the harvest is safely gathered in, but thankful too for the glory that is Hexham Abbey and the treasures which have survived its stormy history.

Beneath this great Christian church is the finest Saxon crypt in England, built largely with Roman stones on some of which can still be traced inscriptions of dedication to their heathen gods.

In the chancel is St. Wilfrid's Chair, the throne or seat of the bishop, which became the Seat of Sanctuary or Frid Stool. In 1870 the Cross of St. Acca, who was Bishop of Hexham in 709–32, was removed to Durham Cathedral, but was quite rightly brought back to the abbey in the 1930s.

Appropriately there is a chapel dedicated to St. Ethelreda, the queen who took the veil and was ultimately canonized. There are many beautiful and interesting paintings of those whose names are forever connected with the building and history of St. Andrew's Abbey—St.

Andrew himself, Queen Ethelreda, St. Oswald, the Christian king of Northumbria and, on the choir screen, many Bishops of Hexham. But most interesting of all and very rare in this country, are four small panels depicting The Dance of Death.

Through the centuries, the abbey that Wilfrid founded has grown into the magnificent building which it is today. From its tower proudly flies the blue and white cross of St. Andrew, Scotland's patron saint, on the English side of the Border! Within its walls are laid up the colours of regiments famous in our history, tombs and gravestones of the great and the humble who have made their contribution to the history of Hexham. The helmet of Sir John Fenwick, who was killed at Marston Moor in 1644, hangs on the north wall of the choir. This Sir John was an ancestor of the Fenwick who was beheaded for high treason in the reign of William III. This Sir John's estates and possessions were confiscated and his horse Sorrel became the property of the king. Dutch William was riding Sorrel when the horse stumbled over a mole hill and threw the king, who died shortly afterwards. The Jacobites toasted 'The little gentleman in brown velvet', regarding the accident as just retribution for one who had sent a gallant gentleman to his death for loyalty to the House of Stuart.

The effigy of Sir Thomas of Devilstone, who died in 1297, lies in Prior Leschman's Chantry; the chantry in which are carvings in stone of St. George and the Dragon, a fox preaching to some geese, a lady combing her hair and a monkey enjoying a meal of buns! Strange decorations for a Prior's Chantry.

As one comes out into the sunlight, either into the Market Place, or by the great door which leads onto the flags, the past and present of Hexham are intermingled. In the Market Place, so busy on a Tuesday when the stalls are set out in the Shambles beside the Pant. The Pant is a covered well, a type only seen in Border Country which would have once been the main supply of water for the dwellers in the houses which cluster round the abbey. One of the ancient monastic buildings is now the headquarters of the local constabulary.

At the east end of the square is the Moot Hall, under which an archway leads to the Manor Office, both buildings dating from about the thirteenth century and no doubt built for purposes of defence, though at one period in its history, the Moot Hall was the Bishop's Palace. For many years the Moot Hall was neglected but now it is used as the Brough Library. The story of the Moot Hall through the ages, if one knew it all, would make a fascinating book. Here, until the year 1838, all courts dealing with the regality of Hexham were held and the rough justice of the Borders was dispensed. From the time of Elizabeth I, all business in connection with the Manor of Hexham was dealt with in the Manor Office and only ceased less than a hundred years ago.

Close to the Manor Office and overlooking the Tyne Valley is an attractive whitewashed house which was the old grammar school; a grammar school with a charter granted by that most far-seeing monarch, the first Elizabeth, who realized the immense importance of education. What Elizabeth's comments would be on the fact that now the boys' and girls' schools have amalgamated are questionable. Before the Elizabethan school was founded there was a boys' grammar school in the town, with not a particularly happy history. In April of 1296, the Scots were burning their way through the northern counties, leaving a trail of ruin behind them. In this raid Hexham suffered badly, the new and glorious abbey was set on fire and only the walls were left standing, but the grammar school suffered most of all; two hundred scholars were burnt alive. A year afterwards William Wallace descended on the town and what little had withstood the sack of the previous year was now destroyed. Worse was to come, within the next few hundred years dispute followed dispute, in those days always settled by the sword, and by the time Robert Bruce arrived in the early part of 1300 there was little left to burn. In all fairness to the Scots, the English were doing exactly the same thing in Scotland whenever they crossed the Border. In comparison with the abbeys on the Scottish side, which, without exception are ruins as a result of English forays, Hexham came out of it fairly well.

Many and varied have been the royal visitors to the town of Hexham. David of Scotland came, who burnt the town, but spared the abbey. Before David, the unpopular English John came to Hexham on three occasions and spent his time looking for buried treasure in the Tyne. By a strange coincidence, close to where King John tried to unearth treasure near Corbridge, hundreds of years afterwards, the precious Corbridge Lanx was discovered!

The most famous royal visitor was the queen of Henry VI, Margaret of Anjou. Although some historians throw doubt on the veracity of the story, authentic or not it is one of the most famous Hexham legends. During the time of the Wars of the Roses, the county of Northumberland was strongly for the House of Lancaster, and it was to the north that Queen Margaret fled to hold her court in the mighty castle of Bamburgh, from whence, so tradition says, she rode out on a May morning, accompanied by the little Prince of Wales, to ride across the county towards Hexham.

The Yorkist armies were already in the district when Margaret's army, under the Duke of Somerset, reached the town, and tradition has it that a house south of Hexham called The Duke's House is so named because Somerset took refuge in an old barn nearby. Somerset who, after the Yorkist victory, was to meet his death on an improvised block in Hexham Market Place.

About three miles south of Hexham, close to the Devilswater, there is marked on the ordnance map the scene of the battle which took place on Hexham Levels and the date 1464. This battle was known as the Battle of Hexham and here the queen's forces were heavily defeated.

In those days long ago The Shire was largely a forest inhabited by lawless men; very different from the well-farmed district of today. The old bridge which spans the Devilswater beside the Linnels was yet to be built, the bridge which bears the date 1530 and the inscription "God preserve Wilfrid Errington, who builded this bridge". Now, where the battle raged and the Red Rose of Lancaster was trampled in the dust, there is some of the most lovely scenery in the county. The old mill at the Linnels; the wooded banks of the little peat-coloured burns and the wild expanses of heather-clad moorland climbing towards the Durham border.

Queen Margaret would have little inclination to admire scenery as she fled from Hexham Levels, her horse becoming lame at the Queen's Letch, a name meaning a slip, which commemorates the accident. It was now when wandering on foot, the Prince of Wales beside her, that legend says Margaret was befriended by the Hexham Robber. The robber, who instead of taking the opportunity of stealing the queen's jewels, guided her and Prince Edward to what is now known in the district as The Queen's Cave, a cave which today is very difficult to find without the aid of a good map. Here in the cave above the Dipton Burn, the queen was fed and sheltered by the chivalrous robber until the Yorkist forces dispersed and she was able to make her way across Northumberland towards the coast, from which she escaped in a fishing boat to France. At Warkworth Castle today the visitor is shown a room where Margaret is alleged to have spent her last night in Northumberland, but unfortunately there is another room at ruined Dunstanburgh which is also shown to the visitor as Queen Margaret's Room!

Whether the story is true or not, the Battle of Hexham was certainly fought. Stragglers from the Lancastrian army would be fleeing for their lives. Through Swallowship and into the wild country towards Harwood Shield on the extreme edge of Hexhamshire Common, men would be on the run. In Dipton Woods and by the banks of the Rowley Burn they would be in hiding. Still a well-wooded country, the forest has gone, but the platitude that history repeats itself is, in this case, true, as there are new forests growing up, planted by the Forestry Commission. The Battle of Hexham Levels is now a memory. It is in the names of the farm houses and little hamlets that it is remembered. Lord's Lot and The Dukesfield; the very names in Hexhamshire are music. Finechambers Mill, Smelting Syke and the strangely named Click 'em Inn not far from the Traveller's Rest and the village of Whitley Chapel are a few of the many more unusual names to be found in The Shire.

The legend of Queen Margaret is still vivid and even in this sophisticated age children still play the parts of a Medieval queen and a chivalrous robber. An old song, rarely heard now, has its origin in this part of Northumberland, "The Hexhamshire Lass".

South of the town is the high ridge of hills known as Yarridge—famous far and wide as the scene of Hexham Races. Surely Yarridge is the most beautiful steeplechase course in the whole of the British Isles. The panoramic views to the south and north are bounded in the far distance by the Pennine Chain and the Cheviots. When the sun shines over Tynedale on a spring day, the silks of the jockeys, the fresh green of the turf and the water jump make Yarridge the most perfect setting for a race meeting. Three meetings a year are held on Yarridge, the most important race being for The Heart of All England Cup at the spring meeting. Nor far away at Slaley lived the huntsman Pigg, immortalized by Surtees in "Handley Cross". When the last race is over and the crowds stream down the steep hill into the town, the narrow streets are jammed with traffic. These narrow streets which add to its charm with their unusual names, about whose origin there are so many different theories: Priestpopple, Hencotes, St. Mary's Chare, always known locally as Back Street; Fore Street, the old name of which was Front Street, Gilesgate and Battle Hill, and the wide and lovely Beaumont Street named after the family of Viscount Allendale. On the north side of this broad street are the extensive and attractive abbey grounds, through which runs the Cockshaw Burn. It is here in the abbey grounds that the war memorial stands, the memorial unveiled in 1924 by Prince Henry, now the Duke of Gloucester. Another war memorial is a stone arched gateway into the grounds, which was given by the late Mr. James Robb as a tribute to the local battalion of the Royal Northumberland Fusiliers. This archway, which dates from the reign of William and Mary, was originally the entrance of The Old White Hart Hotel in Fore Street.

The abbey grounds lead on to another open space which rises towards the west. This is the Sele, and from it there are magnificent views across the Tyne to where the church of St. John Lee stands out so prominently. St. John Lee is literally perched on a high promontory above the river, below it are the flat lands referred to by the Saxon name of haughs, and pronounced "halfs" in Northumberland. Close by the river stands "The Hermitage", a large house named probably from the fact that some local hermit made it his retreat.

Hexham, now the centre of a prosperous farming district, is a busy, important little town, concerned with the present as much as the past. There is a most informative and interesting little book published in 1882, entitled *Hexham Fifty Years Ago*, written by William Robb, the father of the James who gave the town the memorial to the Fusiliers. Mr. Robb, who is of course recalling events which took place in 1832, in the reign of William IV, has many interesting sidelights on the Hexham of those days. It is amazing to discover that there are some things cheaper today than they were in 1832! To travel to Newcastle and back by The British Queen, the coach which started from "The High Grey Bull", cost seven to eight shillings return and took four hours to reach Newcastle! Mr. Robb goes on to say that in view of the cost the coach was not often full, especially west of Hexham, and that some people walked to Newcastle and back to transact their business which he says was reckoned a fair test of a man's physical powers. In 1832 cockfighting was still regarded as a sport, and the Cock-Pit was where the old offices of *The Hexham Courant* stood in Back Street; it is now a sale room. Only a few years earlier bull baiting took place in the Market Place.

In the early part of the nineteenth century one of the most thriving industries was glove-making and "Hexham Tans" as they were called were sent to the London market and even to America. One firm had an output of fifty dozen pairs of gloves a day. The glovers and shoemakers had their own guilds and customs and on occasions marched through the town with bands playing and banners flying. As is to be expected in a district where many sheep are reared there is a large hide and skin trade. There is even a local breed of sheep, the Hexham Leicesters, on no account to be confused with the more aristocratic Border Leicesters. The Hexham breed can be distinguished by their blue noses!

It is illuminating to look through old classified directories of Northumberland to see how industries have changed or died out. Of the saddlers and harness makers listed in the nineteenth century directories, hardly any remain. The blacksmiths have gone and no more do the inns advertise good stabling. There was a very up-to-date café in Hexham in the late 1890s which advertised, as its principal attraction, a w.c.! Of the forty or fifty grocers who traded in Hexham in 1850, most have been pushed out of business by the multiple store. It is pleasant to think that the business founded by our author Mr. William Robb is still in existence although in different premises. The value of money has also changed. After the Pilgrimage of Grace, when the monks of Hexham Abbey clung to the old religion and in consequence were turned out, the elder brethren were allowed forty shillings a year and a gown. The less fortunate were executed and Jay, the Prior of Hexham was hanged. The revenues of the priory at the time of the Dissolution of the Monasteries were £122 11s. 1d. per annum!

Many of the old customs and traditions have disappeared. No longer are the Hirings a great event. In November and May, men and women, lads and lasses would stand about the streets waiting to be "asked" or hired, and to clinch the bargain the new master gave his future servant "arles" as his bond of good faith, the amount of the arles in monetary value depending upon the generosity of the giver. At the live-stock sales at Hexham Auction Marts today, a luck penny is still given by the seller.

The Market Place has witnessed many stirring events through the years, events which have left their mark in the history of the town. Always loyal to the unfortunate House of Stuart, Hexham men would gather in the shadow of the abbey to march out for Charles I in the Civil Wars. Many a Border raider has been imprisoned in the dungeons of the Moot Hall. The stocks which were originally in the Market Place were removed to the Manor Office, the massive square building where in places the walls are eleven feet thick. When the young Earl of Derwentwater came home to Dilston in 1710, there were great celebrations in Hexham and whole oxen were roasted in the Market Place. Five years afterwards the ill-fated earl led out a pathetic little army from Dilston, and many Hexham men who joined him in the Rebellion of the '15 were never to see Tynedale again. For most of them the end of the journey was death on the gallows of the Lancashire prisons.

In 1761 the Riot Act was read in the Market Place. Many of the people, largely miners from the Allendale lead mines rebelled against the new recruiting regulations for raising the Militia. The mob, under the impression that there would be no retaliation from the soldiers, got out of hand and unfortunately blood was shed. An officer and private soldier were shot and some women and children lost their lives. The Militia were ordered to open fire; forty-five men were killed and about three hundred wounded in this unhappy affair. This was the last time blood was shed in Hexham, the Border town which had suffered so grievously in the days when England and Scotland were forever at war with one another. Only the names remind one of the past: Battle Hill, so called because of a skirmish between Scots and English during the Edwardian wars and not, as many think, commemorating the Battle of Hexham fought on Hexham Levels. The thoroughfare of Quatre Bras, and the Monument at the top of Beaumont Street, a memorial to one of the well-known family of Benson who fought in the South African War, are reminders of wars fought far from the valley of the Tyne.

Its stirring history behind it, Hexham is now justly proud of its present. Its Parliamentary division is the largest in the county, stretching from the Durham border to the Scottish. The elections are now conducted on more peaceful lines than in the past, when there were often broken heads at The Hustings! Until 1832, Northumberland returned only two Knights of The Shire, and these members of Parliament can be traced from the year 1298, when Northumberland's representatives were Henry de Dychend and John de Ogle.

The council offices are now in Hexham House, a building which at one time was the property of the priors. It is an attractive house, overlooking a bowling green, beyond which are the abbey grounds and The Sele. Close to Benson's Monument, as it is always referred to in

Hexham, is the principal entrance to the grounds through gates given by the Benson family, who also contributed towards the purchase of the land, which is now planted with flower beds which are a blaze of colour against the background of the trees. Hexham's original water supply came from the heart of The Shire, from the Ladle Wells, an improvement on the old supply from the Pants.

That most lovely of Northumbrian folk songs, "The Water of Tyne", was first heard in the Hexham district some time in the eighteenth century. The words were taken down from the singing of an old man, according to a paper read at a meeting of professional musicians in 1892, and this has been confirmed by that eminent authority, Dr. Whittaker, in his collection of north country songs. One theory is that the song was written after the Rebellion of the '45, but where the singer pleaded with the boatmen to "Scull her across that rough river to me" will always cause controversy. Some say it was where the Devilswater runs into the Tyne; others that it was just before the South Tyne joins the North at Warden where "The Boathouse Inn" is now. This appears to be more probable than the first theory as the Tyne at Dilston is wide and shallow. Haughton Ferry is also claimed to have been the setting where the song was first heard, wherever it was. The song is the most haunting melody. "The Water of Tyne", sung by that most celebrated Northumbrian, Owen Brannigan, sung as only a Northumbrian can, is unforgettable:

> Oh bring me a boatman,
> I'll give any money,
> And you for your trouble,
> Rewarded shall be,
> To ferry me over the Tyne
> To me Hinney, and scull her across
> That rough river to me.

In recent years Hexham has produced one of England's best known poets, Wilfrid Gibson, who died some years ago. Although Gibson's poems have achieved national fame, those with a local background have the strongest appeal to Northumbrians and especially to people born in Hexham and the surrounding district. *Whin*, a collection of this poetry, includes some of the best poems ever written about Northumberland.

Many scholarly and learned books have been written on Hexham and its abbey, from the time of our first historian the Venerable Bede up to the present day. In every history of the county a large section is devoted to this ancient and attractive town that stands above the Water of Tyne.

Long before the abbey was founded, prehistoric people, and after them the Romans, built their camps and forts in Tynedale. Battle cries rang out across the wide river where now the boats are moored on Tyne Green. The bishops and the saints had their hour of glory, kings and queens wrote their names on the pages of history, while still the Tyne flowed on towards the sea. The great flood of 1771 swept away the bridges which succeeded the fords. Above it all, as it does today, towered the "greatest abbey north of the Alps".

The power of the bishops and priors ended with the Dissolution of the Monasteries. The Shire is no longer a palatine, but incorporated in the county of Northumberland. The abbey lands, which extended for many miles beyond Hexham as far as Newbrough in the west and Anick and Acomb north of the river, were broken up and sold, but the love and pride of Hexham Abbey are perhaps stronger now than in the days when bishops ruled over their great territory.

From all over the world visitors come to this little market town in Tynedale to visit the abbey, explore the narrow streets and wander through the lovely parks. The Agricultural Show, though now held in Tynedale Park at Corbridge, and renamed The Tyneside Show, will always to the older generation be known as "Hexham Show". Until 1964 this was the most successful one-day agricultural show held in England. After changing to a two-day event it has in 1968 reverted to its original form although now held on a different date. In days gone by the stock on show would be largely indigenous to the county; the Shorthorns and Blue Grey cattle, Cheviot and Blackfaced sheep and, of course, the "Hexham" Leicesters. Now the foreigners have intruded; the black and white Fresians have ousted the Shorthorns and, saddest of all, the tractors and machinery have superseded the heavy horses and there are very few draught horses when the grand parade goes round the ring. It is in the Hunter classes that the horses hold their own; and the descendants of Border raiders, bearing names only heard in Northumberland, gallop round the ring at the Tyneside Show.

The Tynedale Foxhounds hunt the country north of the Tyne and share with the Border the distinction of having two of the longest masterships in the history of foxhunting. The late Mr. John C. Straker of Stagshaw and the late Mr. Jacob Robson of the Byrness each served for more than fifty years. Both a son and a daughter of Mr. Straker have been masters of the Tynedale and his daughter and grandson joint masters with Colonel Neil Speke. Mr. Jacob Robson was master and joint master of the Border from 1879 until 1933 and his son, Mr. Jacob Robson, Jr., has also served as master and joint master.

Many fairs used to be held in Hexham but with the march of time they have disappeared. Some of the old coaching inns are no more but, whatever changes may be made, for better or for worse, the abbey will always be there, guardian of the town. Sad to say, there are some visitors to the abbey who do not respect its sanctity, a sorry reflection on the twentieth century.

At one time the town was practically surrounded by nursery gardens. Some of these are no more and one can no longer walk through Fell's Gardens on the way to the station, the railway station where long ago, on hiring days, the young men of the town used to derive much amusement from watching the girls struggling into the trains in their unwieldy crinolines!

Gilesgate, the steep street leading from the Market Place, is still known as "Gilligate", for, if a Northumbrian can mispronounce or distort a word, he will do so. It must puzzle a stranger to hear a real Hexham man or woman say that they "have jumped someone in Fore Street", meaning that they have met a friend by chance.

One of the most attractive pictures in Hexham must surely be the brides who marry in the abbey and then come out into the sunshine by the door which leads into the Market Place, their veils blowing in the wind, to face the crowds which always gather when there is a wedding. This must be as impressive and beautiful a setting as any bride could wish for, especially if she is a "Hexhamshire lass".

The busiest of the Northumbrian market towns, Hexham is rapidly expanding. Many new housing estates of the more expensive type have been built to accommodate the number of people who have their business in Newcastle, only twenty miles away, and who, to use a most ugly word, "commute" daily. Fortunately, so far, the town has managed to maintain its country atmosphere. At its two auction marts, weekly marts and special sales are held, while many people in the town are engaged in business connected with agriculture, such as machinery for the highly mechanized farms of the Tyne valley, and seed and corn merchants, whose firms have been established for generations.

A privately owned newspaper, *The Hexham Courant*, is published weekly and records in great detail all the local events. At the west end of the town, on the Allendale road, is the new grammar school, the former buildings being unable to accommodate the increasing number of pupils. Hexham Golf Course, between the Carlisle road and the Tyne, is set in a most delightful position with glorious views towards the meeting of the North and South Tynes at Warden. The club has its headquarters in a mansion, "The Spital", once the home of General Sir Loftus Bates. There is the War Memorial Hospital, opened after the First World War, and the General Hospital at the eastern approach to the town. Hexham is a self-supporting, busy community. Proud of its past, which is inseparable from the history of the abbey, Hexham is also proud of its present. A musical festival, the Tynedale, is an annual event. Amateur dramatic societies flourish in this, the social centre of a widely scattered district. In the winter, hunt balls are held. Cricket,

Roman Baths at Chesters

tennis, and rugby are popular, the Tynedale rugby team having supplied many players of county standard.

However much the life of Hexham may change, the great abbey will forever dominate this town on the "Water of Tyne".

4

Hexham Priory Church where St. Winifred was bishop

III

THE DERWENTWATER STORY

Farewell to pleasant Dilston Hall,
My father's ancient seat;
A stranger now must call thee his,
Which gars my heart to greet.

Surtees, DERWENTWATER'S FAREWELL

The saddest figure in all Northumbrian history is James Radcliffe, third Earl of Derwentwater. Born in the year 1689, James Radcliffe was heir to the great estates which his family owned in Northumberland and Cumberland, estates which he was to enjoy for a few short years only. A grandson of Charles II, his mother Lady Mary Tudor was the daughter of that amorous monarch and Moll Davis, an actress. It was his fated Stuart blood and the fact that he was a Roman Catholic which moulded his tragic destiny, the destiny which led him to his death. On a February morning in 1716 James Radcliffe was beheaded on Tower Hill and the Derwentwater Legend began. So much has been written about this brave and gallant Northumbrian that it is difficult to sift fact from fiction.

The abortive Rebellion of the '15 and the part which Derwentwater played have inspired historians such as C. J. Bates and W. S. Gibson, and in Hodgson's *History of Northumberland*, published in 1827, is much valuable information. Harrison Ainsworth's *Preston Fight* and the romantic *Dorothy Forster* by Walter Besant are two of the best-known novels, the latter although highly imaginative gives a wonderfully detailed description of Northumberland in the eighteenth century. In the Corbridge district the legends still survive. So many different places claim to have hidden the earl when he was a fugitive, from Newbiggin in Hexham Shire, to a cave in Shafto Crags, where it is said the refuge was discovered when a dog was seen with a basket of food tied round its neck making regular journeys to the cave! And under the great staircase of the old Beaufront Castle, which overlooks the Tyne, north-west of Corbridge, and in "The Lord Crewe Arms" at Blanchland, where a priest's hiding hole in one of the chimneys was a Derwentwater refuge.

Of the great castle of Dilston nothing now remains but a ruined tower, built long before the Radcliffes came. In the reign of Henry II there was a castle at Dilston, owned by the family of Dyvelston, a family who gave their name to the Devilswater, above which Dilston stands. The Tynedales, lords of the barony of Langley, succeeded the Dyvelstons as owners of Dilston; afterwards it passed to the Claxtons whose family ended with an heiress who married a John Cartington. They in their turn had only a daughter, this daughter taking as her husband Sir Edward Radcliffe. Of this marriage was born Francis, who was created first Earl of Derwentwater and Viscount Langley by James II, and so the Radcliffes began their short reign at Dilston in Tynedale. The mansion which the third earl built was demolished after his execution. In the present century the chapel has been re-consecrated and services are occasionally held within its ancient walls; more frequent than services are baptisms, as the modern Dilston Hall, the property of Viscount Allendale, was until recently a maternity hospital and many of the babies born at Dilston were christened in the chapel where Derwentwater worshipped.

It was far away from Dilston that James Radcliffe was born, the eldest of a family of four and the child of an unhappy marriage. He was born in London and, at the age of three, was sent to France to the court of the exiled Stuarts. There he was the playmate of his cousin, James Francis, called the Old Chevalier by the Jacobites and the Old Pretender by his enemies. It was for his cousin's cause that Derwentwater was later to lose his life and lands. Loyalty to the House of Stuart brought tragedy and ruin to those who supported it, and the Radcliffe brothers, James and Charles, by reason of the ties of blood and religion, were both to suffer the extreme penalty of death.

Educated in France, intelligent, ahead of his times in outlook and tolerance, even his most bitter enemies failed to find flaws in the character of the man who was to be known through Tynedale as "The Bonnie Earl". Even the renegade vicar of Allendale, who was chaplain to the Jacobite Forces during the Rebellion and who later turned King's Evidence to save his life, wrote in his *History of The Rebellion*, "The sweetness of his temper and disposition, in which he had few equals, had so secured him the affection of all his tenants, neighbours and dependants, that multitudes would have lived and died for him; he was a man formed by nature to be generally loved, and he had a beneficence so universal that he seemed to live for others. As he lived among his own people, there he spent his estate; and continually did offices of kindness and good neighbourhood to everybody as opportunity offered. He kept a house of generous hospitality and noble entertainment, which few in that county do and none come up to. He was very charitable to poor and distressed families on all occasions, whether known to him or not, and whether Papist or Protestant."

It was in 1710, when he was twenty-one, that Lord Derwentwater came home to Dilston, the Dilston he had never seen and the Dilston he would leave for ever in five short years. From all over Northumberland came members of the great county families, the numerous cousins and distant relatives, for the Radcliffes were connected with many of the old families of Northumberland. Swinburnes and Fenwicks, Erringtons, Collingwoods, Shaftos and Widdringtons were among the many who came to welcome the young man home; and from Bamburgh came a young squire and his sister, Tom and Dorothy Forster, whose names were to figure so prominently in the drama of the '15.

Of medium height, speaking without the distinctive Northumbrian burr, so different from the hard-drinking, sport-loving Northumbrian gentlemen, Derwentwater greeted not only those whose names are written in the pages of history, but the humble people, his tenants, the servants on his vast estates—the men he would so bitterly regret "calling out" to wear the fated white cockade of James III in the years that were to be. All was feasting and gaiety at Dilston in 1710. Whole oxen were roasted, the wine and home brewed ales flowed. Huntsmen came back from the chase, mud spattered and weary, to be entertained by their host at Dilston.

The generous kindly young man who rode round his estates, visiting his farms with a good word for all, had a shadow hanging over him, a shadow no bigger than a man's hand. Introspective, taking his responsibilities seriously, and well aware that plots were already being laid to bring back "The King Over the Water" when Queen Anne should die, perhaps he had a premonition that the time was short. The time in which he could learn to love the valley of the Tyne and the great purple moors which sweep over to Blanchland; to visit Beaufront and Capheaton and his ruined castle of Langley which was to be so lovingly restored by one of the earl's most fervent admirers, C. J. Bates, the man who erected the only memorial there is, in all Northumberland, to Derwentwater's Bonnie Martyred Earl.

Riding with James was his wild young brother, Charles, hot-headed and high-spirited, so different from himself. He played bowls at Stamfordham, made plans for the great house yet to be built at Dilston and, the romantic novelists would have us believe, rode over the moors to Blanchland to walk by the banks of the Derwent with the charming Dorothy Forster. Unfortunately for the romantically minded, there is no evidence to show that the two ever had a love affair although, when the standard of James III was raised in Northumberland, he was to be the hero and she the heroine of the most ill-fated unhappy little revolt.

Blanchland is so romantically situated and such a perfect setting for a love affair, that Dorothy would have been less than human had she not been attracted by this good-looking young man, so courteous and different from the wild young men of Northumberland, the Perry Widdringtons and Ned Swinburnes whom she knew. In "The Lord Crewe Arms" which stands at the east side of the square which forms the village, every room is named after those who came out in the '15. Dorothy herself, Derwentwater, Widdrington and Swinburne, Charles Radcliffe and Errington and even the name of the Protestant Chaplain Patten is commemorated in "The Lord Crewe". The public house is named after a great palatine bishop of Durham, Lord Crewe, who married another Forster. The heroine's aunt was Dorothy Forster the elder, whose picture hangs in Bamburgh Castle. The Forsters, once a wealthy and powerful family in the county, owned land at Bamburgh and Blanchland. After the Dissolution of the Monasteries the abbey lands of Blanchland were granted to a John Bellow and John Bloxham, subsequently being sold to the Forsters who, through riotous living squandered their inheritance which was bought by their aunt's husband, Lord Crewe. It was due to the generosity of the bishop that the two young Forsters lived at Blanchland for some time. Love affair or not, there could never have been a marriage between a great Catholic earl and the daughter of an impoverished Protestant squire. Walter Besant, in his novel, gives a most fascinating and graphic description of Blanchland, a village that has changed very little since the days when the Forsters lived there.

The abbey of the White Lands is the greatest treasure of Blanchland. It was in 1175 that the abbey was founded, an abbey which like all those in the Border Country was to have a wild and stormy history. Parties of marauding Scots were often in the district and on one occasion their attempts to find the abbey were foiled by a thick mist which enveloped the valley. The monks in their relief at deliverance from their enemies rang the abbey bells with disastrous results. The Scots, who were lost in the mist at a place known as Dead Friar's Hill on the Durham side of the river, heard the bells and the sound guided them to the doomed abbey, which they burnt and pillaged, killing several of the brothers and riding off with their ill-gotten gains.

Froissart gives an account of the difficulties to be faced by strangers in the Blanchland district. Edward III in 1327, at the head of an army of 60,000 men, on his way to Scotland, was lost in the bogs and mosses of the moors, and when eventually he reached the abbey the king, who was received by the abbot, confessed his sins and ordered Masses to be said. Being also of a practical turn of mind he turned out his horses to feed in the fields near the monastery. Froissart goes on to say that the name Blanchland was used in the days of King Arthur.

A battlemented gateway adds to the charm of this most attractive and historic village, which was designated a perfect village by *Town and Country Planning*. The romance of the '15 still lingers in Blanchland. It was from here that Tom Forster rode over the hills to Dilston to discuss Jacobite plots and plans with Lord Derwentwater; Tom Forster who has been condemned by history as an incompetent, pig-headed fool. Ironical that a man with such a reputation should have been one of two members sent to Parliament by Northumberland in those days!

Above the banks of the Devilswater the great house of Dilston was becoming a reality. The foundations were laid, all was activity and bustle, soon it would be ready—a fitting home for a great earl. Yet the earl was still unmarried. Dilston Hall was no place for a bachelor, there must be a countess to play hostess within its great halls. It was from far away Dorset that Anna Webb came to be the wife of the third earl, to live for such a pitifully short time at Dilston and forever to be blamed by posterity for urging her husband to take up arms for the Stuarts; most unfairly blamed, as, long before his marriage, the earl was already committed to the enterprise which was to be his ruin. Dilston is haunted by the ghost of the poor little countess. She appears wringing her hands and lamenting the incident in which she is said to have flung down her fan, telling Lord Derwentwater to take it and give her his sword.

James and Anna were married on the 10th July, 1712, and by a condition laid down by her father spent two years in the house of Hatherhope, the property of the Webb family. They returned in the fatal year of 1714, the year in which Queen Anne died, bringing the prophecy true which James V of Scotland made after the Battle of Solway Moss, when he heard that his queen had given birth to a daughter, "It came wi' a lass and it'll gang wi' a lass", for Anne was the last Stuart to rule over us. Had a child of Anne's survived her, Derwentwater and his bride might have lived out their lives at Dilston, for the '15 and the '45 would never have been fought.

Rumours that Queen Anne was dead swept through the country. The Jacobite agents were travelling from France to England and Scotland. The time was drawing near when either a Hanoverian prince, the elector of Hanover, would sit on the throne, or as the Stuart supporters hoped and prayed "The King shall enjoy his Own Again". Toasts were drunk to the King Over the Water, as the glasses were passed over the finger bowls, and, across the Border, the Scots, under the Earl of Mar, the turnabout "Bobbing John", were waiting for the order to rise.

In Northumberland there was much activity. Letters and messages were passed to and fro from the houses with Jacobite sympathies. Many and varied were the means used by the messengers. An old holly bush on the road to Slaley is still pointed out as one of the spots where letters were hidden, and most fantastic of all is the legend that the Misses Swinburne of Capheaton disguised themselves as fairies and hid letters under four stones in the Fourstones district, and so gave the village its name!

It was in July of 1715 that Lord Derwentwater parted with his bonnie grey steed, sending the horse to a Mr. Hunter for safety as the Government had decreed that any horses over a certain value and owned

by Catholics were to be confiscated. The letter which Lord Derwentwater wrote to Mr. Hunter is in the possession of Mr. Guy Allgood of
Nunwick in North Tynedale. Surtees has used poetic licence in his
ballad when he says: "And fare you well my bonnie grey steed, That
carried me aye sa' free, I wish I had been asleep in my bed, Last time I
mounted thee".

The last few months of peace and security at Dilston were nearly over.
The countess and her baby son would soon be alone, for on the 1st of
August 1714 Queen Anne died and Lord Derwentwater was a wanted
man. The Government was acting quickly, standing by the Act of Settlement that only a Protestant could sit on the throne of Great Britain.
Already plans were afoot to bring over from Hanover the man whom the
Scots called "The wee, wee, German lairdie", our first King George, who
couldn't speak a word of English! The will the queen was alleged to
have made, in which she nominated as her successor her half-brother,
James Stuart, was missing, if it ever existed. The Jacobites said it had
been destroyed by the Whig Government.

Now Lord Derwentwater's movements are difficult to follow; there are
so many contradictory stories of his whereabouts at this time. Hidden
he certainly was by his faithful friends and tenantry. Some say that he
stood on a hill overlooking Dilston, where he confided to Mr. Errington of Beaufront that it was breaking his heart to leave the land he loved
so well. Events were now moving quickly. In 1715 the Stuart standard
had been raised on the Braes of Mar. The Scottish lords, Nithsdale,
Kenmure, Carnwath and the Earl of Wintoun were "out". It was now
or never for the Northumbrians, and on a golden October day, when
the autumn colours were in all their glory, James, Earl of Derwentwater, rode out from Dilston for the last time. He led a little party of
men over the bridge at Corbridge and eastwards to Nafferton Farm
where a conference was held, and it was decided to declare openly for
James III. Next morning at Greenrigg, between Watling Street and
Sweethope Lough, the little army gathered, and here, with the Wild
Hills of Wanny as a background, where the River Wansbeck rises, the
most fatal decision of this ill-starred adventure was made. Tom Forster
of Bamburgh was created General of the Forces. Tom, who knew
nothing of soldiering and who was much too fond of the bottle, as well
as being endowed with very little brain, was to lead this untrained
army towards London and the hoped-for victory. Their fate was
sealed then, but Tom Forster was a Protestant and it was argued that a
Protestant general, however badly equipped for the position, would
attract more followers to the Cause than a Roman Catholic earl, however well loved and trusted that earl might be. Wearing the white
cockades and led by their general, the army marched for Rothbury
where, in the capital of Coquetdale, James III was proclaimed.

Recruits were now coming in. Lord Widdrington and his two

brothers, descendants of that Widdrington who, when both his legs were cut off at the Battle of Otterburn, fought on his stumps; Swinburne of Capheaton—Ned who was to die in Newgate; Clavering of Callaly and George Collingwood of Eslington Tower near Whittingham who was later to be hanged. Selby of Biddlestone Hall; John Hunter and a Robson from Thropton; Shaftos of Bavington; Charltons of The Bower; and Errington of Beaufront and Mad Jack Hall of Otterburn were some of the Northumbrian gentlemen who took up arms against the Hanoverian king. Many were to pay for their loyalty to James III with their lives. Poor Mad Jack Hall was hanged. Jack, who had already sworn the Oath of Allegiance to George I, was sitting in the Court House at Alnwick when he heard that the Jacobites were "out", and in his haste to join them rushed out of the Court House without his wig!

From Rothbury the army of horse and foot, Catholic and Protestant, a few Irish and Frenchmen, made their way to Warkworth on the coast; and in a room in a public house in Warkworth Market Place, "The Mason's Arms", there is an inscription commemorating the fact that Lord Derwentwater and General Forster stayed there in October of 1715. Here, some forty Scots under the Earl of Home's brother joined the Northumbrians. When they proclaimed the king at Warkworth the army was about three hundred strong. From Warkworth to the ducal town of Alnwick the general led his forces, a general who seems to have done little or nothing to gain information about the state of affairs in the city of Newcastle, otherwise he would never have made the march to Morpeth, for when they arrived it was to hear the disheartening news that Newcastle was all for the Hanoverians. William Cotesworth, the Government spy, had done his work well and the city was closing its gates against the Jacobites. In Morpeth, the boys of the grammar school were given a day's holiday, and prayers for King James were said in Morpeth church. Away on Holy Island a little garrison under Lancelot Errington was endeavouring to signal to a French ship which was reported to be carrying arms for the rebel army. Brave though the garrison was, they were overcome by a party of Government troops from Berwick. Errington and his nephew escaped later from Berwick gaol. Lancelot became a publican in Newcastle and died of a broken heart when he heard of the defeat of the Old Chevalier's son, Bonnie Prince Charlie. Disheartened by the attitude of Newcastle, the army marched to Hexham where Lord Derwentwater saw his home for the last time. Undecided and wavering as they were, much time was wasted at Hexham before the order was given to march north, the object being to join up with the Scots at Kelso.

On the 22nd of October, with pipes playing and drums beating, the two armies joined forces, and from the most lovely town on Tweedside, the town of Kelso, the army marched out. There were nearly two thousand of them, up and down the Scottish side of the Border, aware now that Government troops were on the move. General Carpenter was at Newcastle when Tom Forster and the Scottish lords decided to cross into England at Longtown. From there they passed through the market town of Brampton and on to Alston, where there is still a house in which Lord Derwentwater stayed. By Kendal and the western side of the Pennines they marched into Lancashire, where there were high hopes of recruiting many more to their ranks. These hopes were not to be fulfilled. Badly led as they were, with General Wills and his Government troops at Wigan, they were still convinced that the raggle-taggle army could bring the king into his own again. November and the town of Preston; and the end of their journey was upon them. Preston, ever fatal to the House of Stuart.

There are several conflicting accounts of the battle, the battle that was lost before it was fought. No attempts were made to fortify the town, the way was left open for the Government troops. Bravely as the Scots and English fought, Lord Derwentwater and Charles Radcliffe fighting with them, they had no chance against the well-disciplined troops, and when, without any consultations with his brother officers, Tom Forster met the Government generals and agreed to an unconditional surrender, the Rebellion of the '15 was over. Only one man escaped from Preston, Frank Stokoe of Chesterwood near Haydon Bridge, who afterwards helped to bring Lord Derwentwater's body home.

The vengeance the Government dealt out was sharp and cruel. Many of the rank and file were hanged in the Lancashire prisons. Far away from home died Northumbrians and Scotsmen, while the leaders were taken to London. The Tower and Newgate were waiting for their victims. The gentry rode, with their hands tied behind their backs, and when they neared the capital each horse was led by a trooper of the king's army, while the mob jeered and hurled insults at the defenceless men. To the Tower went Lord Derwentwater and the Scottish lords, Charles Radcliffe and the erstwhile General Forster to Newgate. There were no battle honours for Preston Fight, as in later years there were none for Culloden. And far away in Northumberland women were waiting for news. Who brought the grim tidings to Dilston has never been satisfactorily proved. It could have been Frank Stokoe who came to tell the wife of James Radcliffe that all was lost and her husband a prisoner in the dreaded Tower. Someone brought the news quickly, for soon a coach drove out from Dilston, and in it was a weeping woman and a small boy, a woman who was expecting her second baby whose father would die before its birth. The house where she had known such happiness would be desolate and forlorn; strangers would walk by the Devilswater; only the ghosts of the Radcliffes would haunt Dilston. Untouched by her youth and sorrow, George I refused to listen to

Anna, Countess of Derwentwater as she went down on her knees to him, begging him to spare her husband's life.

The trials of the rebels were a foregone conclusion; beheading by the axe for the peers, and for those of lesser rank the brutal hangings, followed by the barbarous drawing and quartering. Some were to escape; Lord Nithsdale, by the efforts of his wife who smuggled female clothing into the Tower, disguised her husband as a woman, thereby gaining his freedom. But the most dramatic escape was that of Tom Forster. Whatever the verdict of history, Tom was Dorothy's well-loved brother, and it was the intrepid Dorothy who made her memorable journey to London in the bitter winter weather, riding pillion behind the village blacksmith from Warenford, a little hamlet on the Great North Road, not far from Adderstone Mains where this heroine of the '15 was born. Dorothy Forster had never left her native county; young, lacking influence and sister of a condemned man, this brave Northumbrian girl, by her courage and determination, planned the escape from Newgate, which was crowned with success. Her faithful blacksmith forged skeleton keys for Tom's cell, Dorothy having gained possession of the original by bribing the gaoler. A sea captain had been found who for a consideration would take Tom Forster to France—a lucrative trade in which the captains were indulging freely. On the appointed night Dorothy visited her brother as usual and, in the absence of the guards, no doubt fuddled with wine supplied by the prisoner's friends, contrived to get him safely out of the horror that was Newgate.

Dorothy and Tom were never to meet again. He was a proscribed man, who could never return to his native land where the threat of a traitor's death would always hang over him. Dorothy spread a rumour that Tom had died in prison, and an empty coffin was placed in the Forster vault in Bamburgh church, a coffin that bears two dates, for years ahead, in 1737, when Tom Forster actually died, his body was brought home to Northumberland. In the crypt of the most lovely church at Bamburgh lies General Tom Forster and, close beside him, the sister who risked her life to save him, the Dorothy who did not spend the rest of her life grieving for Lord Derwentwater, for she married the blacksmith from Warenford, dying in 1739. The name on the stone slab of her grave is Dorothy Armstrong, but in Northumberland she will always be remembered by her girlhood's name of Dorothy Forster, and in most families of Forster today is a Dorothy.

Charles Radcliffe, too, was to escape from Newgate, living out his life on the Continent and marrying the Countess of Newburgh, returning to England at the time of the '45 Rebellion to be captured on board ship before he landed, and as a proscribed man sent to the Tower. Charles, who in the years of his exile had visited Dilston and been mistaken for the ghost of his brother! The cruel fate which dogged the house of

Radcliffe was waiting for Charles, and on the 8th of December, 1746, he met his death on Tower Hill, the last Englishman to die by the axe, where thirty years before the best and bravest of the Radcliffes died.

Condemned to death by his peers in Westminster Hall, Lord Derwentwater was offered his life if he would recant and change his Faith. Being the man he was the answer was no. His own words express his sentiments. "Some means have been proposed to me for saving my life which I look upon as inconsistent with honour and conscience, and therefore I reject them; for, with God's assistance, I shall prefer any death to the doing of a base unworthy action. I only wish now that laying down my life might contribute to my King and Country, and the re-establishment of the ancient and fundamental Constitution of these kingdoms, without which, no lasting peace or true happiness can attend them—then I should indeed part with my life even with pleasure. As it is, I can only pray that these blessings may be bestowed upon my dear country; and since I can do no more, I beseech God to accept my life as a small sacrifice towards it."

On the morning of the 24th of February, 1716, dressed in a suit of black velvet, a suit that is still preserved, James Radcliffe climbed the scaffold on Tower Hill. Spectators noticed that he flinched and turned pale as the full horror of the situation faced him, but recovering his composure and praying for and forgiving his enemies, James Radcliffe, third Earl of Derwentwater, met his death with the courage of the great gentleman he was. His last request had been that his body should be brought home to Northumberland, a request which was refused, but faithful friends managed to remove the coffin from the Tower and, accompanied by the widowed countess, the little company set out on the long journey north. Hiding by day and travelling by night at length they reached Dilston, where they rested the coffin on "The Earl's Bridge", before they buried him by candlelight above the Devilswater. James Radcliffe had come home. That night, the Northern Lights in the Corbridge district were so bright that for many years afterwards the country people called them "Lord Derwentwater's Lights".

For many years the body of the Bonnie Earl lay at Dilston, a Dilston owned now by the Commissioners of Greenwich Hospital. The little countess died in Belgium, and their son received injuries in a riding accident from which he subsequently died. The daughter, born after her father's execution, married Lord Petre, whose family possess many Derwentwater relics. In 1805 the vault was opened, and the remains exposed to view. It is a true but gruesome fact that a local blacksmith drew some of the earl's teeth and sold them as relics! His heart, enclosed in a silver casket, had been sent to Brussels. The Derwentwater story, as far as Northumberland was concerned, was over for in 1874 the earl's body was taken to Essex and placed in the vaults at Thornden Hall, the home of Lord Petre. He no longer lies in good Northumbrian earth, but the legends and the memories of Derwentwater and the '15 will never die.

A quarter of a century ago, a pageant was performed at Dilston in which the earl was the chief character. For a brief hour they lived again, Tom and Dorothy Forster, Widdringtons and Swinburnes—all those who had made history in 1715.

In 1746, boxes of deeds were discovered at Capheaton Hall, the ancestral home of the Swinburnes, which contained papers relating to the Dilston estates and which had been hidden at Capheaton for safety. These deeds are now in the Public Record Office.

Legend and history, fact and fantasy have gathered round the Earls of Derwentwater, those two men, James and Charles, whose memorial stands by the roadside between Haydon Bridge and Langley. A stone cross, erected in the last century by Mr. C. J. Bates, bears this inscription, "To the memory of James and Charles, Earls of Derwentwater, Viscounts Langley, beheaded on Tower Hill, 24th February, 1716, and 8th December, 1746, for Loyalty to their lawful sovereign".

IV

SOUTH TYNEDALE

Hoot awa' lads, hoot awa'.
Hae ye heard how the Ridleys and Thirlwalls and a'
Ha' set upon Albany Featherstonehaugh.
And taken his life at the Deadmanshaw?
There was Willimoteswick,
And Hardriding Dick,
And Hughie o' Hawden and Will o' the Wa'
I canno' tell a', I canna' tell a',
And mony a mair that the Deil may knaw.

Sir Walter Scott, MARMION

The valley of the South Tyne stretches from the meeting of the waters at Warden Rocks to its source at Tynehead near Cross Fell. Crossing the border from Cumberland at Gilderdale, the South Tyne is one of the few Northumbrian streams which rise beyond the boundaries of the county.

Lying between the great barrier of the Roman Wall and the hills of Allendale, this lovely south-west corner of Northumberland is a land of ancient castles, most of which were at one time within the barony of Langley; the Langley from which the ill-fated family of Radcliffe took their title of viscount. The square tower of Langley Castle overlooks the fertile valley, standing midway between Hexham and Haltwhistle and south of the large village of Haydon Bridge. At the end of the nineteenth century, Langley was a ruin; the once great stronghold of the de Lucys, who rebuilt the old castle of the Tindales in 1360 was burnt within fifty years. Through its succession of owners, Umfravilles, Percys, Nevilles and finally the Radcliffes, Langley's history was stormy. After the execution of James, Earl of Derwentwater and Viscount Langley, the sequestrated estates passed to the Greenwich Hospital. Ruined and neglected, it seemed that the glory of Langley had died with the '15, until in 1882 Mr. C. J. Bates, the historian to whom Northumberland owes so much, bought the estate. Mr. Bates restored Langley to its former state of a fourteenth-century castle. Today the castle is open to the public at certain times of the year, and the view from the battlements is magnificent. To the north stand out the jagged ridges of the Great Whin-Sill, and in the valley below the South Tyne winds its way to the meeting of the waters.

The restoration of Langley is as much a memorial to Mr. Bates as the chapel dedicated to his memory after his death in 1902. In the west tower of the castle is a bell which was once in the cathedral church of St. Nicholas in Newcastle. In the lawless days of Tynedale's past the bells of Langley would ring to warn the country people of approaching danger; today the bell is silent but the sound of the burn can be heard as it rushes through the steep ravine on its way to Haydon Bridge. The road from Langley to this stone-built village is bordered by tall trees, behind which rise the steep slopes of Homildon, as this range of hills is known.

Close to Haydon Bridge, at the farm of East Land Ends, is a little two-roomed cottage, where in 1789 a child was born who was to become famous as John Martin the artist. His best known picture, "The Plains of Heaven", is said to be a view of his native valley. As a boy, John Martin drew pictures in the sand by the banks of the South Tyne, and, for want of better material, painted pictures on calico. In the years to come the works of this village boy were sold for as much as £2,000! John Martin's education was composed of the three "Rs", but the fire of genius burned within him. Apprenticed to a coach-builder in Newcastle, he then became the pupil of an Italian, Boniface Musso, who when he left Newcastle for London took young Martin with him. Many of Martin's pictures are scenes from the Old Testament, "Belshazzar's Feast" being awarded a premium of £200 by the British Institution.

Not only did John Martin paint in oils, he was also an engraver and produced "Illustrations of Milton" for which he received 2,000 guineas. The inhabitants of Haydon Bridge appear to have been extremely indifferent towards their famous son, as when Martin wrote to the secretary of the Reading Room, offering the committee copies of his most famous pictures, the secretary failed to inform the members! Some years later the letter was discovered, and an acceptance sent which arrived on the day of the artist's death. It was in the year 1854 that the boy from Haydon Bridge died in the Isle of Man, where he is buried in Kirk Braddon churchyard. His only memorial in his native village is in the name of a street, John Martin Street.

Haydon Bridge is a large straggling village, famous for its excellent school "The Shafto Trust". A grammar school was founded in 1685 by deed of the Reverend John Shafto and in 1879 reorganized by the Charity Commissioners. Within the last few years the school has become a technical school and draws its pupils from a wide agricultural area, specializing in subjects connected with farming. In 1950 a field day was declared open by Mr. R. D. Shafto of the old family whose best known member is the "Bobbie" of the folk song and who was born in the county of Durham at Spennymoor.

Bobbie Shafto's gone to sea,
Silver buckles at his knee,
He'll come back and marry me
Bonnie Bobbie Shafto.

John Martin was a pupil of the old grammar school.

One of the great events in the history of Haydon Bridge was the opening of the Newcastle and Carlisle Railway, or rather the continuation of it from Hexham to Carlisle. It was on the 28th of June 1836, the year before Queen Victoria ascended the throne, that two trains, one drawn by the engine "Hercules" and the second by the "Samson", left Blaydon at eleven o'clock with the directors and their friends. Shortly before two o'clock, having taken nearly three hours to travel twenty miles, the party arrived at Haydon Bridge! An old account says that flags were hoisted and guns fired to celebrate the occasion, and that the company spent a delightful day "without the slightest accident". More than twenty years later, Queen Victoria's son, the Prince of Wales, passed through Haydon Bridge station on the 19th of May 1857. In historical notes of the district the visit is described thus: "Among the passengers by the train which arrived at 11.45 a.m. from Carlisle was His Royal Highness, the Prince of Wales. He alighted from the train and went into the refreshment room where he partook of wine and biscuits. He also purchased some books from the stall of Mr. John Charlton, Station Master."

It is pleasant to record peaceful events in the history of the parish of Haydon, as, until the nineteenth century, the inhabitants lived dangerously, if they managed to survive at all. Even after the men of South Tynedale became more law-abiding, storms, tempests, floods and sudden deaths seem to have been the outstanding events recorded!

In 1323, a Charter was granted for a market and fair to be held in the village, but as these gatherings so often ended in brawls between various families, they did not add to the peace of the district.

In 1528 a band of Border raiders, Charltons, Dodds, Nobles and Armstrongs, were returning from a raid in the bishopric of Durham, where they had carried off the priest of Muggleswick. The Tyne was in flood and it was impossible to cross by the fords; an attempt to force the gate which stood at the end of the bridge failed, and the band of Raiders, who, judging by their names, were from the North Tyne valley, abandoned their horses on the south side of the river. Many were captured or killed by men led by an Errington, who was constable of Langley. Those who survived were later tried at Alnwick. Hanged from the gallows, their bodies were hung in chains as a warning that the wardens were determined to stamp out the perpetual raiding and lifting between, not only England and Scotland, but the various river valleys of Northumberland. The body of Noble was brought to Haydon Bridge. In spite of the rough justice meted out by the Wardens of the Marches, the raiding continued to flourish, and in 1587 Hunsden, the Queen's Commissioner, wrote to Lord Burghley; "If ever Mr. Ridley or Mr. Heron had done their duties, neither the barrency of Langley nor Hawden Brigges had been either burnt or spoylde for they had both warning of the Scottes coming in by a x j of the cloke in the forenoon, and yet neither of them sent any warning either to Hawden Brigges or Langley, being within iiij myle of Mr. Heron and two myle of Ridley". And later in the same letter "I have very vehement suspicions that Ridley himself, and some other English men have been acquainted with the drawers of the Scottes of Hawden Brigges, which if I find trewe, I will make them hop headless, whosoever they be". Even in 1619, Lord Walden is quoted as saying that "he cannot persuade honest people to live in South Tynedale!"

It was in 1632 that Sir Francis Radcliffe of Dilston bought the Langley barony, and more peaceful times dawned. Some of the rent rolls still survive and it is interesting to read the amounts charged for the rent of farms which are still in existence today. Peel Well, Lipwood Well and Whinnetly were £16 the half year! North of the village on the road to Grindon is a farm named "The Cruel Syke", which legend says ran red with blood after one of the many raids.

Till the cruel Syke wi Scottish blode rins rede,
Thoo mauna sowe corn by Tyneside.

North-west of Haydon Bridge at Chesterwood is one of the many buildings known in Northumberland as Pele houses, the lowliest form of Pele tower. Built for defensive purposes, these houses had accommodation for the cattle on the ground floor and room for the family above. From this arises the expression often heard among farmers of "bringing the cattle into the house". Many of the great castles were originally Pele towers. In the Pele tower at Chesterwood lived Frank Stokoe, the man who escaped from Preston Fight in 1715, and was one of those who helped to bring Lord Derwentwater's body home to Dilston.

Here, high above the valley, about two miles east of Chesterwood, is the old village of Haydon, from the Saxon word meaning an enclosure. It was from this old settlement that the village beside the bridge took its name. The village where the "new" church was built in 1796, and on which the old church at Haydon looks down. Dedicated to St. Cuthbert, it is said to have been one of the many resting places of the bones of the saint, which the monks carried throughout the northern counties for hundreds of years. Occasionally services are held in the old church in which, oddly enough, the font is made from a Roman altar. There is a great deal of doubt as to when this little church

Dilston Castle from which Derwentwater rode out in the '15

was originally built; if the bones of St. Cuthbert rested there, it must have been in existence before the saint found his last resting place in Durham Cathedral in 995. There is a gruesome legend connected with the old church given in detail in William Lee's *Haydon Bridge and District*. It is the old story of the girl who longed for finery which she could not afford. Watching the local tailor making a coat for her master at Altonside Farm, the girl pestered the tailor so much that at length he made a bargain with her. If she would go to the old church at Haydon at midnight and bring back the communion book from the altar, he would make her a coat which would enhance her charms in the eyes of her lover. Accordingly the girl carried out her share of the bargain, but, as she was leaving the church, she heard voices, and hiding behind the door she saw two men dragging what appeared to be a woman's body into the church and burying it under the flagstones. Running out of the church towards her home, the girl tripped and fell, and on recovering herself she saw by the light of the moon that she had tripped over what is described in the story as a "bowarrow", which she recognized as that of her lover! The next night when he came to visit her she showed him the incriminating evidence, at which he trembled like "an aspen leaf" and dramatically said "I bid you farewell, a long farewell". So the girl gained a new coat but lost her lover.

The parish of Haydon ends at the Whitechapel burn, where there stands a typical square Northumbrian farmhouse. It was here that the "Sketch from Whitechapel" was made in 1839. The old man who farmed Whitechapel was the writer's great-great-grandfather. Here on this road which links the cities of Carlisle and Newcastle, and three miles west of Haydon Bridge, a sign post points to "Ridley and Beltingham". There is a steep slope down to the bridge which spans the river, which branches off a "new road", constructed in the last century by the owners of Ridley Hall, as the slope up to the highway was too steep for the carriage horses. This is Ridley country; once the territory of that powerful clan who made their first appearance in Northumberland in the twelfth century: some say the name is derived from the riddling of the corn. These Ridleys, whose name appears so often in Border history, lost their land for their loyalty to Charles I in the Civil Wars. The old verse says:

> So fell the Ridley's ancient line,
> Lord Williams ancient towers,
> Fair Ridley by the silver Tyne,
> And sweet Thorngrafton's bowers.

The most famous of all the Ridleys was Nicholas, about whose birthplace there will always be controversy. Willimoteswick, that strangely

5

Blanchland—the perfect village

named Border tower, once the chief seat of the Ridley clan, stands south of the river at the end of the road from Ridley bridge and claims to be the birthplace of the man who became a martyr; but so does Unthank Hall, a little farther up the valley. There were Ridleys living at both places in the sixteenth century when Nicholas was born, and Ridleys who all had the same Christian names! Willimoteswick appears to have more claim than Unthank, but as there is even doubt about the year in which Nicholas was born, the exact place of the bishop's birth will never be known. There is no doubt whatsoever as to the date of his death. That martyr's death by which he achieved immortality. It was on an October day in 1555 that the man from South Tynedale walked to his death at Oxford. Where the martyr's memorial stands today outside Balliol, two men who held their principles dearer than life, Ridley and Latimer, died at the stake. Educated in the city of Newcastle upon Tyne, Nicholas Ridley eventually became Bishop of London, but with the accession of Mary Tudor Ridley had either to renounce the reformed religion or die, so he chose death. The words with which Bishop Latimer encouraged Ridley are immortal in the history of England: "Be of good comfort, Master Ridley and play the man, we shall this day light such a candle in England, as by God's grace shall never be put out".

In the ghastly manner of the times a bill was made, and rendered to the Government for the burning of the martyrs. It reads as follows:

For three loads of wood faggots for burning Ridley and Latimer—	12s.	
Item, one load of furze faggots—·	3s.	4d.
For the carriage of these loads—	2s.	
Item, a post—	1s.	4d.
„ two chains—	3s.	4d.
„ „ Staples.		6d.
„ Four labourers.	2s.	8d.
	25s.	2d.

Nicholas Ridley's last conscious thoughts were probably of the valley of the South Tyne, or the little chapel of Beltingham where he may have worshipped as a boy, as the church at Beltingham was originally a domestic chapel of the Ridley family.

Tucked away in this south-west corner of Northumberland remote and secluded time has passed Beltingham by. Standing halfway between Ridley bridge and Willimoteswick, the little church stands above a burn making it look like an island, and clustered round the green and the lych-gate are the few houses and the former school. This church, another dedicated to St. Cuthbert, was founded in Saxon days but little of the Saxon building remains. The church we know today was restored at the end of Queen Victoria's reign by the Honourable Francis Bowes-Lyon, who was an uncle of H.M. Queen Elizabeth the Queen Mother. The yew tree in the churchyard would be young when Nicholas Ridley died and the forefathers of men who sleep beneath its shade may well have cut their bows from it to draw at Flodden. The almost perfect leper's squint is still there, to remind us that in the dark ages the outcasts were banned from the house of God.

Sorrows and tribulations as well as happiness are welded into the fabric that is Beltingham. Now all is peace, the battles and feuds forgotten, and the quiet dead sleep on. The years may pass, but in this corner of Northumberland there is no change. The seasons come and go, the heather blooms on Morley Banks, and in the spring the herons build their nests in Ridley woods.

Leaving the peace of Beltingham behind, the road winds its way through the hamlet of Ridley, where above the door of the Pele house can still be seen the target, cut out of the stone, where the bowmen practised long ago. Over the bridge and onto the road west; through Bardon Mill to Henshaw, with its church, where alternate services with Beltingham are held. At Henshaw, in the old school known as "The Team Barns", the farmers used to bring their corn to thresh with flails. There is a new road now which by-passes the little hamlets, and Melkridge with its Pele house is now a quiet little spot; ahead the town of Haltwhistle climbs up its steep bank, the town famous in Border history for the raid at the end of the sixteenth century, when the Liddesdale men, led by the Armstrongs, got their own back on the men of South Tyne. "The Fray of Hautwessel" is graphically described in verse:

> The limmer theives o' Liddesdale
> Wadna leave a kye in the hail countrie,
> But an' we gie them the cauld steel
> Our gear they'll reive it a' awaye;
> Sae pert they stealis I you say;
> O' late they came to Hautwessel,
> And thowt they there wad drive a fray,
> But Alec Ridley shot too well.

In the strange manner of those days, the opposing sides played a game of football before slaughtering one another!

In the church of the Holy Cross, there is a tombstone, six feet long, of John Ridley of the Walltown, brother-in-law of the martyr. It is significant that Alec Ridley who "shot too well" has not a memorial within the church! The Ridleys were not all of the same calibre as the bishop, and it is on record that one of the clan, John, in 1627 made a stackyard in the churchyard. It is rather surprising that he is described in the records as a "gent" of the parish of Haltwhistle. The church is delightful, whatever John Ridley may have done in the churchyard. The oldest part dates from the twelfth century. An effigy of a member of the ancient family of Blenkinsopp is in the chancel. Unfortunately most of the Parish records were destroyed and only go back to about 1700.

How Haltwhistle derived its name will always remain a mystery. There are many theories. "The Holy Hill of the High Water", or "The High Watch Hill or Beacon" are two possible sources, but it is noteworthy that the old people pronounce it as it was in the days of the famous "Raid of Hautwessel". The old tower of Haltwhistle was in a dilapidated condition, and in spite of many efforts on the part of people who wished to preserve the history of the town, it has been demolished and a bungalow built on the site.

It is to the credit of the fighting spirit of the people of south-west Northumberland, led by the then member of Parliament for Hexham, Sir Rupert Speir, that the branch line to Alston has survived until now. This short railway journey is one of the loveliest in the whole country, sweeping over the viaducts at Haltwhistle and Lambley to its terminus at Alston. This is the land of the castles, of Bellister, Featherstone and Blenkinsopp. The land of ghosts and legends handed down through the centuries until they have almost become accepted as facts . . . the White Lady walks at Blenkinsopp; the Grey Man at Bellister; and close to Featherstone, in Pinkingscleugh, the burn runs red with blood on the anniversary of one of the many dark deeds which took place in the "Good Old Days".

A little way south-west of Haltwhistle stands Bellister Castle on a rocky eminence which at some time has been surrounded by a moat. The Blenkinsopp family owned Bellister as early at 1470, and the ruins of it have now been incorporated in a fairly modern house.

The grisly legend of the Grey Man is of a wandering minstrel who called at the castle in the dim and distant past and was given food and hospitality by the then lord of the castle. Regretting his generosity and suspicious that the minstrel was a spy sent by one of his enemies, the Lord of Bellister's manner became extremely cold. The minstrel, realizing that he was no longer a welcome guest and fearing danger, left the castle as quickly as possible. This abrupt departure convinced the Lord of Bellister that his suspicions had been justified, and he ordered his retainers to let loose his bloodhounds. The poor old man was torn to pieces by the hounds near some willow trees on the banks of the Tyne. The ghost of the victim haunted the cruel lord for the rest of his earthly existence.

Blenkinsopp's castle has fallen on hard times. In recent years it has been severely damaged by fire and little but the shell remains. In 1339,

Thomas de Blenkinsopp obtained the royal licence to fortify his manor house of Blenkinsopp. To quote Hodgson, the great authority, "The old family residence stood on the right bank of the hope or valley of Glenwhelt; prior to the Conquest it had probably belonged to one Blencan, from whom the place and township derived its name, for in the oldest writings it is called Blencan, or Blenkenshope". At Blenkinsopp there is a secret passage which is supposed to lead to the neighbouring stronghold of Thirlwall, on the Tipalt Burn.

The castle remained in the possession of the family from which it takes its name until 1772, when Jane, the heiress, married William Coulson of Newcastle. The Coulsons sold Blenkinsopp to the Joicey family, who have also disposed of the castle, and now live at the nearby Blenkinsopp Hall. Though the castle has passed through many vicissitudes, the ghost of the White Lady remains, whoever the owners may be, searching for the traditional chest of gold, which she had hidden from her lord and master. One can hardly blame the White Lady for her actions, as her lord, Bryan de Blenkinsopp, seems to have been a very mercenary character. He vowed at a drinking party that he would never marry unless his bride was so wealthy that it would take ten men to carry her dowry of gold into the castle. By some means or other, of which we are not told, the gentleman was lucky enough to find a lady with the required amount of gold. Unfortunately his bliss was short lived. The lady realized that she had been married for her money and hid the treasure in the castle grounds. Bryan, offended by his lady's behaviour, disappeared and was never heard of again. The lady, regretting her action, as they always seemed to do, became inconsolable and, after her death, continued to haunt the castle and will do so for all time unless someone has the temerity to follow her to the hiding-place and remove the chest of gold, the cause of all the trouble. Not to be outdone by the castle ghost, Blenkinsopp Hall has a black dog which appears if any member of the family is about to die.

The legends and tales of the great pile of Featherstone are even more horrifying, as in one case they are founded on fact. Featherstone today is one of the most impressive castles in Northumberland. Its setting, close to the ford across the Tyne which it guarded, is encircled by the steep hills which rise from the river and the bastion of Tynedale Fell. Sometime before the year 1200 there was a castle at Featherstone. There is mention of a Featherstonehaugh living there in 1212. In all its long history only five families have lived and owned the castle of the Featherstonehaughs, the original owners, who lost their estates in the Civil Wars, when like many Northumbrians they supported the cause of Charles I. Parliament sold the estates to the Earl of Carlisle, but, in 1711, a Featherstonehaugh who was mayor of Newcastle bought the estate of his ancestors. His son however, when he inherited an estate in Sussex, sold it to James Wallace, who eventually by marriage became a Hope-Wallace, and the Featherstone estate remained in the possession of the family until it became a school during the Second World War. It is now owned by Colonel John Clark, who has a long family connection with the district.

The "L"-shaped tower dates from 1330, and although extensive alterations were carried out during the ownership of the Hope-Wallace family, much that is old remains. There are a twelfth-century doorway and thirteenth-century buttresses, which are part of the old "Hall" house, and also a Jacobean postern door in a wonderful state of preservation. Some of the masonry bears Scottish craftsmen's marks.

In the sixteenth century, Richard Featherstonehaugh was a chaplain to Catherine of Aragon and, because of his loyalty to this first wife of Henry VIII, he was executed. Although the family of Ridley were no doubt involved in the murder of Sir Albany Featherstonehaugh, and "took his life by the Deadmanshaw", the verse of poetry from "Marmion", which is quoted at the beginning of this chapter, is not genuine. Surtees composed the lines but persuaded Sir Walter Scott that it was a traditional ballad handed down through the generations. Scott accepted the verse as genuine and by now many people have come to believe that it is!

Another dark chapter in the history of the Ridleys is connected with the family of Featherstonehaugh, and has become one of the best known legends. In Pinkingscleugh, at one time, dwelt a witch named Beardie Grey, who disappeared one stormy night after making the usual blood-thirsty prophecies. There can be seen at night a ghostly wedding party who were "set upon" by the Ridleys of Hardriding near Bardon Mill. The story is that in the old house at Hardriding there long ago lived a Hugh Ridley who was in love with the heiress of Featherstone Castle. The heiress's father had other ideas about a bridegroom for his daughter, and the girl, whose name was Abigail, was married, on her part most reluctantly, to a distant cousin. The Ridleys no doubt knew what was taking place in the little chapel at Featherstone, and they waited until the bridal party went on a hunting expedition as part of the celebrations. In the dark glen of Pinkingscleugh, the Ridley clan waited until the bridal party appeared. The intention was to carry off the bride to Hardriding but, like most of the plans of those days, everything went wrong, and the unfortunate bride, who threw herself between her bridegroom and her lover, was killed and Hugh Ridley, realizing what had happened, according to the story, "put an end to his existence".

A wild and bloody history, yet set in some of the most beautiful and romantic scenery in all Northumberland. Here are "the tumbling burns that run" the land described by Ada Smith, who was born in Haltwhistle and is buried at St. John Lee.

Oh, my heart is fain to hear the soft wind blowing,
Soughing through the tree tops up on northern fells.
Oh, my eye's an ache to see the brown burns flowing
Through the peaty soil and tinkling heather bells.

Beyond Featherstone, near Lambley, is the pathetic little site of the convent of Benedictine nuns, which was razed to the ground by the Scots in 1296. The farm of Wolf Hills near Coanwood is a grim reminder of the wild animals which terrorized this hill country long ago. Near the village of Slaggyford, dominated by the great mass of Williamstone Fell, the South Tyne chatters over its stony bed, past the little church of Kirkhaugh, which stands conspicuously alone in the middle of a field.

South Tynedale in Northumberland ends where the Gilderdale burn forms the county boundary. Tossed between England and Scotland and the last part of the county to become "English", the Scottish influence is still strong in south-west Tynedale, both in speech and custom, and, fight the "Old Enemy" though the South Tyne men did, there was a lot of ganging up with "Ye Scottes".

In the uplands of the South Tyne valley, where the blackfaced sheep thrive on the springy turf, the sheepdogs have the monosyllabic names of the district; Tyne, Moss and Glen have answered to their masters' whistles throughout the generations. At the South Tyne Show at Haltwhistle the blackfaced sheep come into their own. They are "gathered" in the autumn and there are few more lovely sights than the shepherds and their dogs bringing the sheep down from the hills.

In the late summer the hills that climb towards Allendale are purple with heather. Plenmeller Common sweeps on towards Whitfield, and down in the valley the river runs by Haydon Bridge, through Capon's Cleugh to Allerwash, where it is joined by the little burn which winds its way from Newbrough. This village became a "new burgh" in the reign of Henry III who granted a charter for a market to be held at Thornton, where the scanty remains of an old tower are today. In medieval times Edward I and his court spent nearly two months in this pleasant part of Northumberland before continuing their march to the west. The Roman road of Stanegate runs through Newbrough, the recently built old people's houses commemorating this fact in their name.

A great deal has been done to preserve the history of this district by the local Women's Institute, who, under the presidency of Mrs. Norman Newall, compiled a *Scrap Book* which traces the history and important events in the parish in word and picture.

Although housing estates have been built, Newbrough still retains its old world character, with its three "big" houses, and village inn

"The Red Lion". A stone beside the inn is said to be one of the boundary stones, originally Roman altars, which gave the nearby village of Fourstones its name. In a field near the church—which was rebuilt in 1865—is St. Mary's Well, believed at one time to have healing powers, and no reptile could live in its pure waters.

South Tyne is now nearing the end of its course from the Pennine hills: wide and shallow it runs over its stony bed under Warden Bridge to join the Water of Tyne.

V

NORTH TYNEDALE

On Kielder side, the wind blows wide,
There sounds nae hunting horn,
That rings sae sweet, as the winds that beat,
Round banks where Tyne is born.
                    A. C. Swinburne, A JACOBITE'S EXILE

In the wild country that was once part of the Middle March, the North
Tyne is born. In the desolate waste of Deadwater on the frontier
between England and Scotland, in the very heart of the "Raiding"
country, rises this lovely river. A river fed by the countless burns which
flow from the Cheviot Hills, it winds its way to join the South Tyne
at Warden Rocks, where the united rivers form the Tyne. Wild and
bloodthirsty is the history of North Tynedale, this land of the Four
Graynes as the four great families are known—the Charltons, Dodds,
Robsons and Milburns. From time immemorial men have borne these
surnames in North Tynedale. In 1870 Edward Charlton, M.D., published
a history of the Four Graynes, copies of which are still in existence.
The book is dedicated to "The Present Hedesman of the Foremost
Grayne, William Henry Charlton of Hesleyside".

Long ago in the days of the Great Elizabeth, Sir Robert Bowes made
a report upon the state of the Borders which cannot have given Her
Majesty a very good impression of her far Northern subjects!

In his report Sir Robert says: "The countreye of North Tynedaill
which is more plenished with wild and misdemeaned people, may
make of men upon horsbak and upon foote about six hundred. They
stand most by fower surnames, whereof the Charletons be the chiefe.
And in all services or charge impressed uppon that countrey the Charletons, and such as be under their rule, be rated for the one-half of that
country, the Robsons for a quarter and the Dodds and Mylbornes for
another quarter. Of every surname, there be certain families or graves
(graynes) of which there be certeyne hedesmen that leadeth and
answereth for all the rest." The government of the day must have been
thankful that there were only about six hundred of such "wild and
misdemeaned people".

The ancient stronghold of the "foremost grayne" was at Charlton,
near Bellingham. Nothing now remains of the Pele tower, but at

Hesleyside Hall Charltons still reign. West of Bellingham, on the south bank of the river, the oldest part of the house dates from the fourteenth century, though the lands of Hesleyside were Charlton property long before the tower was built. Many additions have been made throughout the centuries, but the house has yet to fulfil its destiny. According to an ancient curse, the home of the Charltons has to be burnt down three times, and then sink.

Two of the greatest treasures at Hesleyside are the famous Spur, and the original plans made by Capability Brown when he laid out the grounds in 1776.

In the Raiding days, when supplies were low in the larder, the lady of the house, instead of suggesting to the men of the family that it was time to ride out and "lift" some of their neighbour's sheep and cattle, used a much more subtle method. The Spur was placed on a dish or *assette* and was solemnly carried into the great hall. North Tyne men would need no encouragement to ride the foray and the lady of Hesleyside could be sure that her larder would soon be well filled with good Scottish beef and mutton.

The Spur of the Charltons measures about six inches and has been preserved by the family. This old Border custom is the subject of a painting by W. B. Scott and is at Wallington Hall, near the little village of Cambo. The Mrs. Charlton portrayed by Scott was, before her marriage, a Dodd. This is one of the many instances of inter-marriage between Northumbrian families and is a warning to strangers who enter the county never to make remarks about any particular family, as so many and interwoven are the relationships.

If the Charltons are the "first hedesmen", then Bellingham is the first town, in fact the capital of North Tynedale. A typical Border town, standing on the east bank of the river, it takes its name from the de Bellinghams, a family now extinct. The pronunciation "Bel-lingjum" is typical of the county, where every similar place-name is "jum", with the exception of Chillingham, which is too much of a tongue twister even for a Northumbrian.

St. Cuthbert's church must be one of the very few in the country which is roofed with stone. Legend has it that the Scots burnt down the church so many times that it was more economical to have a stone roof. Dating from the eleventh century, the church does not seem to have been very well patronized by the wild folk of the valley, if one can believe the old records of 1607. A communion service was held only once a year, the font was broken, the clerk could neither read nor write, and of Bibles and prayer books there were none!

One of the more notorious of the Charlton clan, "Bowrie", who was "out" in the '15, killed one of the Widdringtons in a quarrel near Buteland. The body of the unfortunate victim, it is said, was buried at the entrance to "Bowrie's" pew, and to enter it, the Charlton would have had to step over the grave of the murdered man. Bowrie, as the story goes, never entered the church again. This legend is open to question. The Charltons are one of the oldest Roman Catholic families in the county and, as the murder took place in 1711 long after the Reformation, if "Bowrie" had remained faithful to the old religion he would not have entered Bellingham church in any case!

The most famous legend connected with the church is that known as "The Long Pack". Many and varied are the versions of what happened in the eighteenth century, and the mystery has never been solved of the identity of the body which lies or, some say, was removed from the grave in Bellingham churchyard where the gravestone is in the shape of a pack. Nameless, with rude carvings of the packman's trade, the legend has stirred the imagination of generations. The generally accepted story is that in 1723 there was living at Leehall, a stone-built house between Wark and Bellingham, one of the many members of the Ridley family. This Colonel Ridley had ventured farther afield than most Northumbrians of his day and had amassed a fortune in India. Retiring home to his native land, he refurnished Leehall and, according to rumour, possessed plate valued at £1,000, a vast sum of money for those days. In the winter months, the colonel and his family spent their time in London, leaving behind at Leehall a small staff, which appears to have been rather short-sighted on the part of Colonel Ridley, as he must have been well aware of the reputation of the district for "lifting".

One afternoon a maid-servant, whose name was Alice, was alone in the house when a packman called. That would be no unusual occurrence in those days, but Alice had been given strict orders that no stranger was to be allowed to enter the house. In spite of the packman's pleadings and flattery, she refused him admittance, until at last, worn out by his entreaties, she agreed that he could leave his pack. The man said that he had tramped from Newcastle, and would return for his goods the next day.

Alone in the isolated house, Alice's nerves were on edge. There was something wrong about the pack she felt sure. It was dark by now and, lighting a candle, she examined the pack, which to her horror appeared to move. She rushed out of the house, shouting for help. The only two men about the place, Richard, an old retainer, and a young boy whose name was Edward, listened to her tale of the pack that was alive.

Richard was inclined to dismiss her story as imagination, but Edward, who possessed an old-fashioned gun, which he used for scaring crows, a gun which he had christened Copenhagen, seized his weapon and dashed into the parlour. It was literally a shot in the dark. The boy fired at the pack and immediately groans were heard, and blood gushed through the canvas. Horror stricken as they were, neither

Alice nor the two men lost their heads. Tearing open the pack, they found the body of a young man, a man who was dying. Beside him were four loaded pistols and a whistle. In the language of today, he was the "inside" man. Realizing that this was a plot to rob their master, the intrepid servants made a plan.

The next night, after dark, having gathered together all the able-bodied men they could find (there were no police in those days) and armed with all the weapons they could muster, the whistle was blown and very soon the sound of galloping horses was heard. There on the banks of the North Tyne a very different reception committee from the one they expected was awaiting the packman's confederates. Many men were killed on that dark and lonely night. The bodies of the dead were carried away by their accomplices, and next morning there was little evidence of the attempt to rob Colonel Ridley of his plate. Not one man involved in the plot was ever traced. It is said that there were many "moonlight flittings" and that several local men disappeared. It took a week before the owner of Leehall arrived from London to the scene of the tragedy, and the body of the man in the pack lay at Bellingham for a fortnight, but was never identified. Buried in a nameless grave, the mystery died with him, or is there substance in the story that the body was removed one night by friends of the dead man and that no body lies beneath the grave stone of "The Long Pack"?

Bellingham is not however living in the past. In the autumn, the little town is crowded by farmers from both sides of the Border for the Lamb Sales, and in September the Agricultural Show is held. Many of the officials and exhibitors bear the names of the Four Graynes. Now Charltons, Robsons, Dodds and Milburns show their horses and cattle instead of "lifting" them as they did in the old days. Many times has the story been repeated of the occasion when Robsons had been carrying off sheep from the Scottish side. Some say they were Elliot's and some Armstrong's flocks that were driven down the valley of the North Tyne, and when examined by their new owners were found to have scrapie. Back the Robsons drove the sheep over the Border, leaving a message "that the next time gentlemen came to lift sheep, would the Scots see that they had no disease!"

There is a sad story told in verse, of the trials and tribulations of a shepherd who celebrated a visit to the show, but not wisely, and eventually ended up in the Police Station. The last line tells us pathetically that "He'll gan nae mair back to the Bellingham Show". Before his troubles began the old man started off in great style:

> A's an auld shepherd an A' live oot-bye,
> An a' seldom see out but the sheep and the kye,
> So a' ses to wor Betsy "a' think a' will go,

And hev a bit look at the Bellingham Show."
"Aweel" says the auld wife "if thou's money to spare,
Nae doot its alang time sin ye hae been there."
But the pack lambs selt weel, they've alang time been low,
So A' think A' will gan to the Bellingham Show.

Unlike the unfortunate shepherd, people return year after year to
the show. Elliots and Armstrongs have long forgotten the Robson
feud, and Scottish pipers come from over the Border, many of them
descendants of the men who long ago would never have crossed to
the English side unless they carried back with them Northumbrian
cattle and sheep. The only time there was peace in the Border Country
was in the hay time, when they won their meagre crops of hay and
then, with the Hunter's Moon, the Raiding season opened. Now, instead of riding the raid, the hardy men of the Borders ride with the
North Tyne Foxhounds, which hunt the wild moorlands. There is
some evidence that Robsons were hunting the North Tyne country
in 1720. Members of the Dodd family were masters until 1878. These
men would scarcely recognize their country now, so changed has it
been by the huge forests planted by the Forestry Commission. The once
bare hills are now covered with spruce, many of the huge sheep farms
have disappeared and, lovely though the acres of forest are, they are
an ever present source of regret to the sheep-farmers and the fox-
hunters.

Changed though the scenery is from Bellingham to the Border at
Deadwater, this is still one of the loveliest of the Northumbrian valleys.
North of the grey little town, the Hareshaw Burn empties its waters
into the North Tyne, tumbling over the famous Linn, or waterfall,
which in the last century was a favourite place for picnics. In the wild
days of Border warfare, sometimes North Tynedale came under the
sovereignty of Scotland and sometimes of England; on occasions the
Scottish Courts were held on the English side. One of the few roads
into Scotland from the English side was up the valley of North
Tyne. The men of Hexham took this road on their way to sack Hawick
in 1514.

Ruined Pele towers, fortified farm houses, such as the old Gatehouse
at Tarset, were once the homes of the "wild and misdemeaned people"
who caused the Government so much trouble. Where Tarset Castle
once stood, only a mound remains. This castle once owned by the
Red Comyn, who was assassinated by Robert Bruce, was burnt in
1526. In the lawless fashion of those days, the North Tyne men drove
out of the castle Sir Ralph Fenwick and his men who had been sent
to hunt down and capture one of the South Tyne Ridleys, who was
involved in the murder of Sir Albany Featherstonehaugh. Led by a
Charlton, the Tarset men scattered the forces of Sir Ralph much to

"his great reproache" says the old chronicler. Ridley escaped from justice and Tarset Castle was in flames.

No wonder that until 1770 the good people of Newcastle refused to have any apprentices in the city who came from North Tynedale!

> Tarset and Tarret burn
> Hard and Heather bred,
> Yet-Yet-Yet.

The war cry of the Tarset men must often have struck terror into the hearts of their enemies. Tradition has it that there is an underground passage from Tarset to the nearby Dally Castle, which survives in name only. In one of the many ruined Pele towers, there lived one of the many Milburns who achieved notoriety as "Barty of the Comb". The Scots having made a successful raid on Barty's sheep, the angry Milburn and a crony, Corbit Jack, set off on a reprisal raid, and, lifting some wethers, they set off for home, but ran into a party of Scots on the way. In the skirmish Corbit Jack was killed and Barty wounded. By a superhuman effort Milburn slew his assailant, and, in Barty's own words, the head of the unfortunate Scot "sprang alang the heather, like an onion".

Now where these grim deeds took place the foresters are at work. New villages have been built to house the workers and their families; the population of the valley has increased since the days of about six hundred men on "horsbak and foote". At the head of the valley at Kielder is the headquarters of the Forestry Commission. The offices are in the castle, at one time used as a shooting box by the dukes of Northumberland.

Kielder too has its grim legend, "The Cowt of Kielder". This unfortunate young man, designated Cowt, tempted providence by riding "widdershins" (against the sun) three times round the Kielder Stone, a huge rock which is part of the Border line. The Cowt and his followers were captured by Sir William Soulis and taken to his stronghold of Hermitage in Liddesdale. Here all but the Cowt were bewitched, he having taken the precaution of wearing a sprig of rowan berries in his helmet. Galloping out of Hermitage, pursued by Soulis and his men, the Cowt reached the Liddle Water where he lost his rowan berries. The Soulis men held the wretched young man under the water until he drowned and the pool in Liddle Water is still known as the "Cowt of Kielder's Pool". Retribution overtook the wicked Lord Soulis in a most terrible form; his enemies boiled him alive in a lead cauldron at The Nine Stane Rig.

Every village and hamlet, every burn in the upper reaches of the North Tyne has its grim history or legend. Falstone, Thorneyburn, and Plashetts have been the scenes of many a fray. On the banks of the

Kielder burn, on the Lewis and Chirdon burns, men have fought and died. North Tyne was one of the last of the valleys to be subdued. Now part of the National Park of Northumberland, its boundaries marked by signs bearing the picture of a curlew, North Tyne is peaceful, though as the forest extends there are rumours that as in Ridsdale the wild cats are coming back. The influence of Scotland is strong; in nearly every village is a Presbyterian church. No more when the moon is full do the raiders ride the foray, so vividly described in a verse of W. H. Ogilvie's Ballad:

> Last night a wind from Lammermoor
> Came roaring up the glen
> With the tramp of trooping horses
> And the laugh of reckless men,
> And struck a mailed hand on the gate,
> And cried in rebel glee,
> Come forth! Come forth! my Borderer,
> And ride the March with me!

Long before the raiders, prehistoric man had built his rude settlements and camps, and in the lower stretches of the river from Bellingham to Chollerford, especially in the Gunnerton and Barrasford districts, are remains of the first inhabitants of North Tynedale. The scenery in the lower reaches has a different kind of beauty, the valley widens and the river, fed by its many tributaries, receives the waters of the Rede, at the little hamlet of Redesmouth. The scenery is treeless and somewhat barren until the once important town of Wark is reached, where the Wark and Houxty burns add their waters to the Tyne.

In medieval times, Wark was the capital of North Tynedale. The Courts of the Liberty of Tynedale were held on the Mote Hill, an easily defended position used for their councils by the Celts. From Wark, a road leads to the delightfully named Roses Bower, once a stronghold of the Milburns. High above Wark, across the river, is the village of Birtley, which commands glorious views of the Roman Wall country, and northwards, the hills which are climbing towards the Border. At Birtley are the extensive remains of Early British camps, which, with Countess Park near Redesmouth are some of the most important earthworks in the county. North Tyne's most magnificent castles, Chipchase and Haughton are close to Wark. Chipchase, with its peculiar name meaning "the market" within the hunting ground or chase, is the most beautiful Jacobean house in the county. The original castle, of which only a tower remains, was built in the fourteenth century, possibly by one of the then great family of Umfraville. It passed by marriage into the hands of another ancient and powerful family, the Herons, one of whom, Sir George, a keeper of Tynedale, was killed in the last great Border fray, the Raid of the Redeswire, in 1575. One of the more unusual legends is that after the raid, the victorious Scots made presents of falcons to the English prisoners, in return, the Scots said, for dead herons! At the end of the seventeenth century, Chipchase was sold. It was in the reign of James I that the Jacobean manor house was built. Since those days there have been various additions; the most interesting being the beautiful little chapel in the grounds. Chipchase is now the property of Colonel Taylor.

Lower down the river and on the opposite bank, close to the attractive village of Humshaugh, is the mighty fortress of Haughton, one of the oldest inhabited castles in Northumberland. Haughton dominates the scene; battlemented and romantic, it is the fairy-tale castle come true. A "hall" house was built here before the castle. Sometime in the fourteenth century, the building of Haughton Castle began. Its first owners were the Swinburnes, one of whom, William, was treasurer to Margaret, queen of the Scottish King, Alexander III. Haughton's owners after the Swinburnes were the Widdringtons, another of the old county families.

Battered and burnt by the Scottish Armstrongs, with the aid of some Northumbrians who were as usual involved in a feud against the lords of the castle, Haughton's history is a stormy one, which was the lot of all the Border strongholds. Falling into ruin, deserted and neglected until the end of the eighteenth century, passing through the hands of various owners, the castle was bought in the nineteenth century by an industrialist, the late Mr. W. D. Cruddas. It is due to the Cruddas family that Haughton regained its former glory, and it is difficult to believe that a great deal of the castle has been rebuilt, so cleverly have the restorations been carried out.

In the reign of Henry II an agreement was entered into, for a ferry to ply to and fro across the river, to connect Haughton with the village of Barrasford. From that day Haughton Ferry has been operated by a rope and a pulley! This is one of the many places which claim to have been the setting that inspired the Northumbrian folk song "The Water of Tyne".

Haughton's legend is quite the most blood curdling of all the grim tales of North Tynedale. No two versions are alike, even the date and chief characters change with the different accounts, but it is still widely believed by local people that the castle is haunted by the ghost of an Armstrong who was captured either by a Widdrington or a Swinburne, according to whichever version is accepted. Armstrong had been caught "lifting" and was thrown into the dungeon to await his fate—to hang from the Gallows Tree, when the rough justice of the Border would be meted out: "Hang a man first, and try him afterwards"! Such was "Jethart" (Jedburgh) justice.

A sketch of a Northumbrian farmer from Whitechapel,
near Bardon Mill, 1839

I. Dickinson, lithog

Whoever the owner of Haughton was, he set off for London taking with him the key of the dungeon. On discovering what he had done, this man, who must have had more humanity than was usual in those days, turned his horse north, in the hope that he would reach Haughton before his prisoner had died of starvation. Riding three horses until they dropped (it is always three horses in the best legends) he at last reached Haughton. When the door of the dungeon was opened, there lay the body of Archie Armstrong. Maddened by hunger, he had gnawed the flesh from his arms!

In the last century servants were terrified to come to Haughton, as they believed that the screams of Archie Armstrong could be heard coming from the dungeon. The rector of Simonburn was called in to exorcize the ghost. Of all the lengends, surely this is the most horrible. Does the ghost of Archie still walk, or has his uneasy spirit found rest in the hills of his native Liddesdale? None will ever know.

Simonburn, from where the rector came to exorcize Archie's ghost, is the most beautiful village in all North Tynedale. Surrounded by trees, the houses cluster round the green. Simonburn's character is softer and gentler than the usual Border village. The church, dedicated to St. Mungo, was rebuilt in 1860, but much of the original fabric is still to be seen. Simonburn possesses what are rarely found in Northumberland, effigies dating from the seventeenth century. These are of Cuthbert Ridley, D.D., and his children. It is a relief to know that there were some respectable members of that notorious clan!

The Allgood family of nearby Nunwick have been generous supporters of St. Mungo's church; the beautiful lych-gate is a gift of the Allgoods.

Near Simonburn is one of the many Linns of North Tynedale, on the Teckett Burn. A local poet, Robert Roxby, wrote in praise:

> From winsome Wark to Simonburn
> The trouty streams are fine.

North Tynedale is now merging into Roman Wall country, the valley is wide, the river deep, winding its way by Barrasford, past the trout hatcheries from which the river is restocked; past Humshaugh, with its stone-built houses, on towards the bridge at Chollerford. Hidden away, off the beaten track, there is much that is lovely yet to explore. On the Barrasford side of the river, the road from The Five Lane Ends, passes the entrance gates to Swinburne Castle, a castle which has long disappeared—none of the original structure is left. A manor house was erected at Swinburne, in the seventeenth century and is the property of the Riddell family. The Swinburnes, whose name occurs so often in Northumbrian history, took their name from the nearby burn, the "Swin" or "Swine" burn. The reservoirs of the

6

Haughton Castle—a North Tyne fortress

Newcastle and Gateshead Water Company break the bleakness of the wild moorlands at Hallington and Colt Crag, the stretches of water adding variety to the landscape.

The old North British Railway which ran from Hexham up the valley and over the Border is no more. Even the track has been pulled up and only the piers of the Border counties bridge are left, the bridge that carried "The Scotch Express" across the Tyne, just west of Hexham. No longer do the children run out to wave to the passengers who once travelled on one of the loveliest railway lines in the British Isles.

Early Britons, Roman soldiers, reivers and mosstroopers, "The Four Graynes", have all played their part in the history of North Tyne. Castles and Pele towers, peaty streams and heather-clad hills, farms and forests, legends and bloody Border history have inspired writers and poets, from the doggerel of "Bellingham Show" to the incomparable verse of Swinburne. George Pickering of Simonburn wrote poetry which Burns said he would have given ten pounds to have composed himself. One of the "hedesmen", Wing Commander Charlton, in his *Recollections of a Northumbrian Lady* brings vividly to life the Hesleyside of long ago.

Robsons, Dodds, Charltons and Milburns; names inseparable from the life of North Tynedale, the dry humour of the Northumbrian breaking through the most serious situation. A Robson, when caught red-handed "removing" someone else's sheep and asked who he was, replied, "My name is Robson, I come of a very honest family, but we go in for a bit of shifting". Good British understatement, coming from a reiver.

Until the reign of Henry VII the king's writ did not run in the lawless valley of the North Tyne.

A Charlton of Leehall, at war with Will Lowes of South Tynedale, met his adversary near Sewingshields. Charlton tried to stab Lowes, but missed his enemy and stabbed the horse instead. A ditty commemorating the episode is typical of the Tynedale men, whether North or South:

O, kensta Will Lowes,
O, kensta Leeha'
O, kensta Will Lowes,
The flower o' them a'.

O' had Leeha' been but a man,
As he was never nean,
He wad hae stabbed the rider,
And let the horse alean.

The wardens of the Middle March had one of the toughest posts the Crown could offer. North Tyne men took the law into their own hands and settled their quarrels in their own war-like fashion. Watching the fords, twenty-four hours of the twenty-four in the raiding season, were the setters and searchers. The numerous Gallows Hills are grim reminders of the fate of many a Border raider.

Slaughtering as many cattle as they could spare in the back end, and salting the beef; driving stock into "the house" and seeing in the sky the reflections of the fires where the Pele towers were burning; these things made up the life of a Borderer. Long after the Union of the Crowns and even after the Treaty of Union, lifting was still going on. North Tyne men were no better and no worse than their neighbours, be they Scotsmen or Northumbrians; it was a hard rough life and only the fittest survived.

When the Hunter's Moon is full in October, perhaps the ghosts of men long dead gather, and under the leadership of their chiefs are ready to ride, as they did so long ago. "A Charlton", "A Robson", "A Dodd", "A Milburn", the gathering cries of the Graynes may echo up the lonely glens.

> Over the Borderland, wha' will gan wi' us,
> Saddle your horses an' buckle your blades,
> We will bring back wi' us fat Scottish cattle,
> Good Scottish horses and fair Scottish maids.

From Deadwater to Warden Rocks the North Tyne raiders have written their names on the pages of Northumbrian history.

VI

THE NORTHUMBRIAN COAST

We'll see nae mair, the seabanks fair,
And the sweet grey gleaming sky,
And the lordly strand of Northumberland,
And the goodly towers thereby.

A. C. Swinburne, A JACOBITE'S EXILE

From the mouth of Tyne to beyond Berwick upon Tweed, stretches the "lordly strand of Northumberland", more than seventy miles of the most glorious coastline in the whole country. Forty miles of it is preserved as scenery of unusual beauty. The memorial to Admiral Collingwood, Northumberland's greatest sailor, looks out across the mouth of the river, the industrial Tyne from which so many Tyne-built ships have sailed; while on the cliffs of Tynemouth stand the ruins of the priory, ruins of a once great monastic house, which was stripped of its glory during the Reformation. It was in 1539 that the last prior was compelled to surrender his priory to the Crown, and the work of destruction began. Now the ruins of the church, so boldly etched above the North Sea, are a landmark which is the last and first sight of home for many a seafaring "Geordie". In Scott's "Marmion", he describes the scenery of the Northumberland coast as seen through the eyes of the nuns, as they voyaged north from St. Hilda's Abbey at Whitby:

And now the vessel skirts the strand
Of mountainous Northumberland;
Towns, towers and halls, successive rise,
And catch the nun's delighted eyes.
Monkwearmouth soon behind them lay,
And Tynemouth's priory and bay;
They marked, amid her trees, the hall
Of lofty Seaton Delaval.
They saw the Blyth and Wansbeck floods
Rush to the sea through sounding woods;
They pass'd the tower of Widdrington,
Mother of many a valiant son;
At Coquet-isle their beads they tell
To the good saint who owned the cell;

Then did the Alne attention claim,
And Warkworth proud of Percy's name;
And next they crossed themselves, to hear
The whitening breakers sound so near,
Where, boiling through the rocks, they roar
On Dunstanburgh's caverned shore;
Thy tower, proud Bamburgh, marked they there
King Ida's castle, huge and square,
From its tall rock look grimly down,
And on the swelling ocean frown,
Then from the coast they bore away,
And reached the Holy Island's Bay.

Many of the goodly towers and castles are now in ruins; of the great castles only Bamburgh has been restored to its former glory, but the scenery, from beyond Blyth, has changed very little since those long ago days which Scott so graphically describes. The golden miles of sandy beaches have mercifully been spared the fate of many of the better known coast lines of the south country, which have been commercialized and littered with caravan sites and "Olde Tea Shoppes". Now that the greater part of the coastline has been scheduled as being of unusual beauty, its character will be preserved and saved from the despoilers of the twentieth century.

Part of the great coalfield of Northumberland fringes the coast for some miles, but even the collieries cannot spoil the glorious natural scenery of this part of the once mighty kingdom of Northumbria. When the little port of Amble is left behind (which is situated at the apex of the triangle of industrial Northumberland) there is nothing man-made to mar the beauty of this incomparable coast. Ugly though the colliery districts undoubtedly are, without the coalfield Northumberland would not have enjoyed prosperity and, unlike many of the industrial areas in England, the industry does not spread over the county. It is concentrated within the triangle which stretches from Amble to north-west of the city of Newcastle. Close to the coast, near Seaton Delaval, at Hartley New Pit, occurred the greatest colliery disaster in the history of the Northumberland coalfield. It was in 1862 that 204 men and boys lost their lives in the Hartley Pit disaster. Many times has the tragedy been described, when on Thursday, the 16th of January, while men were going down below in the cage, a beam which supported the pumping engine at the pit-head, snapped and crashed down the shaft, entombing the men below. For days the rescue parties struggled to free the trapped men. When they did manage to clear the shaft, it was too late. The black damp, locally known as "stythe" had done its dreadful work. A pathetic poem was written by Joseph Skimpsey, a miner himself:

> Oh, father, till the shaft is rid,
> Close, close beside me keep;
> My eyelids are together glued,
> And I, and I must sleep.

A fitting epitaph, from a man who knew only too well what his "marrers" had suffered while they waited below for the rescue that came too late. The word "marrer" referring to the man a pitman works beside, is still in everyday use.

The Industrial Revolution, which was to leave in its train disasters such as that at New Hartley, was hundreds of years ahead when, in about the year A.D. 627, the first Christian king of Northumbria, King Edwin, built a chapel of wood on the Tynemouth headland. Destroyed by the Danes in one of their many invasions of the north-east coast, the little church was in ruins until the eleventh century, when monks from Jarrow on the Durham side of the Tyne started the building of the priory, which they dedicated to St. Mary and St. Oswyn. It was here that Oswyn, King of Deria (the old name for Northumbria south of the Tees) who was later canonized, was buried in 651. The Scottish king, Malcolm Canmore, who was killed at Alnwick, and his son Edward were buried within the precincts of the priory in 1094. Ironically, David of Scotland, when he invaded Northumberland in 1138, held the monks of Tynemouth to ransom and, to save their possessions, they had to hand over a large amount of money to the Scottish king!

Two queen consorts of England, the wives of the first two Edwards, came to Tynemouth and it was from here that Edward II and the imposter, Piers Gaveston, fled to Scarborough. Legend and history have gathered round the ruins of Tynemouth's priory and castle; the castle of which little remains. Barracks, now removed, were built on the foundations, though an original gateway has survived. The castle was built as a source of protection for the priory. After the Dissolution of the Monasteries, the fortifications were strengthened, the function of the castle and garrison then being to guard the mouth of the Tyne. In the Civil Wars, Charles I inspected the garrison, but in 1644 the Scottish armies under General Leven attacked the castle and the garrison, which was at the time suffering from the plague, surrendered. The fighting days of Tynemouth Castle were over, and from 1681 onwards it fell into decay. Tynemouth is an attractive place today, with some beautiful old houses, and the charming King Edward's Bay.

The long sands stretch towards Cullercoats and Whitley Bay, where on St. Mary's Island is one of the many lighthouses, which guide the ships along the Northumberland coast. Beautiful though the coast is, there are treacherous rocks such as the notorious Black Middens at Tynemouth, where many a ship has foundered. The fisherwives, in their distinctive costume, no longer sell the catch at the cottage doors in Cullercoats. The row of fishermen's houses has been demolished in very recent times. Cullercoats has a lovely bay, but the character of the old village has disappeared, and Whitley Bay is what was described at one time as a seaside "resort", a resort which is extremely popular with visitors from Glasgow. Between Whitley Bay and the port of Blyth the most interesting place is Seaton Sluice. A favourite haunt of artists in the past, Seaton Sluice with its red roofs and artificial "sluice", constructed at the instigation of Sir Ralph Delaval, was at one time a thriving port, defended by a battery. Now the neighbouring collieries are "worked out" and Seaton Sluice has a forlorn and neglected appearance. Close to this once picturesque village is one of Northumberland's greatest houses, Seaton Delaval Hall, the seat of a powerful family, who by their extravagances and eccentric behaviour gained the title of "The Gay Delavals". Their story has been told countless times by historians and novelists. The line of the Delavals has died out on the male side, but through a marriage with the Astley family, a descendant of "The Gay Delavals", Lord Hastings, is the owner of the hall today and improvements and restorations are in progress. On certain days, this Vanbrugh masterpiece is open to the public.

The Delavals are first mentioned in Northumbrian history in 1121, and until 1818 they held lands in various parts of the county. Related through marriage to William the Conqueror, this ancient family was of Norman descent. A Delaval was present at the signing of the Magna Charta. It was in the eighteenth century that the escapades of the Delavals made the family notorious. The last "respectable" member appears to have been Admiral George Delaval, the man who employed the architect, Sir John Vanbrugh, to build his great house at Seaton Delaval. Of the original house of this Norman family, no trace remains. Standing at the end of the long avenue, from which the sea is visible, is today the finest example left of Vanbrugh's work in the North of England. Northumbrians say it is even finer than Yorkshire's Castle Howard! Unfortunately the hall was badly damaged by fire in 1752 and 1882, and some of Vanbrugh's work was destroyed. Built between 1718 and 1729, both the admiral and the architect died before it was finished. From then on until the death of Edward Hussey Delaval, who led a much more exemplary life than his immediate predecessors, the gay Delavals laid the foundations of the many legends connected with their name.

The latter part of the eighteenth and the early part of the nineteenth centuries was the age of practical jokes, in which "gentlemen" of the times indulged, but the Delaval's ideas of jokes shocked even the sophisticated society of their day. When house parties were entertained at Seaton Delaval, after the guests had staggered to their rooms the ingenious host, who had had pulleys attached to the beds and trap doors conveniently placed underneath, plunged the astonished guests into baths of cold water! Other contraptions were collapsible walls between the bedrooms, and lords and ladies, often wigless and in a state of dishabille, were horrified to find themselves facing their equally embarrassed fellow guests. An invitation to a Delaval house party must have struck terror into the hearts of the recipients. Many invitations must have been declined on the ever convenient grounds of ill health.

Four of the daughters of the house were famous beauties, the most beautiful being Lady Tyrconnel whose portrait hangs at Seaton Delaval today. Naturally such a famous house has a ghost, a ghost which unfortunately for the romantically minded is an optical illusion. A small room which overlooks the courtyard is named "The Ghost Chamber", and here can be seen the Grey Lady. When the sun is setting, it strikes a piece of broken glass which strangely reflects the figure of a woman onto the window. Poor Grey Lady watching and waiting for the return of an unfaithful lover. The church, dedicated to Our Lady and known as St. Mary's, is a wonderful example of Norman architecture and contains interesting effigies and memorials to the family, a family which on many occasions met with tragic deaths. In the park is a mausoleum to the memory of John Delaval, who died in 1775 when he was only twenty. A stone obelisk is said to mark the place where a Delaval was thrown from his horse and killed. The Gay Delavals are now a legend, but their lovely house lives on.

North of Blyth, the River Wansbeck empties its waters into the North Sea, the only "beck" in the county. Beyond the conspicuous Newbiggin Point is the village of Cresswell, from which another of the old Northumbrian families takes their name, the Cresswells of Cresswell. This family has been in the district since the reign of King John. The fortified tower which bears their name looks out over the magnificent curve of Druridge Bay. A short distance inland is the village of Widdrington, associated with another of the oldest families in Northumberland. Nothing is left of the old tower, crenellated in 1341 by Gerard de Widdrington. When James VI of Scotland crossed the Border to become James I of England, his first halt, after he left the town of Berwick, was at Widdrington.

The great bay of Druridge ends at Hauxley Point, and out to sea lies Coquet Island, an island at the mouth of the River Coquet, where, long ago in A.D. 684, an abbess of Whitby met the greatest of the Northumbrian saints, St. Cuthbert. Where the cells of the Benedictine monks once stood is now the modern lighthouse. At Amble the coalfield ends and a short distance up the River Coquet is the historic and beautiful village of Warkworth. Standing at the top of Castle Street are the ruins of the once great castle where so many of the scenes in Shakespeare's *Henry IV* were set. This was the home of the Percys; nearby Alnwick was the fortress. Here at Warkworth lived the most famous of them all, Harry Hotspur. There was a castle at Warkworth in 1139, but it is with the house of Percy that the history of Warkworth, like that of Alnwick, begins. Edward III bestowed the castle and surrounding lands on the second Lord Percy of Alnwick, and until the eclipse of the family, when they disappeared from the Northumbrian scene for two centuries, it was their home. Here during the Wars of the Roses, Queen Margaret is said to have found shelter, and tradition says it was from this part of the coast that she escaped to France in a fishing boat.

With the return of the Percys to Northumberland in the eighteenth century, the work of restoration began. It was undecided for some time whether Alnwick or Warkworth was to be their principal seat. The decision was in favour of Alnwick, and Warkworth's castle was left in ruins. In this century some rooms in one of the towers have been made habitable for members of the family. Ruined Warkworth Castle may be, but in the springtime when the daffodils are ablaze on its grass grown fortifications, it is one of the loveliest sights imaginable. The little town has never lost its character, the fortified bridge over the river, which bears the Percy arms, has narrowly escaped the executioner's axe of twentieth century "progress". This is one of the few fortified bridges in England. In the church of St. Lawrence which was founded in Saxon times, a terrible massacre occurred in 1174. The Scots, under Earl Duncan, put to death men, women and children who had taken refuge within its walls. In the church, which was built upon the Saxon foundations, the Jacobite army in 1715 attended a service. The then vicar of Warkworth refused to pray for "James III" and the service was conducted by a chaplain of the Rebel army.

The land beside the river, where at one time the bowmen may have practised on the south bank, is known as "The Butts". The river scenery at Warkworth is some of the loveliest in all the course of the Coquet. The wooded banks rise steeply from the river. High above is the famous Hermitage, which is reached by a flight of steps. A door cut in the rock leads to three rooms, the chapel, the confessional and the dormitory. The ceiling is groined and there is an effigy of a female figure. Bishop Percy has told the story of the Hermit of Warkworth in verse, which is the old, old story of the maiden whose pride led to her death. A daughter of the house of Widdrington, she was loved by Sir Bertram of Bothal. Bertram was dining with Lord Percy at Alnwick when he received a message from Isabel Widdrington, that she would not marry him until he had proved himself in battle. As there was always plenty of fighting going on in the Border country, Percy and Bertram set off for Scotland. Bertram was wounded in a fray and taken to the castle of Wark on the Tweed. Isabel, hearing of her lover's misfortune and regretting her challenge, left the Tower of Widdrington to make the journey to Tweedside. On the way she was captured by a

Scotsman who had also wished to marry her, and imprisoned in his Pele tower. The news reached Wark, and Bertram, having recovered from his wounds, was determined to rescue Isabel. When he reached the place of her captivity, he heard her voice as she was leaning from a window and he saw a man in Highland dress climbing up the wall of the tower. Bertram, assuming the worst (no one ever seems to have been given the benefit of the doubt in those days) drew his sword, and as Isabel and the Highlander descended by a rope ladder, Bertram killed the man with his sword. Like all the best heroines of legend, the unfortunate girl had thrown herself in front of the dying man who, as she tried to make the lord of Bothal understand, was her brother. Bertram, who seems to have been more than usually impulsive, refused to believe her, and Isabel, now bleeding to death from wounds she had received while trying to save her brother, died at her lover's feet. Not unnaturally overcome by remorse, Bertram gave away all his possessions to the poor and hewed the cave above the Coquet, and spent the rest of his life in penitence for his rashness. More prosaic writers are of the opinion that the Hermitage was the work of one of the Earls of Northumberland. Bishop Percy's ballad gives the more romantic version.

A very different little town from Warkworth is Alnmouth, which stands at the mouth of the river which rises far away in the Cheviot hills, flows through the parklands of Alnwick and gives its name to Alnmouth, the old pronunciations of which are "Alemouth" and "Yellmouth". Alnmouth is at its best when the tide is in, and seen from the north it has the appearance of an island. Red-roofed, with the grey stonebuilt houses which withstand the winds that blow off the North Sea, Alnmouth is completely unspoiled. The notorious pirate Paul Jones attempted to bombard the little town from the sea. In the old days, Alnmouth was the port for Alnwick, and a place of importance. Saxon remains have been found in the district. In 1789, the shaft of a Saxon cross was unearthed on Church Hill. Alnmouth claims, with other places in Northumberland, to have been the scene of the Synod held in 684, when St. Cuthbert was elected Bishop of Lindisfarne. The course of the river has changed in the last two hundred years, and many other changes have taken place in the years since Alnmouth was a busy port, exporting large quantities of corn. In 1850, the railway station was Lesbury, later Bilton Junction and eventually Alnmouth. In the year 1850, Queen Victoria was travelling by train to Berwick to open the Royal Border Bridge. The inhabitants of Alnmouth and district called a meeting and, to quote from the Record of the Proceedings, "resolved that an humble address be presented from this ancient borough, (which had its existence in the days of Her Majesty's Saxon ancestors) to her Majesty Queen Victoria on her passage through this parish". Much time and thought must have been spent in the composition of the verbose address, which was eventually presented to the queen by a deputation, consisting of "Mr. William Dickson, chairman, Mr. Downes, Lieut. R.N. Mr. John Young, Mr. Robert Simpson and Mr. Patrick Thorp Dickson". The excitement in Alnmouth on the 29th of August, 1850 must have been tremendous. When news was received that the royal train was at Newcastle, a message was sent from Lesbury station by "electric telegraph". Five minutes later a message reached the deputation on the station platform to say that the queen herself would receive the address. At two o'clock, the pilot engine puffed its way into the gaily decorated station, closely followed by the royal train itself. Sir George Grey, Bt., a Secretary of State, presented the deputation to the queen and the address was handed over to Her Majesty who must have been somewhat astonished by its contents which read more like a lecture on how to rule the country than an address of welcome! Within a short time Victoria was to be busily engaged at Berwick, and so perhaps she never read the fulsome address where the references to "You Gracious Majesty" run into two figures. Copies of the address are still in existence and make delightful reading.

Very little remains of the Saxon church which gives its name to Church Hill. The later Norman church was in a bad state of repair in 1738 and was already a ruin, which was finally destroyed by a gale which swept the district on Christmas Day 1806. A new church was built in the centre of the village and opened for worship in 1876. Though no longer a port, Alnmouth has a thriving boat-building industry.

In 1852, Mr. William Dickson, who headed the deputation which presented the address to Queen Victoria, published a detailed and comprehensive history of Alnmouth. Mr. Dickson, who was a Justice of the Peace for Northumberland and an F.S.A., wrote four chapters of his History "For the Perusal of The Members of The Archaeological Institute of Great Britain at Newcastle, at the August Meeting for 1852". Mr. Dickson can therefore be regarded as an authority and his information is of great value. A reproduction of a print, dated 1783, is included in this most interesting book, and shows the ruinous state into which St. John's Church had fallen. Between Alnmouth and the ruins of Dunstanburgh Castle are two of the most interesting villages on the coast, Boulmer and Craster; while a little way inland are Howick Hall and Fallodon, the latter for all time associated with the memory of Sir Edward Grey.

Boulmer, once notorious for smuggling, is now two villages, the old Boulmer and the new. The new village is the result of the Royal Air Force and a Warning Station is established here. In the past, Boulmer had a shocking reputation. Here the Northumbrian and Scottish smugglers collected the supplies of illicit liquor, brought from the continent by the sea captains who were involved in "rum running" activities. In some of the older houses hiding-places have been discovered where the casks were stored, and in the last century, casks of spirit were sometimes dug up on the beach. The pen of a Compton Mackenzie is needed to describe this Northumbrian *Whisky Galore*.

Very different is the history of Howick Hall. Built in 1782, the modern house succeeded the ancient tower, mentioned in the county records in 1416. Howick has long been in the possession of the Grey family. Sir Evelyn Baring, who married Lady Mary Grey, was created Lord Howick of Glendale, and now lives at Howick Hall. Surrounded by trees, Howick is famous for its wonderful display of daffodils. The grounds are open to the public in the spring, and as the many visitors approach Howick through the great avenue of beech trees they are greeted by a carpet of yellow daffodils. The Greys have produced many public spirited members in their family. The two most famous are Grey who was Prime Minister at the time of the Reform Bill, and whose monument stands at the top of the street which bears his name in Newcastle, and Sir Edward, born at nearby Fallodon, from which he took his title when he was created a peer. Foreign Secretary in 1914 when the First World War broke out, the words he spoke when it was apparent that war was inevitable will be quoted as long as history is written: "The lamps are going out all over Europe". A lover of the country, especially of birds, Lord Grey created a bird sanctuary at Fallodon. Towards the end of his life, this man whose name is engraved in history became blind, and he died at Fallodon in his beloved Northumberland. One of the best biographies ever written, *Grey of Fallodon* is by a fellow Northumbrian, G. M. Trevelyan.

Craster is a typical fishing village, famous for its kippers! The way in which Craster kippers are cured is a well-kept secret; whatever the method, the flavour is delicious. There have been Crasters at Craster since 1272. Now Mr. Oswin E. Craster has his home in the ancient Tower of Craster, of which there is mention in 1415. Georgian additions have been made to the old tower, a house lived in by the same family for nearly five hundred years. Few counties can boast of such old families as does Northumberland. In 1962, when Queen Elizabeth the Queen Mother was staying at Alnwick Castle, she embarked at the little harbour of Seahouses for her visit to the Outer Farnes. She was assisted into the fishing boat or "coble" by the Duke of Northumberland, whose family of Percy came to Northumberland in 1309, and Sir John Craster, whose family made an even earlier appearance in Northumbrian history. Surely a record which few counties can equal!

The coastal scenery from Craster to Dunstanburgh is particularly impressive; the great Whin-Sill of Northumberland rises here in columns from the sea bed. The most striking scenery is at Cullernose Point, from where the mighty ruins of Dunstanburgh are clearly visible.

When Dunstanburgh was built in 1314 it must have been almost impregnable. Standing on the edge of the steep cliffs, where the sea dashes against the rocks, attack from the sea was impossible.

Dunstanburgh's history is principally royal. Built by a son of Henry III, the Earl of Lancaster, it remained in royal hands until the Wars of the Roses, when the castle was severely damaged by the artillery. Queen Margaret and Henry VI were at Dunstanburgh, and it is one of the places which, with Warkworth, claims to have sheltered the Lancastrian queen on her last night in Northumberland. Dunstanburgh never recovered from the damage inflicted on it by the opposing armies of York and Lancaster, and in 1538 it was reported to be "a very reuynus howse, and of smaylle strengthe". Subsequently passing into the hands of Sir William Grey of Wark and the Earl of Tankerville, the great ruins are now scheduled as an ancient monument, looked after by the Ministry of Works. A favourite subject for artists, Dunstanburgh has been painted by Turner and the Northumbrian artist T. M. Richardson. A romantic legend connected with Dunstanburgh has been told in verse by three different poets, each poem having a different title! "Sir Guy the Seeker" is the title given to the poem by M. G. Lewis; "The Wandering Knight" by James Service of Chatton and "The Coral Wreath, or the Spellbound Knight" by W. G. Thompson.

From Dunstanburgh to Tweedmouth the coast is rich in sheltered bays; Embleton and Beadnell, separated from one another by Newton Point, are increasingly popular with visitors, for here is some of the best sailing between Tyne and Tweed. Once peaceful little villages, busy with their own affairs, they have now been "discovered". Their old world character is disappearing, especially at Beadnell where there is an extensive caravan site. From Seahouses, the fishermen go out in the cobles; boats peculiar to Northumberland, specially built for the conditions which prevail on this rocky stretch of coast.

North of Seahouses, standing high above the sea, is the most theatrical of all the castles of Northumberland; "King Ida's castle, huge and square", the mighty Bamburgh. Second only to Alnwick in its importance, Bamburgh with its wealth of history and legend demands a chapter of its own. Northumberland is narrowing now, a spit of land between the North Sea and Scotland. Budle Bay and Fenham Flats, where the wild duck abound; Beal with the Causeway which at low tide links the mainland with Lindisfarne, the Holy Island; the sands of Goswick where the main railway line to Scotland and the Great North Road run parallel—the old and the new are here intermingled. All that is left of the castle of Haggerston is the tower. There is no record of when this was built. The old house of the Haggerstons was destroyed by fire in 1618. Licence to crenellate the original house was granted to Robert de Haggerston in 1345 by Edward III. The Haggerstons of Edward III's day would be astonished if they could see their castle now.

The grounds surrounding the tower are the headquarters of a caravan club!

The end of "the lordly strand of Northumberland" is almost within sight, divided from the town of Berwick by the River Tweed. Northumberland penetrates for three miles beyond the Scottish river, until high above the red sandstone cliffs the Border is reached. On railway and road are the signs which mark the Border line, England and Scotland! From mouth of Tyne to Berwick Bounds, the seventy miles of Northumberland's incomparable coast-line runs its course.

VII

ALNWICK AND THE HOUSE OF PERCY

> But up spoke proud Lord Percy then,
> And O but he spake hie!
> I am the lord of this castle,
> My wife's the lady gay.
>
> *Sir Walter Scott*, BATTLE OF OTTERBURN

Alnwick Castle, the greatest of all the Border fortresses, has been the property of the Percy family since 1309. Before the Percys came, the building of the Norman castle had begun. It was sometime in the twelfth century, when the lands of Alnwick were owned by a de Vescy, that the foundations of the castle were laid.

The Scottish king, Malcolm Canmore, met his death near Alnwick in 1093. William Wallace and his forces were attacked by the castle garrison in 1297, but it was with the coming of the first Percy that the real history of Alnwick and its castle began. The Percys came to England in the train of William the Conqueror, originating, it is said, from a village in Normandy called Percée, meaning a clearing in the wood. Nine hundred years later in 1940, a descendant of these Norman Percys, George, ninth Duke of Northumberland, was killed near the village of Pecq on the Scheldt Canal in Flanders.

Settling first in Yorkshire and Lincolnshire on lands granted to them by the king, the first "Northumbrian" Percy was Henry, first Lord of Alnwick, who founded one of the greatest families of all, not only in Northumberland but in the United Kingdom. Today in Alnwick lives His Grace Hugh Algernon, tenth Duke of Northumberland, Lord Lieutenant of the County and Knight of the Most Noble Order of the Garter. There is a legend in the county that this most ancient order of chivalry had its origin in Northumberland. Edward III, in 1349, was encamped at Wark Castle on Tweedside where a ball was held. The Countess of Salisbury lost her garter while dancing, which drew forth ribald comments from the courtiers. The king, to cover the lady's embarrassment, held up the garter on the point of his sword and uttered the words which are now the motto of the Order: "*Honi soit qui mal y pense*". Doubtful though the truth of the story is, it is a good Northumbrian legend!

It was Sir Henry de Percy, the first lord of Alnwick, who set about the restoration of the Norman castle of the de Vescies. In Sir Henry's lifetime the keep was reconstructed, the postern and constable's towers built, until, with many other additions, Alnwick Castle became the strongest fortress on the English side of the Border. From the days of Sir Henry until the sixteenth century, when there was little or no peace on the Border, Alnwick was the scene of many wild and stormy deeds. The early Percys were great fighters, and on the rare occasions when there was a truce between England and Scotland, they seem to have found life too dull and went off to fight in the many continental wars in which England was so often embroiled! A Percy fought at Crécy, returning to Northumberland in time to lead his men against the Scottish King David at the Battle of Neville's Cross near the city of Durham, where the Scots were defeated.

Standing as Alnwick does on the highway to Scotland, the Great North Road, and as the crow flies only sixteen miles from the much disputed Border line, the castle was always in the centre of the many conflicts. English and Scottish kings crossed the great drawbridge. Edward III of the Garter legend, stayed within the safety of the great walls, on his marches to and from Scotland, guarded by the Percy "Lions". Where the River Aln, from which Alnwick takes its name, flows through peaceful pastures, armies once made their camps. The jingle of horses' bits, the tramp of armoured men resounded then below the castle walls.

The history of the Percys is to a great extent the history of England. As mentioned in the previous chapter, Alnwick Castle was the fortress, while nearby Warkworth on the coast was the "home" of this family whose best known and most romantic figure was Harry, the son of the first earl, the man immortalized by Shakespeare as "Hotspur". The sobriquet signifies his impulsive disposition. Like many famous writers Shakespeare changed times and dates to fit his characters into his plays, but most of the episodes in Henry IV are based on fact. One scene in part two of the play is "Before Northumberland's castle of Warkworth". From the age of twelve, when Harry Hotspur distinguished himself at the siege of Berwick, until he fell fighting at Shrewsbury, he was a soldier.

The great enemies of the Percys were the Douglases. This feud has only been healed in this century by marriages between descendants of these two famous families, who in years gone by did their best to annihilate one another! Restless, always "spoiling" for a fight, Shakespeare, in a few words, conveys vividly the character of "Harry". Harry of Monmouth, "Prince Hal", says of Hotspur. "He that kills me six or seven Scots, washes his hands and says to his wife, 'Fie upon this quiet life! I want work'. 'O my sweet Harry,' says she, 'how many hast thou killed today?' 'Give my roan horse a drench,' says he, and answers, 'some fourteen', an hour after, 'a trifle, a trifle!' "

The Whin-Sill rises from the sea at Cullernose Point

In 1388, the Douglases had crossed the Border and were laying waste to Northumberland.

> It fell about the Lammas tide,
> When the muir men win their hay,
> The doughty Douglas bound him to ride,
> Into England, to drive a prey.

> For they hae burnt the Dales o' Tyne
> And part of Bamburghshire, and three good towers
> On Redeswire Fells, they left them all on fire.

Having penetrated into the bishopric of Durham, the Douglases laden with booty, turned their attention to the city of Newcastle, where Hotspur already was. In single combat with the Percy without the city walls, Douglas captured the pennon of Hotspur and bragged that he would fly it from the battlements of his castle of Dalkeith. This was an insult to Hotspur's pride, and he swore to pursue the Douglas until he had avenged his honour. It was from this incident that Hotspur and Douglas wrote their names in the pages of Northumbrian history. On the 19th of August, 1388, the Battle of Otterburn was fought in the moonlight. Burning as they went, leaving the village of Ponteland in flames, the Scots marched the thirty miles from Newcastle to within fifteen miles of their own country. In the valley of the Rede, where the Otterburn joins it and where later the burn was to run red with blood, the Scotsmen waited. The Douglas is said to have had a premonition that he would not survive the battle, and Scott, in his epic of this most bloodthirsty of Border battles has Douglas say:

> But I hae dreamed a dreary dream,
> Beyond the Isle of Skye,
> I saw a dead man win a fight,
> And I think that man was I.

This battle, fought between Hotspur and Douglas so long ago, inspired the minstrels and poets for centuries after, and has kept green the memory of Otterburn. Froissart, the French writer, gives a graphic description of the battle which he received from eye-witnesses. The "Ballad of Chevy Chase", which is legendary (a combination of three battles, Otterburn, Homildon Hill and Piperden which were to follow) is set to music, and on official occasions the tune is played by the piper of the Duke of Northumberland, the only English duke with the right to have his own piper. Chevy Chase is played on the sweet sounding Northumbrian pipes, and every year in the town of Alnwick a Pipers' Gathering is held.

The verse quoted at the beginning of this chapter is from Scotts'

7

Bailiffgate, Alnwick, where the warriors kept watch

ballad, and really applies to the encounter between Hotspur and Douglas at Newcastle, but it is appropriate to Alnwick where still a Percy reigns. In the lonely hill country of Ridsdale where the battle cries rang out—"A Percy", "A Douglas", it was the Douglas war cry which was victorious on that moonlight night. Hotspur and his brother Ralph were taken prisoner; the premonition of the Earl of Douglas came true, he died on the field of Otterburn. The spot where he fell, in a little plantation north of the present-day village, is the inappropriately named Percy Cross. Hotspur paid due ransom to his Scottish captors and returned to his own country to see the defeat of Otterburn turned into a Percy victory at Homildon Hill near Wooler, where the Douglases were heavily defeated.

The fighting days of the great "Champion" of the county were drawing to an end. Rebelling against the English king, the Percys led out their followers in the "rising" which bears their name, and far away from his father's lands of Alnwick, Harry Hotspur fought his last battle at Shrewsbury. The Northumbrian speech has a peculiarity which legend says it owes to this great fighting Percy. It is said that Hotspur had a speech defect, and was unable to pronounce the letter r, and that the Northumbrians of his day imitated their hero. It is extraordinary but true, that even today the countrymen make the r guttural, as the long ago Hotspur is said to have done!

Violence and sudden death were taken as a matter of course in the days of Border warfare, and very few of the first Percys died in their beds. When the Lancastrians and Yorkists were waging war against one another, Alnwick, then defended by Sir Ralph Grey (the third Earl of Northumberland having died at the Battle of Towton), surrendered to Margaret of Anjou, and on Hedgeley Moor between Wooler and Alnwick, in 1464, Sir Ralph Percy died for the Lancastrian queen. Close to the spot where the battle of Hedgeley Moor was fought is a sandstone pillar, known as Percy's Cross, which may originally have been Roman. Percy's Well, a spring near the cross, tradition says, is where Sir Ralph Percy drank to quench his thirst.

Of the many royal visitors to Alnwick, surely one of the most pathetic was the thirteen-year-old Princess Margaret Tudor. In 1503, this child set forth from London to marry James IV of Scotland; a man seventeen years older than his bride! Greeted at Durham by the fifth Earl of Northumberland, known as the "Magnificent", the Tudor princess was escorted to his castle of Alnwick where she spent two days. In the earl's deer park the little bride shot a buck, and then went on her way to Berwick, with the earl in attendance, to be greeted on the Border at Lamberton Toll by the Scottish lords. In ten short years, the brothers of the Magnificent Earl were to fight against Margaret's husband on Flodden Field. More than four hundred years afterwards another Princess Margaret was entertained at Alnwick in very different circumstances.

Henry, the sixth earl, Warden of the March, had a chequered career. Unhappily for him he loved the woman who was to become the second wife of Henry VIII, Anne Boleyn. Forbidden by the king to pursue his courtship, Henry poured out his soul in poetry which Surtees, the ballad-monger, attributes to the unhappy earl:

> What's life to me, Northumberland's proud heir?
> Life without her is life without a sun;
> Why should the fates thus ever place me here?
> Why am I doomed life's cheerless course to run?
> But thee fond maid—to starry heights upborne,
> Whose name my lips to 'plain the scance can move,
> Thee, like Philomela, will I ever mourn,
> Anna, my first, my last, my only love!

When Anne Boleyn was brought to trial, Henry VIII, with the sadism inherent in this Tudor monarch, commanded Henry Percy to serve on the commission. Henry avoided this unpleasant task by pleading illness.

The seventh earl's life was to be even more unhappy than that of Anne Boleyn's lover. Thomas Percy, because of his support of the Catholic Mary, Queen of Scots, and his part in the Rising of the North, was beheaded at York in 1572. During his lifetime, the ill-fated Thomas had carried out restorations at Alnwick, the Alnwick which was soon to be deserted by the Percy family for nearly two hundred years. The cousin of the ninth earl was one of the conspirators in the Gunpowder Plot, and as a result suspicion fell upon the whole family, and Henry Percy, in spite of his innocence, was imprisoned in the Tower of London for fifteen years. A highly intelligent man, devoted to the study of chemistry and astronomy, he is known to posterity as "The Wizard Earl".

In 1670, with the death of the eleventh Earl of Northumberland while in Turin, the earldom became extinct. This last Earl of Northumberland left a daughter, who married as her second husband Somerset, known as the Proud Duke; it was their granddaughter Elizabeth, heiress to the Northumberland estates, who married Sir Hugh Smithson, a Yorkshire baronet who changed his name to Percy and became the Earl of Northumberland in 1750, and in 1766 was created first Duke of Northumberland. And so after some two hundred years, Alnwick regained its glory.

The castle was now in ruins, Cromwell's army having done its worst, as it seems to have done wherever it was; but surely it excelled itself at Alnwick. Six thousand Scottish prisoners were thrown into the second bailey, three thousand survived! Two thousand more were to die on their enforced march to Durham.

The first duke began the work of restoration not only of the castle but of the estates, which had been sadly neglected. Today, the administration of the vast estates is a model for all landowners. Wherever the duke has property, be it in the Alnwick district, North or South Tynedale, even where the once proud castle of Prudhoe on the Tyne was engulfed by the vast expansion of I.C.I., a record is kept of every "parcel" of land, and entered in the records are details of every tenant on the duke's estates. Alnwick Castle is not only the past of Northumberland, it is very much the present, a combination of all that was good in the old days, and the best of the new. In the Muniment Tower are the records of long ago, written on vellum. The household books are there, and judging from the Percy records, the servants fared well in what are often referred to as "The Bad Old Days".

The household in 1569 numbered 166 persons; this number excluded the officials of higher rank. Provision was also made every day for fifty-seven visitors who might receive refreshment within the castle walls. How the number of fifty-seven was arrived at is not explained; it seems a curious number. The average cost of feeding this enormous household was £3 11s. 6d. per year, which would be the equivalent of £30 today. When one takes into account that a loaf of bread in 1569 cost about a farthing, and meat less than a halfpenny a pound, this was a most generous allowance. Moving from one castle to another in the sixteenth century was a major operation; even the glass from the windows was taken from one residence to another! Four gallons of wine and nearly forty gallons of beer were consumed every day, yet the yearly quantity of candles used was only 91 dozen. No doubt, having consumed such vast quantities of liquor, the household would be ready for an early bed!

Algernon, the fourth duke, transformed the castle. It was he who brought Italian craftsmen to a Border fortress. From without, the castle is still a fortress, but within, the influence of Duke Algernon is dominant.

It is impossible to describe the treasures which are gathered together in Alnwick Castle. It has been, and very rightly, described as "the Windsor of the North", and every Northumbrian should be proud of the great heritage within his county. Only recently some of the priceless works of art have been on exhibition in the city of Newcastle. On certain days the castle is open to the public, when the treasures can be seen, and there is an excellent "official guide". Alnwick Castle is not a museum, it is a home, lived in by His Grace and his family. Part of the castle is now a Training College for Teachers, and surely such surroundings must inspire those students, who are not even Northumbrians, to a pride in a castle and a family which has played such an outstanding part in the history of the country.

The old customs and traditions are maintained at Alnwick; on Shrove Tuesday, the traditional game of football is played in the Pastures, and the first player who retrieves the ball from the River Aln is rewarded. The first salmon to be caught in the River Coquet at the opening of the season is presented to the duke. At Newburn on the River Tyne, a token rental of a red rose is presented to the duke or his representative.

On the Lion Bridge over the Aln, where the "new" road was constructed after the old coach road was abandoned, is a figure of the unmistakable emblem of the Percys: a lion with a stiffly horizontal tail. Though the stables at Alnwick no longer resound to the neighing of the coach horses, there is still a state coach which was used by the third duke when he was ambassador extraordinary to Charles X, King of France. It is with pride that Northumbrians recall the fact that at the coronation of Queen Elizabeth II, the Sword of Mercy was carried by the present duke, and the Mistress of the Robes to the Queen Mother was Helen, Duchess of Northumberland.

Within the walls of the Duke's Park is a country of its own. Three thousand acres of enclosed land, with every variety of scenery; good "mixed" farming, afforestation, highlands and lowlands. The wall surrounding the Park stretches for nine and a half miles. To enter the Park, permission must be obtained from the Estate Offices, except on Wednesday afternoons and Sundays, when it is open to all. Capability Brown was responsible for part of the lay-out of the Park, and the first duke's "folly", the Brislee Tower, was the work of Robert Adam. This extraordinary erection, ninety feet high, is pseudo-Gothic, so beloved of the builders of the eighteenth century. From this height the first duke could survey his vast estates, from south of Alnwick to the Scottish Border. Seven castles can be seen from the Brislee Tower; not only the Percy strongholds of Warkworth and Alnwick, but mighty Bamburgh, the ruins of Dunstanburgh, Chillingham, the seat of the Earls of Tankerville, Holy Island Castle on Lindisfarne and the ruins of Ros. The first duke had an inscription made on his folly which translated reads as follows: "Look around! I have measured out all these things; they are my orders, it is my planting; many of these trees have been planted by my own hand."

Within the confines of the Park, William the Lion was taken prisoner in 1174. Within this "county within a county" is what remains of Hulne Abbey. Here, among the ruins of a Carmelite monastery, the flowers bloom and down below the River Aln winds its way to the pastures of Alnwick. The old story is that a Northumbrian knight, one Ralph Fresborn, had taken monastic vows, and was discovered on Mount Carmel by a de Vescy of Alnwick, and given permission to return to England on condition that he would build a monastery. When Fresborn saw the hill on which the Brislee Tower now stands, he was so much reminded of Mount Carmel that he chose a site for his Abbey of Hulne where he could look across to Brislee Hill and be reminded of Mount Carmel. Whatever prompted the builders of

Hulne Abbey, a lovelier site could not have been chosen. The ruins today are poignant in their simplicity.

The monks of old replenished their larder from the river below, and there are remains of fish-ponds where no doubt the fish were kept until needed for the abbot's table. Bakehouse, brewhouse, mill, the ruins of the domestic offices show how self-supporting these settlements were. Hulne too has suffered from the pseudo-Gothic; there is a tower, used now by shooting parties, but it in no way detracts from the charms of Hulne with its ruined church which measured 118 feet in length. There is everything within the three thousand acres of Park—a wishing well, rare trees planted by former dukes, one Douglas Fir is 120 feet high, and still within the Park and close to the town of Alnwick is all that remains of the abbey of Alnwick, founded in 1174 and which had an uneventful history—now little but the gatehouse remains. Early British remains have been discovered not only in the Park but in the surrounding district, and many of the relics unearthed in the camps are preserved in the castle.

Dominated though Alnwick is by the history of the house of Percy, the town itself has a life and history all its own. A Border town, where, until the beginning of this century the County Court was held, Alnwick was at one time contained within its defending walls. The names of the streets today bear out its history; Bondgate Within, Bondgate Without; Narrow Gate, Pottergate, are all reminders of the past. The traffic between two capitals, London and Edinburgh, passes through the Hotspur Gate. Built in 1450, it not only commemorates the Champion of the County, Harry Hotspur, but was used at one time as the County Gaol—in more recent times the town band practised within its walls. Judging from the thickness of these, the townspeople would not be disturbed by the efforts of the band! Alnwick is very conscious of its history and traditions; a curfew is still rung, and the freemen have considerable powers and rights. On Alnwick Moor, a freeman of the town, if he so wishes, can claim a piece of land which is his property for life. To drive over Alnwick Moor and see these smallholdings is reminiscent of Scottish crofting country.

Alnwick was the headquarters of the 7th Battalion Royal Northumberland Fusiliers of which, before the disbanding of the Territorial Army, the Duke of Northumberland was Honorary Colonel. The 5th Foot were called Northumberland Fusiliers after the second duke who commanded the 5th Foot in the American War of Independence. There was also a Drill Hall for the local troop of the Northumberland Hussars with which the present duke served in the Second World War.

Entering Alnwick from the south, the first thing to catch the eye is the imposing tenantry column or folly, topped by the Percy Lion, which is generally known as the Farmers' Folly. The story goes that it is so called because, since the farmers' rents had already been remitted, the duke said that if they could afford to erect a column like that they could afford more rent—and put them up again. The truth is that it was put up by the tenantry who were known as the Percy Tenantry Volunteers which the duke founded during the Napoleonic Wars to repel any invasion on the Northumbrian coasts by Bonaparte (like the Home Guard of the last war). The inscription on the column reads: "To Hugh, Duke of Northumberland, K.G. This column is erected, dedicated and inscribed by a grateful and united tenantry. Anno Domini MDCCCXVI." On each side of the column is inscribed the motto of the house of Percy—*Esperance en Dieu.*

The first three Edwards passed through the town on their way to harry Scotland—Alnwick town, like the castle, was always a storm centre. The ancient church of St. Mary and St. Michael has happily weathered the storms, and there is even a memorial to the wife of the last de Vescy.

Alnwick is now the centre of a thriving agricultural area, where the land is noted for the beef-cattle it produces. From Alnwick the roads radiate into the many pleasant villages of north Northumberland, roads which climb to heights where there are some of the most glorious views in the whole country. From Alnwick to Bridge of Aln, where the road drops down into the Vale of Whittingham is one of the loveliest.

On the battlements of the castle are still some of the original stone figures, dating from the Middle Ages. Their purpose was to give the impression that the defenders of Alnwick were always on the watch for their enemies. When restorations were carried out, some of the figures were renewed. In the moonlight, when the outline of the "watchers" stand out so sharply, the watchers who keep perpetual vigil throughout the ages, Alnwick has a dreamlike quality impossible to describe in words. Weeks could be spent within the castle, and still the visitor could not assimilate everything. The Italian workmanship, the wonderful carvings, the damask hung walls and the works of art which have been collected by various members of the Percy family. A frieze depicts the legendary Battle of Chevy Chase, and in the library is the first book printed in the English language and the priceless Sherborne Missal. There is a hair net, made from the chestnut hair of the unhappy Mary of Scotland, the queen for whom the seventh earl lost his life. One can also see Canaletto's pictures of the castle and of Northumberland House in London; a Van Dyke of Algernon, the tenth earl; Warkworth Castle by the Northumbrian artist T. M. Richardson, and these are only a few of the priceless works of art which hang on the walls of Alnwick. Modern sporting scenes of Northumberland by Tom Carr are of particular interest, and there is a characteristic painting of the present duke as master of The Percy Hounds. This pack became The Percy in 1878, since when it has been the property of the Dukes of Northumberland.

In the town of Alnwick are two well-known schools for boys and girls, appropriately named "The Duke's School" and "The Duchess's School". The latter was formerly in a house which stands on land once owned by the ill-fated earl of Derwentwater, but as the accommodation became inadequate, a large modern school has been built. Old prints of the town in the possession of His Grace reveal how peaceful and charming the old town must have been. After the end of hostilities between England and Scotland, peace came to Northumberland and the stormy days of the constant troop movements were over. The kings who rode through Alnwick are now history; Plantagenets, Yorkists, Lancastrians, a Tudor princess, the Martyr King, Charles I and his bitter enemy Cromwell have passed through its gates, and from the north came the Scottish armies. Now royalty comes in peace to Alnwick; the most beloved visitor of all, a descendant of Robert the Bruce who became the consort of King George VI, Queen Elizabeth the Queen Mother, who, whenever she visits Northumberland is entertained at Alnwick Castle.

In 1886 it must have been a delight to shop in the town. A delightful little history, *Eglingham and its Vicinity* by E. J. Wilson, contains the following advertisements: "J. J. & A. Cockburn, Wholesale and Family Wine, Spirit, Ale and Porter Agents, of 39 Bondgate Street, advertise The Spirit of the Day, Old Highland Whisky, as supplied to the principal nobility and gentry of the County at 15/– and 17/6 a gallon, or 2/6 and 3/– a bottle. Nett Cash!" Davison and Patten, the chemists, claim to have had eighty years' experience in stomach disorders, and their pills, priced at $7\frac{1}{2}d$. and 2/9 per box had, according to description, almost magical properties. Had one been tempted to indulge in too much of Messrs. Cockburn's "Spirit of the Day", Davison's pills were the answer. "When the stomach is weak, the Digestion bad, and Liver Out of Order, these pills should be taken in preference to all others. Under their use the Complexion improves, the Skin appears soft and healthy and the most invigorating effects are produced. Their special action on the Stomach and Liver, and their purifying influence on the Blood, account for these happy results." The Alnwick tradesmen of the last century could hold their own with the high pressure salesmanship of today. In 1886, the Star Hotel in Fenkle Street still advertised itself as a coaching house, and at "The Nag's Head", horses and conveyances were on hire. An "ordinary" was held on Mondays and Fridays. There have been many changes in the town since 1886; chain stores have made their appearance, Bingo is played in The Northumberland Hall and yet in spite of this so-called progress, Alnwick still retains an old world atmosphere with its narrow cobbled streets and grey stone houses so typical of a Border town.

Hotspur's name is commemorated everywhere; the local Women's Institutes form part of "The Hotspur Group"; Shakespeare's hero is commemorated by street names in the county, not only in his native town of Alnwick; in Tynemouth, where much of the land is Percy owned, there is a Hotspur Street.

To Northumbrians everywhere there is only one "duke", the tenth Duke of Northumberland, Earl of Northumberland, Baron Warkworth, Earl Percy, Earl of Beverley and Lord Lovaine, Baron of Alnwick. A fitting epitaph for the house of Percy is a verse of poetry from Frederick C. Palmer's "The Ghosts".

O come with me, Ghosts walk tonight
Victims of bloody Border fight
Who made our English history
Grey phantom Percies lead the way
Against the Douglas chivalry,
Grey ghosts of ancient mystery.
Lo! Watch them sweep o'er Flodden Field,
Where all the flower of Scotland died;
Death cannot slay the splendid pride
Of those who fell but scorned to yield,
Who fought in vain, except to earn
Their name upon the scroll of fame
And write in blood each hero's name
Upon the stones of Otterburn.

VIII

BAMBURGH AND THE FARNES

Thy tower proud Bamburgh, mark'd they there
King Ida's castle, huge and square,
From its tall rock look grimly down,
And on the swelling ocean frown,
Then from the coast they bore away,
And reached the Holy Island's bay.

Sir Walter Scott, MARMION

It was in the year 547 that Ida the Flamebearer, King of Northumbria, built the first fortifications on the huge rock of Whin-Sill, which rises 150 feet above the North Sea. These early fortifications were of wood, enclosed by a hedge, and the settlement was known as Dinguard and became the capital of the kingdom which stretched from the Humber to the Forth. King Ethelfrith, the grandson of Ida, gave the fortress to his wife, Queen Bebba, who renamed it Bebbanburgh, from which the name Bamburgh is derived. Sir Walter Scott, who never worried about facts, was about 700 years ahead when he described "King Ida's castle, huge and square", as it was not until the reign of Henry I that the stone keep was built!

Until the unification of the kingdom, Bamburgh was a royal city. Here the Northumbrian kings were crowned; one of them, King Edwin, giving his name to Edinburgh, "Edwin's Burgh". Like all the northern strongholds, Bamburgh's history is a stormy one. In the early days it was burnt by Penda, the heathen king of Mercia. Tradition says that St. Aidan watched the attack from the Inner Farne, and prayed that the heathen king would be defeated, and that as the saint prayed, the wind changed its direction and the royal city was saved.

When the Norsemen invaded the north-east coast Bamburgh suffered severely and lay in ruins until restorations were carried out by Henry I and Bamburgh became Crown property, which it remained until given by James I to Claudius Forster, an ancestor of the Jacobite heroine, Dorothy. When King John laid waste to Northumberland, Bamburgh was one of the few castles which held out against this most unlikeable of English kings, and whose two visits left unpleasant memories.

In 1330 Queen Phillipa the intrepid consort of Edward III, defended

the castle against the Scots, and the damage suffered in the defence
was such that repairs amounting to the sum of £300 had to be carried
out! Bamburgh has every right to its title of "Royal". It was from the
early fortress that the Christian queens of Northumbria sent forth the
missionaries, queens who had converted their heathen husbands to
Christianity; and many of the heathen Northumbrians were baptized
by St. Paulinus. Henry III was among Bamburgh's royal visitors;
also Edward I, who summoned the puppet king of Scots to meet him
at Bamburgh; but perhaps the most famous of all was Margaret of
Anjou, the warrior queen of Henry VI, who held her court here during
the Wars of the Roses. It was from the great rock of Bamburgh that
the Lancastrian queen rode out on a May morning to fight her last
battle in Northumberland, which was a disaster for the house of
Lancaster, the Battle of Hexham.

Northumberland's "Champion" Harry Hotspur, was constable of
the castle in 1403. Kings and queens, warriors and saints have played
their part in the long history of mighty Bamburgh, whose past is
inextricably woven with the Holy Island of Lindisfarne, which was
the cradle of Christianity in the north. Bamburgh, together with
several other parishes, once formed a sub-division of Northumberland,
"Bamburghshire":

> And they hae burnt the dales o' Tyne,
> And part of Bamburghshire,
> And three good towers on Redeswire fells,
> They left them all on fire.

So sings the chronicler of Otterburn.

The Holy Island of the Northumbrian saints is part of Islandshire,
yet its history is associated with Royal Bamburgh. Holy Island today
is reached by a causeway from Beal, but like the pilgrims of old the
traveller is dependent on the tides. Here to this little island, now popular
with holiday makers, long ago there came a missionary later to be
canonized as St. Aidan. From the island of Iona off the west coast of
Scotland he came, at the invitation of Oswald, king of Northumbria,
who was also canonized. It is recorded that when the Scottish missionary arrived he was unable to understand the language of the islanders,
and had to receive instruction from King Oswald. The language
spoken on Holy Island today is still unintelligible to the foreigner!

On the Holy Island, later to be known as Lindisfarne, Aidan and his
monks built a church which was added to through the centuries and
became the priory of Lindisfarne, of which now only the ruins remain.
Created Bishop of Lindisfarne, St. Aidan died in the royal city of
Bamburgh, but his body was brought to his "Holy Island" and buried
in the church he had built. Perhaps even more famous than St. Aidan,

and certainly the most dearly loved of the Northumbrian saints, is Cuthbert, "the shepherd laddie" who tended his flocks near Doddington in Glendale, where today can be seen Cuddy's Cave, one of many in the county. Legend says that the man who was to become Bishop of Lindisfarne saw a vision of St. Aidan in the arms of angels ascending into heaven, and that Cuthbert then decided to dedicate his life to the service of God. Receiving his training at the abbey of Melrose and at Ripon in Yorkshire, he spent three years on Lindisfarne and in his retreat on the Inner Farne, which is one of the islands, now the property of the National Trust, which make up the group known as the Inner and Outer Farnes. How it would please the gentle saint, who loved all birds and animals, to know that his beloved Farnes are now bird sanctuaries.

St. Cuthbert was consecrated Bishop of Lindisfarne at York, and thereafter devoted his life to prayer and meditation, building an oratory and cell on Farne Island where the little church stands today. It was on this island that he died in 687 and his body was taken on the first journey to Holy Island—Lindisfarne. Many years passed before the saint's bones found their last resting place in the great cathedral of Durham, robed in royal garments, a contrast to the simple clothing St. Cuthbert had worn in life. The Venerable Bede says that when the coffin was opened nine years after St. Cuthbert's death, the body was still in a wonderful state of preservation. The peaceful islands of the saints were invaded by the Norsemen, and the monks fled to the mainland with the coffin bearing the remains of St. Cuthbert. The saint was to travel farther after his death than he had ever travelled in life. Through the northern counties, back to Holy Island, to Chester-le-Street, where the coffin rested for more than a hundred years, until the monks received a sign from the local wise woman, who told them to follow "the Dun cow home", the old name for Durham, the island on the river, which brought them to where the great cathedral stands today, and where at last St. Cuthbert was to lie undisturbed.

There in the finest Norman cathedral in England, some say in Europe, lies the man whose writings give the most graphic description of the life of St. Cuthbert—Bede himself.

Holy Island is still a place of pilgrimage for all Christians, who come to pray in the beautiful church of St. Mary which dates from the thirteenth century. Old customs and traditions are maintained on the island, and every bride married in St. Mary's has to jump the "petting" or "louping" stool which stands at the east end of the church. The better the "loup" (jump) the better the luck! At Holy Island weddings, shot guns are fired over the bridal couple.

The island's castle is Lutyens at his most romantic. Built in 1550, this castle, which held out for the Jacobites in the Rebellion of the '15, had fallen into ruin, and was eventually used by the coastguards until bought by the owner of *Country Life* in 1902, and restored by Sir Edwin Lutyens. Open to the public on certain days, this castle in miniature is reminiscent of Grimm's *Fairy Tales*.

Recently an industry has been revived on Holy Island, the brewing of mead, which was practised by the monks so long ago—the remains of the brew house are still to be seen. Not only mead, bearing the name Lindisfarne, but liqueur and honey are also produced, and are finding markets far away from the coast of Northumberland. The label on these Lindisfarne products is copied from the Lindisfarne Gospels which were written about A.D. 700 and are now preserved in the British Museum.

During the Civil Wars, the king's ships anchored in the island's harbour, while Charles himself stayed at Goswick farther up the coast. In 1908 the Prince and Princess of Wales, later King George V and Queen Mary, visited the island, and in 1958 a reigning monarch, Queen Elizabeth II accompanied by the Duke of Edinburgh, landed from the Royal Yacht *Britannia*.

Lindisfarne, or Holy Island, by whatever name it is called, is part of the history of England, while the castle of Bamburgh, restored and inhabited, is the most impressive landmark on the coast of Northumberland. Seen from any one of the little islands, where the visitors from Seahouses are landed from the cobles, Bamburgh is at its most magnificent. North-west, the line of the Kyloe hills can be seen, backed by the mighty mass of Cheviot, and the great stretches of golden sand sweep down the coast which Bamburgh dominates. For less than a hundred years Forsters of Adderstone lived in King Ida's castle, Forsters who were wardens of the Eastern March and members of Parliament for Northumberland, but who by wild living and reckless gambling impoverished their estates.

In 1704, Lord Crewe, a bishop of Durham, who had married Dorothy Forster the elder, as she is known, as his second wife, bought the Bamburgh estates, and it is due to this bishop that Bamburgh was restored to its former glory. Although Lord Crewe died in 1722, he had formed a trust to carry out not only the work of restoration but to endow charities which bear his name and are still in existence today. Many who are unaware of the generosity of Lord Crewe, associate his name only with two inns, "The Lord Crewe Arms" at Bamburgh and "The Lord Crewe Arms" at Blanchland! Lord Crewe's directions were largely carried out by Dr. John Sharp, Archdeacon of Northumberland, who was also a generous benefactor of the Crewe Trust. In the days of the archdeacon there was a dispensary for the poor of Bamburgh, and thirty-four small girls (why thirty-four is not explained) were boarded in the castle, and kept until they reached the age of sixteen when they went into "service". These little girls wore a distinctive uniform and received free education.

Many of the charity's functions were connected with the sea. A life boat, a bell to warn shipping, food and lodging for the shipwrecked, burial for victims of disasters, were all provided at the expense of the charity. Since the advent of the Welfare State, the charity has been administered in different ways, one of which is to give assistance to ministers of the Church of England who are in need.

In the nineteenth century one of Tyneside's great inventors, who founded "Armstrong's Factory" at Scotswood, and who became the first Lord Armstrong, bought Bamburgh from the trust and carried out "improvements" which are deplored by many historians. The castle is now divided into flats, of which one is retained by the present Lord Armstrong.

Open to the public, the castle has much of interest for the visitor. There is an armoury, with a large collection of weapons, a well which is 150 feet deep and of great antiquity, dating probably from about A.D. 774, discovered in 1770. Among the many interesting portraits of the Forster family, is one of the lovely wife of Lord Crewe and her more famous niece Dorothy, and also Dorothy's brother, General Forster, who led the Northumbrian Jacobites in the '15. There is also an engraving of the ill-fated Earl of Derwentwater.

The view from the battlements of Bamburgh Castle is one of the finest in all the county. Out to sea lie the Farnes, those rocky islands where so many ships have foundered, and where the grey seals breed, the only breeding ground on the north-east coast. The seals are a tourist attraction of the first order, and a source of controversy far beyond the boundaries of Northumberland, a controversy in which the writer has no intention of taking part. The authority Grace Hickling has written an admirable book for those who are interested in the seals and their habits.

Sea birds of many kinds inhabit the islands, now protected; at one time the eggs were collected and sent to London. Bird watchers from far and near come to these islands, which have their own distinctive names; Brownsman, Staple Island, the North and South Wamses, the Nameless Rock, the Big and Little Harcars and, most famous of all, the Pinnacle Rocks, and the Longstone, the name of which is for ever associated with Bamburgh's heroine Grace Darling.

In 1815, the year of Waterloo, there was born on the 24th of November, Grace Horsley Darling, the seventh child of William Darling and his wife, whose maiden name was Horsley. The Darling family had been and continued to be lighthouse keepers for generations, and at the time of Grace's birth her father was keeper of the light on the Brownsman. Her early years were spent among the birds and flowers which she loved, for compared with the Longstone, the Brownsman is a fertile island. When Grace was ten years old, William Darling became keeper of the Longstone, and there the girl, whose name was to become famous throughout the country, spent her uneventful life.

It was a wild and stormy night on the 7th of September, 1838, when a coastal steamer, *The Forfarshire*, on her way from Hull to Dundee, was driven off her course. *The Forfarshire* was off Berwick when the force of the gale drove the ship southwards towards the dreaded Farnes, and the doomed ship struck the Big Harcar, a huge basaltic rock, which with the Little Harcar lies between the Wamses and the Longstone. Forty-three people perished in the raging seas, and it was due to the bravery of Grace Darling and her father that they were able to save nine lives. Many times has the story been told of how this frail girl, with the aid of her father and mother, launched the coble (now in the museum at Bamburgh) and father and daughter risked their lives to rescue those survivors marooned on the Big Harcar. William Darling's account of the rescue which he sent to Trinity House conveys more than any of the more dramatic and sensational descriptions published at the time of the courage of himself and his heroic daughter.

Dear Sir,

In answer to your request of the 29th ult., I have to state that on the morning of the 7th September, it blowing gale with rain from the north, my daughter and me being both on the alert before high water securing things out of doors, one quarter before five my daughter observed a vessel on the Harkers Rock; but owing to the darkness and spray going over her, could not observe any person on the wreck although the glass was incessantly applied, until near seven o'clock, when the tide being fallen, we observed three or four men upon the rock; we agreed that if we could get to them some of them would be able to assist us back, without which we could not return; and having no idea of a boat coming from North Sunderland, we immediately launched our boat, and was enabled to gain the rock, where we found eight men and one woman, which I judged too many to take at once in the state of the weather, therefore took the woman and four men to The Longstone. Two of them returned with me, and succeeded in bringing the remainder, in all nine persons safely to The Longstone about nine o'clock. Afterwards the boat from North Sunderland arrived and found three lifeless bodies.

At the inquest held at Bamburgh it was revealed that *The Forfarshire* was unseaworthy, and this resulted in a demand by the public for the regular inspection of sea-going craft. The rescue gained nation-wide publicity and the heroine of the hour was inundated with offers of marriage. An invitation to appear at the Adelphi Theatre in London at £20 a week was refused and Grace Darling remained the unspoilt, unassuming girl who charmed all those who met her. The sum of £700 was raised by public subscription, and artist's impressions of the rescue were sold all over the country. Some of these pictorial records are in existence today. The great and the humble paid tribute to Grace Darling—she was received at Alnwick by the Duke and Duchess of Northumberland.

There was little time left for this gentle Northumbrian girl to enjoy the rewards of her bravery. Symptoms of consumption were already apparent and in spite of "changes of air" at Wooler and Alnwick, where Grace received much kindness from the duchess of that day, Grace Darling died in the village where she was born on the 20th of October, 1842. Her body was laid to rest in Bamburgh churchyard, within sight of the North Sea. An ornate memorial to her memory was erected a little north of her grave, a memorial which can be seen from the sea, and in 1844 another memorial was erected in St. Cuthbert's Chapel and bears this inscription, "To the Memory of Grace Horsley Darling, a native of Bamburgh and an inhabitant of these islands". In 1938 a museum was opened and relics of the heroine are on view, pathetic little relics, school books, some of her clothes, as well as the famous coble.

The church of St. Aidan, close to the museum, is one of the loveliest churches in Northumberland. Mainly dating from the thirteenth century it is one of the largest parish churches in the county. Of the Saxon church built for St. Aidan, there are no traces left, but everywhere, in the stained glass windows and in the memorials, there are reminders of Northumbrian saints and heroines. A modern stained glass window, presented in 1936, depicts on the right side St. Cuthbert surrounded by flowers, shells and birds, with a background of the castles of Bamburgh and Lindisfarne. In the crypt, rediscovered in 1837, lie the bodies of Bamburgh's other heroine, Dorothy Forster and her brother Tom. Tom Forster died at Boulogne in 1737, and his body was brought to his native Bamburgh in 1738. The crypt at that time appears to have been the vault of the Forster family. The Forsters of Bamburgh and Adderstone intermarried, which makes their pedigrees difficult to trace. The famous Dorothy was baptized at Bamburgh in 1686, and died in 1767, outliving most of her contemporaries who had been "out" in the '15. At Bamburgh, as on Holy Island, the bride has to jump the "Petting Stool", the difference being that the Bamburgh stool is of wood, while that on the island is of stone, said to be the plinth of a cross dedicated to St. Cuthbert. An effigy of Grace Darling lies within the church, where Northumberland's most famous heroines, Grace and Dorothy, found their last resting place.

The War Memorial at Bamburgh is unique, a cross placed in a hollow of the great rock on which the castle stands. Bamburghshire! History and romance, legend and glorious scenery, the castle by some

believed to have been The Joyous Garde of King Arthur's Knights, stands solid on its rock, towering over the village which lies below, the most theatrical of all Northumberland's castles.

As is to be expected of such a romantic district, there is a famous legend: "The Laidley Worm of Spindlestone Heugh". Nearly every county in the country has a "worm" legend; possibly the most famous is "The Lambton Worm" which is connected with the county of Durham. The Laidley Worm may not be so well known, but it has a place in the history of Northumberland. A little way inland from Bamburgh, on the River Waren which flows into Budle Bay, is Spindlestone. It is the age old story of the wicked stepmother, in this case a queen, who, jealous of her stepdaughter, Margaret, transformed the poor girl into a "laidley worm" (a loathsome serpent), whose evil deeds terrorized the surrounding countryside. A vicar of Norham circulated a ballad which he claimed was the copy of a manuscript written in 1270 by a local ballad-monger, Duncan Fraser, who lived on the Muckle Cheviot. This claim is open to question, but whoever was responsible for the following verses gives a wonderful description of the Worm's activities:

> For seven miles east, and seven miles west,
> And seven miles north and south,
> No blade of grass was seen to grow,
> So deadly was her mouth.
> The milk of seven streakit cows,
> It was their cost to keep,
> They brought her daily, which she drank
> Before she went to sleep.
> Word went east, and word went west,
> Word is gone ower the sea,
> That a Laidley Worm in Spindlestone Heugh
> Would ruin the North Countree.

As with all the best legends, Princess Margaret had a brother, The Childe Wynde, who unfortunately was abroad at the time of the transformation. However, in due course news reached him of the Worm's "gannins on" and he set sail for home, taking the precaution of tying bunches of rowan berries to the masts of his ship, as an antidote to the witchcraft practised by the wicked queen. All the queen's attempts to drive off Childe Wynde were unavailing, and he landed safely in Budle Bay.

> The sea was calm, the weather clear,
> When they approached nigher;
> King Ida's castle well they knew
> And the banks of Bamburghshire.

8

The Royal Border Bridge, Berwick upon Tweed
Surrey's artillery crossed Twizel Bridge on the way to Flodden

Childe Wynde had some trouble in persuading his sister to cast off
her role of worm and become human again, but at last she saw reason
and, as far as is known, lived a normal life afterwards. The last verse of
the poem testifies to the truth of the story:

> Nor dwells a wight in Bamburghshire
> But swears the story's true;
> And they all run to Spindlestone,
> The rock and cave to view.

The cave has gone, where it is supposed to have been is now a quarry,
but tradition says that a large stone, The Spindlestone, is that to which
Childe Wynde tethered his horse, while entreating his sister to become
a human being again.

A legend of a very different type, and one which is probably based
on fact, is that St. Cuthbert's favourite birds were the eider-ducks,
and that for centuries these birds were called "St. Cuthbert's Chicks".
In many pictures of St. Cuthbert he is holding a head in his hand,
which legend says is that of the Northumbrian king, Oswald, who
defeated the heathen at the Battle of Heavenfield. It is also widely
believed that the head of St. Oswald was placed in the coffin of St.
Cuthbert.

An interesting old house between Bamburgh and Seahouses is
Monks House, which was built on a piece of land given by Henry II
to the monks of Farne, to build a storehouse for their provisions. At
one period the house was a public house, St. Cuthbert's Inn. Today it
is still occupied, surely one of the oldest inhabited houses in the county.

There is something to interest every type of visitor to Bamburgh
and The Farnes. For the bird watchers the islands are a paradise; not
only are there the almost tame St. Cuthbert's Chicks, but among the
many breeds of birds to be seen are cormorants, shags, oyster-catchers,
herring gulls, kittiwakes, guillemots and puffins. The grey seals seem
to be aware of their tourist value and obligingly pose for photographs.

For the historian there is everything from ecclesiastical history to
local legend, and nowhere is the glorious strand of Northumberland
more beautiful than on this stretch of coast, where the winds blow off
the North Sea. At sunset the great castle of King Ida is so theatrical
that one can almost see King Arthur and his knights and believe in The
Joyous Garde.

Holy Island is a shrine; it has been said that every Christian should
visit Canterbury, but surely every Christian should visit this island
of the saints! The name Lindisfarne is derived from "farne", which
means land, and "lindis", the stream by the land.

The fairy-tale castle on the island is also now the property of the
National Trust.

The islands and their historic remains are safe from the vandalism of the twentieth century. On a tiny island, close to Lindisfarne, St. Cuthbert's Isle, there are some remains of a little church where the saint used to worship. Tradition says that at nightfall St. Cuthbert can be seen, counting the beads which bear his name.

Every stick and stone here is history; so many legends have gathered round the Northumbrian saints that it is impossible at times to be sure which is legend and which is history. St. Cuthbert, St. Aidan and many lesser known men of God, kings and queens and the fisherfolk of Northumberland have played their part in the story of Bamburgh and The Farnes.

The writer's most vivid memory of Bamburgh is of a summer day some years ago when, with a party of seventy old gentlemen, she visited the royal city of King Ida. Up the steep road to the castle these gallant old gentlemen climbed, and then made their way to St. Aidan's Church. A member of the party was an organist and, seating himself at the organ, he played that most moving and beautiful hymn, based on the twenty-third psalm, "The Lord is My Shepherd". It was an unforgettable experience to hear seventy voices, some rather old and shaky, raised in praise in this historic and beautiful church. The words of this hymn are surely a fitting epitaph for the saints, for the Bamburgh heroines and for all the nameless and forgotten people who have contributed to the history of Northumberland.

> Where streams of living water flow
> My ransomed soul he leadeth
> And where the verdant pastures grow
> With food celestial feedeth. . . .
> And so through all the length of days,
> Thy goodness faileth never,
> Good shepherd, may I sing thy praise,
> Within thy house for ever.

IX

BERWICK AND TWEEDSIDE

Tweed says to Till,
"What gars ye rin sae still?"
Says Till to Tweed,
"Though ye rin wi' speed
An' I rin slaw,
Where ye droon yin man, I droon twa."

Anon.

In days gone by the geography of the British Isles was described as: England, Ireland, Scotland, Wales and Berwick upon Tweed. Tossed thirteen times between England and Scotland, this ancient Border town, with its red-roofed houses standing high above the River Tweed, is the cause of more confusion to the historian than any other town in the kingdom. Politically, Berwick is part of Northumberland, yet it is one of the royal burghs of Scotland! As recently as 1958 the mayor and burgesses of this once important port petitioned the Lord Lyon King of Arms for the restoration of its ancient rights, which were granted in November of that year. Now Berwick is registered in Scotland as a Scottish burgh, with its arms and shield which bears the motto: *Victoria Gloria Merces.*

Wherever one goes in Berwick its dual nationality is apparent. The police are administered by the Northumberland Constabulary; several banks are Scottish; England extends north of Tweed to beyond Berwick Bounds, yet the Tweed is a Scottish river to the end of its course. Most anomalous of all is that, until a very short time ago, a Scottish regiment was stationed in the town, the King's Own Scottish Borderers! Berwick is geographically neither England nor Scotland: it is the county of Berwick upon Tweed, with a character of its own.

The importance of Berwick's strategic position was obvious as long ago as Saxon days, its name "Bere", or "Bar", "Wic" signifying its commercial value as a grain port. Once Scotland's most important port, its position resulted in its being the most disputed town in the two kingdoms. Until 1482, when the dispute was finally settled and Berwick became part of the English kingdom, it was constantly changing hands as the fortunes of war fluctuated between English and Scots. It is not surprising that there are few old buildings in a town which has been the scene of so many sieges and sackings by the armies of both countries. The great Elizabethan walls, which succeeded the earlier Edwardian fortifications, are in such a wonderful state of preservation that Berwick upon Tweed today is the finest walled city in the kingdom. From the Scotsgate which guarded the road to the Border, it is possible to walk round the walls of the town much as one could have done in the days of Elizabeth I. It is ironical that the English queen gave the orders to strengthen the defences of the most northerly outpost of her kingdom, which, within a few short years, was to be united with the Auld Enemy by the succession of James VI of Scotland to the throne of England.

Tradition says that it is due to James VI and I that the beautiful "old" bridge across the Tweed was begun in 1611 and opened in 1624. When the king left Edinburgh in 1603 on his journey south, he crossed the Tweed by an old wooden bridge which was in such a shocking state of repair that King Jamie enquired if there was "nae man in the toon wha could build a brig", and his remarks were said to have made such an impression on the townspeople that they built a stone bridge to replace the wooden one which had so much displeased His Majesty.

Berwick is a town of bridges; and the most impressive approach is by the great railway viaduct: the Royal Border Bridge. Robert Stephenson, the celebrated Northumbrian engineer, was responsible for this link between London and Edinburgh. Standing 120 feet above the river, which here widens out into its estuary, it took three years to construct the 1¼ miles and twenty-eight arches which span the Tweed. Since 1850, when the bridge was opened by Queen Victoria, great expresses have thundered over the Tweed; trains with romantic names such as The Flying Scotsman, The Heart of Midlothian and The Talisman.

The opening of the Border Bridge by Queen Victoria was not one of the happiest of royal events. Much work and preparation had gone into the arrangements for the royal visit, but Her Majesty's train stopped only for ten minutes and the loyal people of Berwick were denied the opportunity of seeing their sovereign. Perhaps the welcome the queen had received earlier in the day at Lesbury had been too much for her!

In 1928 Victoria's great-grandson, the Prince of Wales, now Duke of Windsor, came to open the new road bridge over the river which, in deference to the prince, is named the Royal Tweed Bridge.

Unfortunately, with the coming of the railway, most of the remains of Berwick Castle were demolished. Now only a fragment of this once great stronghold clings perilously to the heights above the river. The early history of Berwick's castle is somewhat obscure. Mentioned first in 1167, it was probably rebuilt in the reign of Henry II. British

Railways have placed on record in the railway station that: "This station stands on the site of the Great Hall of Berwick Castle. Here on November 17th 1292 the claim of Robert Bruce to the throne of Scotland was declined and the decision in favour of John Baliol was given by King Edward I before the full Parliament of England and Scotland, a large gathering of the nobility and populace of both England and Scotland."

Berwick, the royal burgh, might also be described as the Royal Road. English and Scottish monarchs have led their armies through its ancient gates, some on the road to victory, others on their way to death and defeat. Edward II, that unworthy son of the "Hammer of the Scots" rode at the head of his troops through the city on the way to Bannockburn, where the English army suffered their heaviest defeat at the hands of the Scots. It was on a June day in 1314 that Scotland, under the leadership of Robert Bruce, inflicted such casualties on the English army that those who survived fled from that fatal field and joined the English king in full flight for the Border. Weary and exhausted, they passed through Berwick, little dreaming that nineteen years were to pass before Bannockburn would be avenged within the bounds of Berwick. On the 19th of July, 1333, the English, under Edward III, defeated the Scots at the Battle of Halidon Hill. The Scots were no match for the strange new weapon the English used on that July day. This was the longbow, which the English archers fired with such deadly aim, not only at Halidon Hill, but later at Crécy.

One of the greatest of Scottish patriots, William Wallace, laid siege to Berwick in 1297 and his name is commemorated in that part of the town known now as Wallace Green. After the capture of Wallace and his ghastly death, one of his limbs was sent to Berwick and no doubt exhibited to the townspeople. Laid to waste by the kings of both countries, its inhabitants massacred and their homes burnt, it is amazing that so much of this "debatable" town has survived, although after the Union many beautiful Georgian houses were built, some of which are still inhabited.

Savage indeed were the punishments meted out in the days of Border warfare. The Countess of Buchan, who had crowned The Bruce at Scone, was captured near Berwick and the wretched woman was confined in a wicker cage, which was hung outside the walls of the castle. For four years, some say six, this unhappy woman endured this dreadful punishment, which she happily survived. The stocks which at one time stood outside the Town Hall, are now within Castlegate, a grim reminder that this form of punishment was in use until 1857. Part of the body of the Earl of Northumberland, who was killed at Bramham Moor, was exhibited in Berwick in the same savage manner as that of Wallace. In the Wars of the Roses, Henry VI surrendered Berwick to the Scots and for twenty-one years it was Scottish yet again. With what bitterness the Scots must have given up this Key to their Kingdom for the last time in 1482.

With the Union of the Crowns peace at last came to the town above the Tweed and, with peace, its decline in importance as a port. Now Berwick is the centre of a great agricultural area; the fertile farms of Tweedside are world famous and at the auction marts at Berwick and Belford the home-bred cattle and sheep of Tweedside come under the hammer.

The name of Tweed is synonymous with salmon; some of the most expensive "beats" in the country are on the Tweed. At Horncliffe one can stand on the suspension bridge and watch the salmon netted. The Chain Bridge, as it is locally known, claims to be the first suspension bridge to be erected in either England or Scotland.

Among the many royal visitors to Berwick was the Princess Margaret Tudor, who married James IV of Scotland. She spent two days in the town on her way to Lamberton Toll. At one time runaway marriages were performed at the Toll and it was sometimes called the Gretna Green of the Eastern March.

Oliver Cromwell was at Berwick during the Civil War. He was never a welcome visitor as his troops left behind such havoc and destruction. To Berwick came John Churchill, whose first ennoblement was that of Baron Eyemouth, a title taken from the fishing village north of the Border. John Churchill, later the great Duke of Marlborough, was at Holyrood Palace in attendance on James, Duke of York, and made the journey to the Border town to meet his wife, Sarah, on her way from London to join him. Sarah was later to gain fame and notoriety as Duchess of Marlborough, Mistress of the Robes, Keeper of the Privy Purse, Groom of the Stole and practically ruler of the country.

Berwick has the doubtful honour of having been the headquarters of the only general in the history of the British Army who ever brought the news of his own defeat. After the Jacobite victory at Preston Pans in 1745, General John Cope galloped by way of Lauder and Coldstream to Berwick with the inglorious tidings. This was the event which inspired the well-known song:

> Hey, Johnny Cope, are ye waukin' yet?
> And are your drums abeatin' yet?
> Hey, Johnny Cope, are ye waukin' yet
> To gang for the coals in the mornin'?

Berwick has been aptly described as an exciting town, not only because of its wealth of history, but for its planning and scenery. The grey stone houses with their red roofs, the steep streets, or "gates" and the magnificent circuit of its walls combine to make the capital of the

Eastern March a truly romantic place. The harbour and pier give Berwick the added attraction of a fishing port and the tang of the sea is always in the Berwick air. The Kings' Own Scottish Borderers have gone but they have left behind their Regimental Museum and their undying history. It was a soldier of this Scottish Regiment who piped his comrades "over the top" at the Battle of Loos, a deed which gained him the Victoria Cross. Piper Laidlaw's name is engraved in the annals of the regiment whose march past is to the tune of "Blue Bonnets over the Border".

There were no pipers left to play a lament in 1513 when the body of James IV was brought to Berwick after Flodden.

The old custom of Riding the Bounds is still carried out with due ceremony every first of May yet, although Berwick is justly proud of its past and maintains many of its old customs and traditions, the people of the town live very much in the present. On the south bank of the river, at Tweedmouth, the old custom of crowning the Salmon Queen was revived in 1945. Originally this was a religious festival but it is now a social event. Held in the third week of July the celebrations include a carnival, athletic sports and a ball in the Corn Exchange at Berwick.

Many houses have been built in the last few years and the town is becoming a mixture of the old and the new. The most lovely old house is the Governor's on Palace Green, which is now occupied by the Ministry of Labour. The Customs House on the Quay Wall is a delightful example of Georgian architecture.

This part of the country is hunted by the North Northumberland Foxhounds whose kennels are near Etal. The North Northumberland hunt over country which is a mixture of moorland and grass, although a great deal of the grass country was ploughed during the last war and this trend has continued.

How interesting it would have been if Charles Dickens, when he stayed at the King's Arms Hotel in Berwick, had left a written impression of nineteenth-century Berwick. Dickens gave two of his celebrated readings in the Assembly Rooms; and evidently enjoyed his stay more than did Burns, who formed a poor impression of Berwick and its people. John Knox paid several visits to the town where, at one time, his mother-in-law lived. No doubt the great reformer took the opportunity to "thunder" from the pulpits. The parish church is believed to be one of the only two churches built during the Commonwealth, which, no doubt, explains its austere type of architecture. A curfew is still rung every night of the week except Sunday and, at one time, the Scotsgate was locked every night at ten o'clock. The names of the gates and bastions of the walls evoke the past: the Cowport, through which the townspeople drove their cattle to the pastures; the Ness Gate, which is of nineteenth-century origin, and the Shore Gate, which is much older, still survive. The Bell Tower was where the warning was sounded when danger was approaching. Meg's Mount Bastion and the King's Mount indicate their functions against attack. The Berwick speech, as might be expected, is a mixture of Scots and Northumbrian which is best described as "Tweedside".

A nineteenth-century historian gives a glowing account of the advantages of being a prisoner in Berwick Gaol! Advantages which it is doubtful if any prisoner appreciated. Views of "the German Ocean, Bambro' Castle and Holy Island" are promised; and though the cells are on an upper floor one can only assume that the Victorian writer was speaking without first-hand experience of Berwick, or any other prison in the nineteenth century. Much modernization and improvements have been carried out in this building, which is the fourth to stand on the same site. Queen Elizabeth II came to honour the ceremony when the alterations were completed.

An unusual link with royalty is that the firm of Cowes, who claim to be the original makers of the famous Berwick Cockles, were "Purveyors to H.R.H. the late Princess Mary Adelaide of Teck". History does not relate how the mother of the late Queen Mary acquired a taste for these mint-flavoured sweets, or "bullets" as sweets are called in Northumberland.

Many excellent and scholarly books have been written about this fascinating outpost of Northumberland, a town unique in the United Kingdom, which is neither Northumbrian nor Scottish. Berwick upon Tweed is a law unto itself, even to the extent of not having yet signed a peace treaty with Russia at the conclusion of the Crimean War. Berwick's name having been omitted from the treaty, the legend has now grown, with many variations, until it has become history.

Above the Royal Border Bridge for some miles Tweed is the boundary between Northumberland and Scotland. This is one of the loveliest stretches of a beautiful river. Scott, who could paint a picture in words, has sung of Tweedside in "Marmion":

> Day sat on Norham's castled steep,
> And Tweed's fair river broad and deep
> And Cheviot's mountains lone.

The Northumbrian waters of Till join the water of Tweed at Tillmouth. The historic bridge at Twizel, across which Surrey took his artillery on the way to Flodden, still stands; this peaceful, fertile land was once a battlefield, a cockpit between the two countries. Here Northumberland was laid waste by both Scots and English. Only the foundations of Wark Castle remain and the ruined keep of "Norham's castled steep" is evidence of the bloody warfare which once raged here.

Norham is one of the most delightful of the Tweedside villages with its long main street, its ancient cross and the ruins of the once powerful fortress, while the river flows deep and wide towards the sea. Here, on the 14th of February, the salmon nets are blessed to inaugurate the season which is a source of wealth and industry to the district. It was in Norham's beautiful and ancient church that, a short time ago, a daughter of the Earl of Home, then Foreign Secretary and later Prime Minister, was married. It seemed a fitting end to the old feuds, the daughter of one of Scotland's oldest families, married in a Northumbrian church. The Earl of Home, now Sir Alec Douglas-Home, owns land in Norhamshire; for this is another instance of a sub-division of Northumberland into a shire, such as is found at Bamburgh and Islandshire.

So interwoven are the histories of Northumberland and Scotland that it is sometimes difficult to stick to the political Border. In Coldstream, on the Scottish side, where Sir Alec Douglas-Home's family has lived since before Flodden, was raised a regiment which is part of the English Army. This regiment, commanded by General Monk, was instrumental in bringing about the restoration of Charles II and became the Coldstream Guards, which has strong links with Northumberland. In 1968 the regiment was given the Freedom of Coldstream. It was across Coldstream Bridge that Robert Burns first set foot on English soil and, from the remarks Burns is reported to have made, this part of Northumberland pleased him more than Berwick which he visited later.

At Norham, both in the church and the ruined castle, the influence of the great See of Durham is evident. It was not until 1882 that Newcastle became a bishopric with its diocese embracing Northumberland. Norham Castle was part of the County Palatine of Durham and the last outpost of its prince bishops. In the days of Border warfare Norham Castle was maintained by the Durham bishops, not the English kings. In 1121 the foundations of the castle were laid by Bishop Flambard. Besieged on several occasions, many additions were made to the bishop's castle. Of the days of Norham's glory Scott again paints one of his word pictures:

> The battled towers, the donjon keep,
> The loophole grates where captives weep,
> The flanking walls that round it sweep
> In yellow lustre shone.
> The warriors on the turrets high,
> Moving athwart the evening sky;
> Seemed forms of giant height;
> Their armour, as it caught the rays,
> Flash's back against the western blaze,
> In lines of dazzling light.

From the time of Bishop Flambard, until 1583, Norham was maintained as a defence; then, gradually falling into ruin, the great days of Norham were over. David of Scotland successfully stormed its walls on two occasions. Regained by Bishop Pudsey for the English, this bishop carried out repairs; and the very unpleasant King John stayed at Norham four times. Edward I was a visitor to Norham during the negotiations with the Scots in the days of Bruce and Baliol. An event in Bishop Percy's narrative poem "The Hermit of Warkworth", in which the name of Marmion first appears, inspired Sir Walter Scott to write his epic. James IV inflicted severe damage on the long-suffering stronghold before Flodden, using the famous cannon, Mons Meg, which is now on the ramparts of Edinburgh Castle, with such effect that the garrison surrendered. Described in verse more than any other North-umbrian castle, Norham, even in ruins, is impressive. In autumn when the leaves are changing colour on the tree-lined banks of Tweed, the ruined castle stands above the river as though brooding over its past glories.

The church, dedicated to St. Cuthbert, was built at about the same time as the castle, on the earlier site of a Saxon church. Very little of the original Norman building is left. Twice burnt by the Scots, drastic restorations were made in the last century, but its wonderful arcade, which was spared during the restoration, is magnificent, and is larger than a similar arcade in St. Andrew's Priory Church at Hexham. In early days Norham was a place of great importance as here was one of the principal fords across the Tweed and a flourishing market was held. This charming village is extremely popular with fishermen and to many who have never seen the once mighty castle its name is familiar. Sir Walter's verse spread the charms of Norham far beyond the boundaries of Northumberland.

A few miles up Tweed is the village of Wark. Only grass-grown foundations remain of the once proud castle, the scene of the Garter Legend. Here at Wark, in its glory as important as Norham, kings and queens held their courts. Battered and burnt by the opposing forces, Wark's importance as a Border stronghold was brief and stormy. Built some time in the early part of the twelfth century on the site of Saxon foundations, the castle was granted a charter by Henry I. Besieged by David of Scotland, burnt by the English King John, sacked by the armies of Wallace in 1297, taken by Bruce in 1313, there is little, if any, record of peace at Wark until the famous episode of "The Garter". The first three Edwards, on their journeys north, all stayed within its battle-scarred walls. Shortly after the castle was built, Stephen, one of the least known of all English sovereigns, made Wark his head-quarters.

In 1419 Wark, then in Scottish hands, was taken in melodramatic fashion by a Northumbrian Ogle and his men. These dauntless men crawled through a sewer, which led from the Tweed into the kitchen of the castle. Taking the Scots by surprise the Northumbrians killed the entire garrison and Wark was once more under English command. On their way to Flodden the Scots left Wark in ruins, and though, after the English victory, it was repaired by the Earl of Surrey, it never regained its importance and, after the union, it fell into complete ruin. The history of Wark, even for a Border fortress, is exceptionally bloody, and is expressed in the old rhyme:

> Auld Wark upon the Tweed
> Has been many a man's dead.

Beyond Wark the road runs on by the side of the river towards the much disputed Border line that through the ages has been the cause of so much bloodshed and misery. Seen through the mists of time, romanticized by poets and novelists, the battles of long ago have achieved a glamour with the passing of the years which they never had in reality. The misery and suffering are glossed over; only the heroism and the glory are remembered. In reality life in a Border county, before the Union, was the survival of the fittest. Women and children were bereft of husbands and fathers and their homes burnt to the ground. Hundreds of nameless men died in the eternal struggle between the two countries.

At Carham on the Tweed, where a stream divides Northumberland from Scotland, a battle was fought in A.D. 833 between the Danes and the English. Leland tells us that "in the 33rd year of Ecbright the Danes arrived at Lindisfarne and fought with the English at Carham, where eleven Bishops and two English counts were slain and a great number of people". Near to Carham are the extensive remains of Early British camps and a bronze sword, now in the British Museum, was discovered in the nearby Tweed.

Leland in his prosaic remark that "a great number of people" were killed, with true British understatement, sums up the history of Berwick and Tweedside. Wilson's *Tales of the Borders*, now regarded as a chronicle of the times, are tales of ordinary people, while Sir Walter Scott, in verse, immortalized Tweedside. May the Berwick of today long remain "different"; it is its greatest charm. Queen Victoria made a big mistake in missing a visit to the red-roofed town. On the hill where the English bowmen took their revenge for Bannockburn the view is dramatic of river, sea and, in the distance, the Cheviot Hills; while below the town of Berwick today goes about its lawful occasions.

Berwick is so close to the Border that it seems appropriate and permissible to conclude this chapter with a verse from a Scottish song: "Blue Bonnets Over The Border".

This was the stirring tune which Piper Daniel Laidlaw played at Loos, when the men of the 7th Battalion King's Own Scottish Borderers went over the top.

> March! March! Ettrick and Teviotdale!
> Why the deil dinna ye march forward in order?
> March! March! Eskdale and Liddesdale!
> A' the blue bonnets are over the Border!
> Many a banner spread
> Flutters above your head
> Many a crest that is famous in story!
> Mount and make ready then,
> Sons of the mountain glen,
> Fight for the Queen and the old Scottish glory!

X

GLENDALE AND FLODDEN

I've heard them lilting at our ewe milking
Lasses a' lilting afore break of day;
But now they are moaning on ilka green loaning,
The flowers of the forest are a' wede away.

Jane Elliot, THE FLOWERS OF THE FOREST

In the north-west corner of Northumberland which is Glendale,
was fought the saddest battle in all the Border's stormy history; the
Battle of Flodden Field. It was Flodden's tragic story which inspired
Jane Elliot to write the haunting lament, still played by the pipers:
"The Flowers of the Forest". On a September day in 1513 "all the
flower of Scotland" died on Branxton Hill, which is the site of the
battle, always referred to as Flodden.

Within the boundaries of romantic Glendale, which takes its name
from the River Glen, are some of the most varied scenery and most
dramatic views in all Northumberland. Glendale, which marches with
Scotland on its western border, is bounded on the north by Islandshire
and Norhamshire; on the east by Bamburghshire and on the south by
the valley of the Coquet. Dominated by the Muckle Cheviot, the
highest hill in all the Cheviot range, Glendale is a land of wild moorland
from where the rivers and burns flow down to the plain near Wooler,
to that great tract of level land which in the Ice Age may have been
the bed of a lake.

The rivers and burns have enchanting names. Most famous of the
Glendale rivers is the Till which, for the first part of its course from
where it rises on Scotsman's Knowe, is the Breamish which means
"the bright water", until joined by the Glen into which have run the
peaty waters of the College Burn. It becomes the Till at Bewick Mill,
the old couplet saying:

Foot of Breamish and head of Till
Meet together at Bewick Mill.

The Till meanders through the plain by the lovely villages of Ford
and Etal to join the Tweed at Tillmouth. Many are the castles and
Pele towers on the banks of Till, and Till can boast of one of the most

interesting and ancient bridges still in existence, the famous Twizel Bridge, which dates from the early fifteenth century, and over which the English artillery crossed on the road to Flodden.

Two of the most magnificent views in Glendale are from the cairn on the summit of Cheviot itself, which stands 2,676 feet above sea level, and from Dod Law, a hill crowned by the remains of an early British encampment, as are many of the Cheviots and the surrounding hills. From the top of Dod Law Glendale is spread out like a map. Down in the plain is the little town of Wooler, standing on the water which bears its name. To the south-west tower the giants of Cheviot, Hedgehope and Bloodybush Edge and the unmistakable Yeavering Bell with its conical peak; and south-eastwards on the very edge of Glendale is the castle of Chillingham, famous for its herd of wild white cattle, the only herd of wild cattle which still survive. The grey little market town of Wooler is a typical border town; capital of its district. It was famous in the past for the many cattle fairs which were held there and, in the last century, Wooler gained fame as a health resort where goats' milk was drunk by those in search of health. It was to Wooler that Grace Darling came in the last stages of her fatal illness. In the Rising of the '15 Lord Derwentwater and the Jacobite army spent a short time in the town, and in the '45 Prince Charlie sent a small party to commandeer quarters in order to confuse the Hanoverian Commander, General Wade, as to where the prince's army intended to cross the Border.

One of Northumberland's most notable daughters, Josephine Grey, the social reformer, was born at Milfield House, about six miles from Wooler. Her father, John Grey, was well known as an agriculturist and later became agent for the Greenwich Hospital Estates in South Tynedale. Part of Josephine Grey's childhood was spent at Dilston on the Devil's Water. This woman, who did so much valuable work in the nineteenth century to combat the social evils of the day, is more generally known by her married name of Butler. At the end of her long life she returned to her beloved Northumberland and is buried in Kirknewton churchyard under the shadow of Yeavering Bell.

On Milfield Plain, which is part of the bed of the prehistoric lake, was fought one of the many battles between Scots and English. In the month before the tragedy of Flodden, some Scots, under the Earl of Home, were returning from a raid into England where they had burnt several villages. Laden with booty which they had "lifted", Home's men were surprised by a band of English under Sir William Bulmer of Brancepeth in County Durham. The Durham men were victorious and for long years afterwards the Scot's name for the road through Milfield was "The Ill Road". Many years after the rout of Home's men, General Monk waited at Milfield with his forces before his momentous march south which brought about the Restoration.

In the twentieth century, hundreds of years after the days of Border strife, it was from Glendale that stone was quarried at Doddington to form the base of the Scottish War Memorial in Edinburgh Castle. In the church at Branxton, close beside Flodden Field, the War Memorial to the men who died in the First World War bears the names not only of Northumberland's Fusiliers but men of the Cameronians (Scottish Rifles), the Royal Scots and the Seaforths. It was in this church of St. Paul, built some time in the twelfth century and where a Norman arch has survived, that the body of James IV rested on the night after Flodden. From Branxton the body was taken to Berwick before starting on the long journey south where it finally found a resting place at Sheen in Surrey.

> Dool and wae for the order sent our lads to the Border,
> The English for aince by guile won the day:
> The flowers of the forest who fought aye the foremost,
> The prime of our land are cold in the clay.

Since those far off days Englishmen and Scotsmen have fought side by side, and what could be more appropriate than the memorial at Branxton where Northumbrian and Scottish names are on the Roll of Honour, a fitting memorial to the "Flowers of the Forest".

Branxton Church in its simplicity is one of the most delightful small churches and perhaps one of the least known in Northumberland. Close to it is the well immortalized by Scott in "Marmion" as Sybil's Well. It is doubtful that this well existed at the time of Flodden but fact and fiction have become so interwoven that it is extremely difficult to separate the two. The moss-grown well bears an inscription:

> Drink weary pilgrim, drink and stay
> Rest by the well of Sybil Grey.

The story of Flodden has been told by historians countless times, but so overshadowed have the authentic accounts become by "Marmion" that many people accept Sir Walter's famous epic as correct. Tradition and legend have gathered round the hillside in Northumberland, so that today the battlefield is hallowed ground. Every year in early August a wreath is laid upon the cairn, surmounted by the granite cross that stands on Piper's Hill which was erected in 1910. This ceremony is held in August to coincide with Coldstream's Civic Week, and was inaugurated about twenty years ago.

From the Scottish side of Tweed the "Coldstreamer" (a young man chosen by the people of Coldstream) rides at the head of a cavalcade of horsemen, sometimes a hundred strong, and after the laying of the wreath the cavalcade climbs the steep ascent to the summit of Branxton

Wooler and the Cheviots from Dod Law

Hill where a service is held, and an address given to pay tribute to Scots and English who fought and died so long ago on Flodden Field.

In 1964, the address was given by the Lord Lieutenant of Berwickshire, the Earl of Haddington, K.T. The service is impressive in its simplicity, and as the last notes of the lament are played, those who stand on Branxton Hill in England, looking towards Scotland, realize that, inappropriate though the date of the ceremony is, nothing could be more appropriate than the inscription on the memorial: "To the Brave of Both Nations 1513".

It was in the early summer of 1513 that King James IV of Scotland made the fatal decision to invade the kingdom of his brother-in-law, Henry VIII. James was dissatisfied with the dowry he had received with his English bride, Margaret Tudor; Henry was occupied with a war in France, and to the Scots king it seemed a golden opportunity to invade England. Legend affirms that the Queen of France sent James her glove, accompanied by a love letter, urging him for her sake to attack the English on their own ground and so relieve the pressure on France. James IV was very much a Stewart and such an appeal, if the French queen actually made it, would arouse his sense of gallantry. Whatever the decisive factor was, the Scottish armies assembled at Edinburgh. The official reason given for the invasion was to avenge the death, in a brawl which involved a Heron of Ford Castle and Sir Robert Kerr, warden of the Eastern March on the Scottish side.

None of the chroniclers agree as to the strength of the Scottish army, the numbers varying from sixty to one hundred thousand. How many fought on that September day is not known, but the numbers of the Scottish dead were at least ten thousand. With pipes playing and drums beating, the doomed army marched for the Border, and on the 22nd of August, when Tweedside would be looking its loveliest, the river was forded near Coldstream.

The fortresses of Wark, Norham and Etal were burnt by the advancing Scots and King James made his headquarters in a Heron stronghold, the castle of Ford, close to the Till. King James has been accused by some, rightly or wrongly, of dallying at Ford with Lady Heron, who was young and attractive; while others say that Lady Heron encouraged Jamie's advances in order to prolong his stay and thus give the English armies more time to rally their forces, under the Earl of Surrey, who was the king's representative while Henry was in France.

James was never able to resist a pretty woman and no doubt he was content to while away those September days, the last of his life, with the Lady of Ford Castle. The marriage between Scotland's king and the Tudor princess had failed to keep the peace between the two countries and Queen Margaret shed few tears for her husband. The

9

Chillingham Castle

romantic legend that she was anxiously waiting at Linlithgow, in what is now called Queen Margaret's Tower, for news of her husband is a figment of the imagination. Waiting she certainly was but not for news of the king. She was waiting for the Earl of Angus, "Archibald Bell-the-Cat", who quarrelled with his king before the battle and left his two sons to die at Flodden, while he himself was later to marry the royal widow.

While Jamie was dallying at Ford, the English were moving rapidly. The famous Stanley archers had landed at Tynemouth and, joining with the forces of the Bishop of Durham and the Percys, were marching across Northumberland. One of the many unanswered questions connected with this most disastrous Scottish defeat is why the Scottish military commanders allowed the English artillery to cross Twizel Bridge. Some say it was mistaken chivalry on the part of King James; others that it was lack of military knowledge. Whatever it was, it was one of the many blunders made in that fateful September, which was to lead to Black Friday, as the 9th of September was called for many years after Flodden. The Earl of Surrey was one of the ablest and one of the most ruthless of Henry's commanders, a member of the Howard family, this man, who led the English forces to victory, has left a black record of cruelty behind him. Close to Wooler there are the ruins of the house which Surrey made his headquarters. To reconstruct the actual battle, one would need the ability and the pen of a man such as Sir Brian Horrocks. The English army numbered about thirty thousand, foot soldiers and cavalry; Surrey himself commanded the centre on the site where Branxton Vicarage stands today. King Jamie set fire to Ford Castle when he said goodbye to Lady Heron, an action which is out of keeping with his chivalrous character. Perhaps the susceptible James had realized that Lady Heron was only playing a part!

The Scots took up their position on Branxton Hill, and, whether it be authentic or not, Scott's description of the scene in "Marmion" is unforgettable:

> From Flodden Ridge
> The Scots beheld the English host
> Leave Barmoor Wood, their evening post
> And heedful watched them as they crossed
> The Till by Twizel Bridge.

Friday, the 9th of September, 1513, is a date that is forever one of Scotland's most bitter memories. It was about four o'clock in the afternoon that the battle began. By nightfall Flodden was history. Bravely though the Scotsmen fought and died, they were not only out-manoeuvred but out-generalled by Surrey's army. Rushing down the hill to meet the onslaught of the English archers, the Scots kicked off their brogues in an effort to steady themselves on the slippery slope. Hundreds of the Scottish corpses were found barefooted when the gruesome task of counting the dead was carried out.

No man ever died more bravely in battle than James IV of Scotland. With the flower of his army dead or wounded the Stewart king fought on, surrounded only by a handful of his countrymen, until at last he fell, mortally wounded. Scotland lost not only her king, but twelve earls, Crawford, Montrose, Lennox, Argyle, Errol, Athol, Morton, Cassilis, Bothwell, Rothes, Caithness and Glencairn; fifteen lords and chieftains; bishops and abbots and a natural son of the king. Almost every noble family in Scotland was in mourning for a member killed on that September day when the evening sun shone on the living and the dead, the great and the humble, who had followed their king to the end. More than five thousand Englishmen found their last resting place in Glendale. The English, too, paid dearly for their great victory.

> We'll hear nae mair lilting at our ewe milking,
> Women and bairns are heartless and wae,
> Sighing and moaning on ilka green loaning,
> The flowers of the forest are a' wede away.

is Scotland's incomparable lament for Flodden.

Glendale can not only boast that within its boundaries is the most famous of Northumberland's many battlefields, but also the highest hills in the Cheviot range and the Wild White Cattle of Chillingham. The Cheviot valleys have a beauty which is peculiarly their own. The College Valley is particularly beautiful. Wild and remote, this valley has a pack of foxhounds which bears its name. These hounds hunt the hill foxes, which are a menace to the Cheviot and Blackfaced sheep which are grazed here.

The Cheviot sheep are indigenous to this part of Northumberland. In the days of the Clearances in the Scottish Highlands, when the landowners evicted the crofters to make way for the coming of the sheep, a Northumbrian Robson was responsible for the importation of this breed to the Highlands. They are now known as "North Country Cheviots" to distinguish them from the native sheep of the Cheviot country.

On the old maps the spelling of College included a "D" which is sometimes used today. The burn rises at the foot of Cheviot and flows northwards to Kirknewton, where it joins the Glen. This is the country hunted by the hill pack, which was established some thirty-five years ago.

The Cheviots are largely grass-covered, with heather and bracken towards their summits. In Cheviot itself are two deep ravines, Henhole and The Bizzle, both somewhat terrifying in their grandeur. These ravines are a favourite sanctuary for ravens, whose presence adds wildness to the scene. In the Cheviots, too, are herds of wild goats which roam the lonely moors of Kidland.

Where the College Burn and the Glen unite is the village of Kirknewton. Within the church is a most curious carving representing the Virgin and Magi. The Wise Men are apparently wearing kilts! The church dates from Norman times but has twice been restored. Yeavering Bell, the Cheviot with the most delightful name of all, towers above the valley. Recently investigations have been carried out by air to obtain photographs of the extensive "city" which is thought to be that of Edwin, a Christian king of Northumbria. Bede records the fact that Edwin's palace was at Yeavering, and among the many discoveries have been a Bronze Age cremation cemetery and several pottery urns.

Almost under the shadow of Yeavering is Coupland Castle. This is one of the very few fortified castles built after the Union, probably in 1619. The Couplands were once a well-known Glendale family but the castle was built by the Wallace family. With two or three changes of ownership, Coupland has been altered and restored, but its ghost haunted the castle until 1925. Who, if anyone, exorcized the ghost or what put an end to its "goings on" is not recorded. Owned now by the Aitcheson family, the grounds of Coupland Castle are at times open to the public. The lovely walled garden is the creation of the late Sir Walter Aitcheson. On the summit of Yeavering Bell are the extensive remains of an Early British camp from where the watchers would light their fires to warn the many other hill forts of approaching danger.

At the foot of Dod Law, in the village of South Doddington, is all that remains of the Pele tower, or Bastle House, which claims to be the last fortification built (by a Grey of Chillingham) before the Union. The crumbling tower is in a farm yard and is sadly neglected.

At the foot of Cheviot, on its southern side, is the Harthope Burn which flows between Hedgehope and Cheviot. Approached from Langleeford, this is the easiest ascent of the hill which fails only by 300 feet to qualify as a mountain. The top of Cheviot is boggy land and there is nearly always some snow lying, even in summer time. Wild and beautiful in summer, but dangerous and cruel in the storms and blizzards of winter is the Cheviot Country.

Within sight of Cheviot is Chillingham. Chillingham Castle, owned by the Earl of Tankerville, is now uninhabited. A licence was granted to Sir Thomas de Heton in 1344 to crenellate the castle which later passed into the possession of the Grey family of Wark on Tweed and thence by marriages to the Bennets, the family name of the Earls of Tankerville. The glory of Chillingham is its setting. Backed by the steep height of Ros Castle with its remains of earthworks, Chillingham Castle looks out across the Till towards the Cheviot Range. Now rapidly falling into decay, Chillingham in its heyday must have been one of the most romantic of the Border castles.

Today the fame of Chillingham is the herd of Wild White Cattle, unique in the British Isles, which roam the park. There is always the fear that, should enough heifer calves not be born, the strain will die out. The animals have all the characteristics of their wild ancestry and have never become domesticated. The king bull is chosen by the herd, and as long as he is fit and strong he reigns over his subjects, but when infirmity and old age creep upon the king he is banished from the herd. Should the banished leader attempt to return to the herd, he is in danger of being gored to death by the new king. When a calf is born the cows are most dangerous and will attack a stranger on sight. Permission has to be obtained from the park keeper to visit the herd. The cattle have a black muzzle; the inside of the ear and part of the outside are red and the horns are white with black tips. A society has now been formed, whose object is to make every effort to preserve the herd. In days gone by the local people used to join in shoots to keep down the numbers of the cattle!

In October 1872 the Prince and Princess of Wales (later King Edward VII and Queen Alexandra) visited Chillingham and a shoot was arranged for His Royal Highness. There is a detailed and graphic description of the days' events in a most informative little book by E. J. Wilson, published in 1886. Mr. Wilson tells us that on the 16th of October the prince had the honour of shooting the king of the herd. It seems to have been carried out with much pomp and ceremony, as though it had been a lion hunt! Mounted on a shooting pony and attended only by his host, two keepers and his own Highland ghillie, the prince rode into the park in which, near one of the sheds, a cartload of hay was standing, ready to be distributed among the cattle, as it was hoped that the cattle would follow the cart and that His Royal Highness, being concealed among the provender, might be thus enabled to get within reach. Much time and energy were spent in the efforts to entice the king of the herd within range of the royal sportsman's rifle, until at last the bull, which by this time must have been a sitting target, was, according to the report, shot in the head. As was usual in Victorian days, a gruesome photograph of the victor and vanquished was taken. The Prince of Wales posed near the carcase and he was presented with the head of his victim. History does not relate what was done with the gory trophy but we do know that the carcase, which weighed "upwards of sixty stones, was distributed among the deserving poor of Wooler". No doubt "the deserving poor" were all in favour of royal shoots.

Chillingham church possesses a most beautiful monument to the memory of one of Chillingham's original owners, Sir Ralph Grey and his wife, Elizabeth. Dating, like so many Northumbrian churches, from the twelfth century, this church is dedicated to St. Peter and has been restored and altered on many occasions.

Glendale is indeed rich in attractive villages and Chatton, which is very close to Chillingham, is one of the most pleasing, with its rows of cottages and peaceful atmosphere; though long ago Chatton suffered heavily from the inroads of the Scots and the present vicarage is incorporated in a Pele tower.

If one sticks closely to "wards" and divisions, which the present writer does not, the lovely valley of the Breamish, above Ingram, is not within the confines of Glendale, but this Cheviot valley has more in common with this north-west corner than it has with its own ward of Coquetdale. The road to Ingram leaves the Wooler road north of Powburn and wanders up the course of the river to Hartside, where the gated road begins. These gates are often tied to prevent those who have no respect for other people's property from defiling the country-side with their masses of litter and broken bottles. Indeed the Ingram valley has become too popular, especially at weekends! Above Hartside, on the Linhope Burn, is one of Northumberland's loveliest waterfalls, Linhope Spout, which drops over the steep crags into a pool fifty-six feet below.

On practically every eminence in this district are the remains of prehistoric man; Greave's Ash, Megrim's Knowe and Chesters were all important camps. Tomlinson, in his *Comprehensive Guide to Northumberland*, defines Ingram as meaning "the home of the ancient people of the land". Although many people decry the older historians, it must be remembered that since their books were written many discoveries have been made and more revolutionary theories advanced. At the time of publication these older writers used the material available to them then.

The old tower of Crawley stands out conspicuously on its height above Powburn, which is on the main road to Wooler. The Devil's Causeway passes through the garden of the Plough Inn. Crawley Tower is built on the site of yet another Early British camp, in a commanding position above the Breamish. One of the many Northumbrian Herons was granted permission by Edward III to fortify his tower house of Crawley. In the survey of 1541 Crawley is summarily dismissed as being in need of repair, which is not surprising as this was long before the Union made an end to raiding and reiving.

A legend connected with this Border tower is that one tenant on the estate had a horse on which he had ridden many a foray into Scotland. The owner of Crawley, hearing of the prowess of the horse, offered the man his whole estate in exchange for the horse but, so much did this nameless Borderer value his horse, he replied "I can find lands when I have use for them but there is nae sic beast on yon side of the Cheviot nor yet o' this side, an' I wadna part wi' him if Crawley were made of gold!" Such was the value of a good horse in the raiding days. The view from Crawley Tower is another of the many glorious "map-like" views of Northumberland, which embraces the Vale of Whittingham and the rolling hills of Coquetdale.

Lilburn Tower and Ilderton are two of the many fascinating places of interest which lie south of Wooler. Lilburn has been the home of the Collingwood family since 1793. This famous family numbers amongst its sons George, who was "out" in the Rebellion of the '15, and who paid for his loyalty to the Stuart cause with his life. This George, who is mentioned by name in "Derwentwater's Farewell", lived at Eslington Tower, near Whittingham. The most famous of the family was the admiral, who, though born in the city of Newcastle, where Milburn House stands today, had his roots in the county. The family name is commemorated in "The Collingwood Arms" at Cornhill. Like many old families the Collingwoods have a prophecy, which is told in verse:

> The Collingwoods have borne the name
> Since in the bush the buck was ta'en;
> But when the bush shall hold the buck,
> Then welcome faith and farewell luck.

Dobson, the architect who was responsible for the design of many of Newcastle's public buildings, was also responsible for the modern house at Lilburn. The old tower, which is now a ruin, dates from the time of Edward II and was once the seat of the Lilburn family.

From the little village of Ilderton another Northumbrian family took their name; a family which unhappily has practically died out. This is a land of ancient families. In the churchyard at Ilderton is the Roddam mausoleum. The Roddams, now Holderness-Roddams, claim to be one of the few pre-Conquest families in Northumberland.

On the very Border of England and Scotland are the little towns of Yetholm and Kirk Yetholm. At one time the Yetholms were the headquarters of the gypsies. In the days of the vagrants the many tinkers who travelled Northumberland were designated by the local name of "muggers" because they sold pottery mugs.

Every visit to Glendale reveals something new; it is so rich in history and scenery that it is impossible to do justice in words to all the many villages, castles and camps within its borders. Wark on Tweed and Carham, although included in the Tweedside chapter, are part of Glendale ward.

Perhaps of all the villages, Ford, with its memories of King Jamie and Flodden, is the most interesting and today Ford is a model village.

The castle of the Herons, which received such rough treatment from the Scottish armies, has been restored and is the property of Lord Joicey, who lives at nearby Etal. The castle itself is rented to the Northumberland Education Committee which holds courses within its historic walls. Ford's ghost is, of course, that of James IV, who, so the story says, can be heard girding on his armour in The King's Chamber. Like so many of the castles and fortified houses of the Borders, Ford is named after its first owners, one of the now many extinct families. Held by the Herons until 1536, Ford passed by the marriage of a Heron heiress into the possession of the Carrs of Etal. Battered and burnt by the Scots, the castle fell into ruin after the Union. Changing hands once more the castle became the property of the Gay Delavals and the pseudo-Gothic "improvements" were carried out. Later, when in possession of that most gifted member of the Delaval family, Louisa, Marchioness of Waterford, further renovations were made, in much better taste than that of her predecessors. Standing on a slope above the village, the castle dominates the scene. The modernized cottages line the village street and the water of Till flows close by.

Ford owes much of its interest and charm to the Marchioness of Waterford, who adorned the walls of the village school with murals of her own creation. Taking local people as her models, Lady Waterford depicted them as characters from the Old Testament. The baby who was the model for the infant Moses lived to be a very old man and died within living memory. No longer used as a school, the room decorated by her ladyship is now used for village functions, among them the Women's Institute, who, surely of all Northumberland's numerous W.I.s, meet in the most unusual and attractive setting. The murals have recently been restored and are a lasting memorial to a lady, who in her youth was a famous beauty.

The many visitors to Ford are enchanted by the old forge whose doorway is built in the form of a horse shoe.

On a summer evening, when the sun is setting, the battlements of the castle stand out like etchings. This fortress, which has seen so much history, was the last place in Northumberland to shelter Scotland's king, who, like so many of the Stewart line, achieved his immortality by his manner of dying.

All Glendale's history, as is that of Tweedside, is overshadowed by the carnage of Flodden. In Sir Walter Scott's dramatic description of the battle he conveys an unsurpassed picture of the last moments of the king.

> . . . The squadrons sweep,
> To break the Scottish circle deep,
> That fought around their king.
> But yet, though thick the shafts as snow,
> Though charging knights like whirlwinds go,

Though billmen ply the ghastly blow,
Unbroken was the ring.
The stubborn spearmen still made good
Their dark impenetrable wood,
Each stepping where his comrade stood
The instant where he fell.
No thought was there of dastard flight;
Linked in the serried phalanx tight,
Groom fought like noble, squire like knight,
As fearlessly and well,
Till utter darkness closed her wing
O'er their thin host and wounded king   ("Marmion")

XI

THE MORPETH DISTRICT

Hi' canny man hoy a ha'penny oot,
Me father's in jail, and we canna get him oot.
We'll have some fun, there is ne doot,
Hi' canny man, hoy a ha'penny oot.
Harry Nelson, HI' CANNY MAN HOY A HA'PENNY OOT

In the sixteenth century, Leland, the historian, visited the town of Morpeth and his description has been preserved. "Morpet, a market town, is XII long miles from New Castle. Wansbeke, a praty ryver, rynnithe threge the syde of the towne. On the hyther syde of the ryver is the principall churche of the towne. On the same syde is the fayre castle standing upon a hill, longing with the towne to the Lord Dacres of Gilsland. The towne is long and metely well buylded with low housys, the streets pavyed. It is a far fayrar towne than Alnwicke."

Of the "fayre castle", which was built sometime after the Conquest, little now remains. Whether or not Morpeth is a "fayrar" town than Alnwick is a matter of opinion. The two towns are entirely different. Alnwick is dominated by its great castle, while Morpeth is a busy, bustling market town, intersected by the River Wansbeck, which is here crossed by an imposing bridge, the work of the celebrated Scottish engineer of the eighteenth century, Thomas Telford. Would that there were more contemporary accounts such as Leland's to help the twentieth-century writer. There are two different accounts of the burning of Morpeth Castle. One is that King John, in his efforts to break the power of the Northumbrian barons, was responsible; the other is that the people of Morpeth themselves set fire to the castle rather than allow it to fall into the hands of the English king. The latter has more ring of truth, as John was hated bitterly by the Northumbrians, whose county he laid to the sword. Passing out of the de Merley family by the failure of the male line, the castle became the property of Lord Greystoke, and by yet another failure of the male line, it passed eventually through the Dacres to the great family of Howard, one of whom was created first Earl of Carlisle. The heir to the earldom of Carlisle has the courtesy title of Lord Morpeth, and the beautifully laid-out gardens which rise above the south bank of the Wansbeck are Carlisle Park.

A royal visitor to Morpeth Castle was the Tudor Princess Margaret, who became the queen of James IV. After the tragedy of Flodden, the widowed queen married the Earl of Angus, and crossed the Border into Northumberland, where she gave birth to a daughter at the castle of Harbottle in Coquetdale. Considering Harbottle too wild and primitive a place, the Countess of Angus made the journey from the Coquet Valley to Morpeth Castle, where she stayed for some time. This baby girl, born in Northumberland, grew up to marry the Earl of Lennox and become the mother of Darnley.

In 1644, the castle is described as "a ruinous hole, not tenable by nature, far less by art". The writers of the past were certainly outspoken. The scene has changed since then, from the heights of "the ruinous hole" the ground drops sharply to the river, through the beautiful park, where the flower beds are a blaze of colour and the Wansbeck is spanned by numerous bridges.

Two of these bridges, High Stanners and Low Stanners, take their unusual names from the stony unenclosed ground which here borders the river. Until the Second World War, the children of Morpeth used to sing their traditional song, on the Stanners, a verse of which is quoted at the beginning of this chapter. If a "canny man" hoyed (threw) a coin to the children, they would dook, or dive into the river to retrieve it. When Montrose and his army were marching south in the days of the Civil Wars they besieged the castle above the river. Perhaps they were responsible for the ruinous plight of the once proud de Merley stronghold.

One of the many explanations of the town's name is that it was the moor path, but again there are many differences of opinion about the correct origin. In 1835, the town became a municipal borough, and apart from the industrial boroughs of Tyneside and Blyth and Berwick upon Tweed (which is a law unto itself), Morpeth is the only market town in the county which has a mayor. The old custom of ringing the curfew is still carried out, and every four years the "bounds" of the Borough are ridden by a company of horsemen, led by the mayor. Again Morpeth and Berwick have a tradition in common for they are the only two Northumberland boroughs where the bounds are beaten, or ridden.

This busy town, which is fringed by the Great Coalfield of Northumberland on the east, is most fortunate in its approaches by road. From the south by way of the Great North Road, the industrial area is left behind at Seaton Burn, and the road runs through agricultural scenery with only distant views of the pit heaps on its eastern side. Two massive figures of white bulls surmount the stone pillars at the entrance to Viscount Ridley's estate at Blagdon.

Stannington village, now by-passed by the new road, had until a short time ago as the name of its inn "The Howard Arms", a reminder that the Morpeth district was once largely owned by that family. Now the name has been changed to "The Ridley Arms". Stannington church, which is situated some distance from the village, west of the North Road, has a church tower which stands out as a landmark for many miles in this rather flat part of the county. "Twelve long miles", to quote Leland, and then the outskirts of Morpeth begin. The road sweeps under the overhanging slopes, a mass of daffodils in spring, past the County gaol, and though Northumbrian wrongdoers are now sent to prison in Durham, the town is still the headquarters of the Northumberland Constabulary. In the dialect of the county, the policeman is the "pollis". The narrow main street of the town is part of the Great North Road, and the Morpeth pollises have a busy time at weekends, dealing with the traffic on its way to and from the coast. The town is rightly proud of its Town Hall which was designed by Vanbrugh for an Earl of Carlisle. The Clock Tower, in Oldgate, dates from the fifteenth century and is a type of clock tower or belfry rarely to be found in England. Restorations have been carried out during the years, but the tower still remains one of Morpeth's most interesting buildings. Here in Oldgate for a time lived Lord Colling-wood of Trafalgar fame.

The grammar school has a long and honourable history. It was founded in the reign of Edward VI. There is a fascinating account of its rules and regulations in *The History, Topography and Directory of Northumberland* published in 1855. Education has indeed changed since the Morpeth boys attended their school in the days of Queen Victoria. According to statutes passed in 1811 and 1818, and which were apparently still in force when the *Directory* was written, the cost for a paying pupil was £1 1s. a quarter. The sons of the freemen received a free education. "The master must have the degree of Master or Bachelor of Arts, and be skilled in the Latin and Greek languages, and produce testimonials as to his conduct and doctrine. The usher must possess similar qualifications as the master, but need not possess a degree. The course of instruction prescribed embraces the principles of the Christian religion, the Church catechism, Latin, Greek and English Grammar, the rudiments of Hebrew, and out of school hours, writing and arithmetic, geography and mathematics and other instructions." The income at the time of the charity commissioner's report amounted to £224 2s. 3d. but by a recent decision of the vice-chancellor of England this school has become entitled to lands in the township of Netherwitton of the value of £1,500. If this curriculum had been in force since the founding of the school, how delighted the boys must have been in 1715, when the Jacobite Army on its march towards Newcastle granted them a day's holiday.

The bells of Morpeth church rang out when James III was proclaimed; the rector, who said prayers for the Stuart king, hastily substituted the name of Hanoverian George when the news came that Government troops had reached Newcastle!

The church of St. Mary's is close to the castle, and dates in its oldest part from the fourteenth century, but so many additions and restorations have been carried out that very little of the original church remains. Morpeth church has a singularly attractive setting, and an old custom which survives here, as it does in many parts of the county, is that when a wedding takes place, the church gates are tied as the newly married pair come out of church, and until the bridegroom has paid toll they must stay behind the tied gates.

In the churchyard is a gruesome reminder of the days of the body-snatching. This is a watch tower, dating from 1831, which was about the time when the notorious Burke and Hare, and others of their kind, raided the churchyards in many parts of the country. Like so many country towns within easy reach of a thickly populated area, many housing estates have sprung up within the last few years, yet in the town itself are some delightful Georgian houses. Morpeth still has a country atmosphere, and although the functions of the Hirings have died out, those at Morpeth are still advertised as they are in Newcastle, and the country people come in from the surrounding districts. To travel in a local bus from the town on a Hiring Day is an experience, and the high spirits of the passengers are evidence of the good cheer to be had in the old inns of the town. One of the traditional Northumbrian folk dances is the rousing "Morpeth Rant".

Morpeth is a Parliamentary borough and returns a member to Westminster. A famous lord chancellor of England, Lord Eldon, and his bride, Bessie Surtees, with whom he eloped from the old house on Newcastle Quay-Side, stayed in "The Queens Head" at Morpeth on their way back from a runaway wedding at Coldstream in Scotland. This old coaching house has a wonderful seventeenth-century fireplace, above which are the arms of the family of Pye. In the coaching days, the inns of Morpeth did a thriving trade, and although many of them have been modernized they have long histories.

On New Year's Day, the Morpeth Hounds hold their meet in Castle Square. This pack was established in 1818, by Sir Matthew White Ridley, and hunts over the predominantly grassy country of the Morpeth district. The Morpeth Parliamentary division is itself sharply divided; east of the Great North Road is the densely populated coalfield, yet within it are some delightful and historic villages. The rest of the division is rural, and it is rich in picturesque villages and unspoilt scenery. The town has a pipe band which is famous far beyond Morpeth. The Morpeth men do not play the small pipes of their county as their pipes are Scottish.

In east Northumberland live the pitmen, these men who until not so long ago lived in the rows of back-to-back houses which are now fast disappearing. The pitman is a completely different man from the countryman of Northumberland—in his own traditions, his distinctive speech and a type of humour which delights in telling stories against himself. East Northumberland is the land of the whippets, the Bedlington terriers, the pie- and onion-eating competitions, quoits and Association football; the "other" Morpeth country is the farming, foxhunting fraternity. This is the country of squires and great houses, yet these two vastly different types of Northumbrians uphold equally the reputation of Northumberland as one of the most hospitable and kindly counties in the kingdom. The visitor is given the same generous hospitality by "the Quality", to use the old term, as is dispensed, though in a different way, by the pitman's wife, and this writer speaks from experience of both. The "foreigner" from the South would need a phrase book to understand the pitman's English. "Howay in, and hev yer teas, and sit yerself doon on the cracket" would be a puzzle for any "incomer". The "cracket" is a wooden oblong stool, with a hole in the centre, in which a finger is inserted to lift it. There are still some to be seen in the colliery houses, though with the march of time the old furniture is being "hoyed out" and there are no "desk" beds left. This was a piece of furniture which could fold up and enclose the bed; in the old days, there was so little room in the back-to-backs, that a desk bed was a necessity.

The Northumbrian miner is the best of his kind; there have been fewer strikes in these coalfields than in any in the kingdom. Fond of sport and not above a bit of poaching, these men, who with their ancestors helped to make the county industrially wealthy, can be seen in their hundreds at Newcastle Races. Dressed in their best navy-blue suits, many still wearing cloth caps, these men by their support of the Northumberland Plate, have given to this race the local name of "The Pitman's Derby". It is held in Gosforth Park, which is only three miles beyond the city boundary of Newcastle, and is one of the most attractive race courses in the country. Within the 800 acres of Gosforth Park is not only the race course, but a golf club and a bird sanctuary. At the end of Race Week, which is the last full week in June, the Pitman's Derby is run. In 1962, this meeting was graced by the presence of the Queen Mother. Just off the Great North Road, on the way to Morpeth, where there are notices warning motorists of subsidence due to coal-mining, is this delightful park, where even from the top of the grandstand only one pit-heap is visible. In recent years, the June meeting has become so fashionable that it has been described as "The Ascot of the North". Newcastle Races were originally held on the Town Moor, which is a huge expanse of open space, where the freemen of Newcastle still have a right to graze cattle.

On this moor, in Race Week, the largest fair in the country is held. Known locally as "The Hoppings" the miners and their families flock in from the colliery districts to celebrate their annual holiday. Though the tradition of the Race Week holiday is on the wane on account of the introduction of holidays with pay, the miners and shipyard workers go further afield, but many are still faithful to the traditional visit to "The Plate" and "The Hoppings".

On New Year's Day a very different kind of race is run from Morpeth to Newcastle. In this race, the competitors are men instead of horses, and they leave Morpeth with much flourish and ceremony.

The town of Bedlington, which is the centre of the shire or division which bears its name, is a typical Northumbrian mining town. Second only in size to Ashington, Bedlington could be described as the centre of the colliery districts. Here in June is held the Miners' Gala or picnic, where the miners and their families come to listen to the speeches of their leaders or, in many cases, simply for a day out. The miners' picnic is a tradition; the colliery brass bands play, and the banners of the various Lodges are carried in procession. Vast quantities of beer are drunk, the women and children wear their "Sunday best", and the pitmatic speech of east Northumberland is heard in all its richness. Sitting on their "hunkers" (haunches, a word derived from the Icelandic, to crouch) the pitmen of Northumberland crack (talk) with their marrers (friends). Some of the politicians from the South who come to speak at the Gala must wonder if they have come to a foreign land!

Bedlingtonshire at one time was the property of the Bishops of Durham, and the patron of the living is still the Dean and Chapter of Durham Cathedral. The church of St. Cuthbert is about a thousand years old, and is one of the many in Northumberland where rested the bones of the saint to whom it is dedicated. The main street of the town is wide and pleasant with its interesting old market cross. A native breed of dog, the Bedlington terrier, is famous. Not far from Bedlington and close to the mining village of Pegswood, is one of Northumberland's lovely and unspoilt villages—where the road drops down steeply to the banks of the Wansbeck, is Bothal, with its church and castle. The name is from the Anglo-Saxon, *bottell*, meaning an abode. Bothal is mentioned as early as 1166, when it was held by the Bertrams; like all Northumbrian castles, Bothal has suffered many vicissitudes, passing by marriage eventually to the Dukes of Portland. Bothal is very peaceful, which is surprising in the midst of the coalfield. In this part of the county a phrase book is necessary for the visitor, who would never find the village of Ulgham, unless he had been warned that the local pronunciation is Uffam!

The country west of Morpeth is a complete contrast to that east of the Great North Road. Here in rural surroundings, as yet unspoilt by progress and purely agricultural, is some of the softer scenery of Northumberland and villages rich in history. The charms of Hartburn, Mitford, Meldon, Bolam Lake and Whalton are difficult to describe in words. At any time of year this countryside is beautiful, but is perhaps at its loveliest in the spring, when the churchyard at Mitford is a mass of snowdrops and the lilacs and laburnums line the wide street of Whalton.

Mitford on the Wansbeck has the ruins of a castle, a great house where members of the Mitford family still live, and a church of exceptional beauty. One of this ancient family was the author of *Our Village*. Originally Norman, the church was restored in 1874, when the tall spire was added. One of the recent vicars of Mitford was a McLeod from the Isle of Skye, and a picture of Canon McLeod, as he was, hangs in Dunvegan Castle.

The river scenery near Mitford is delightful, with the Wansbeck flowing between tree-covered slopes towards Morpeth, while farther up the river is the appropriately named Hartburn, where the burn or stream of that name joins the river which rises in the wild country of the Wanny Hills. Hartburn church is of such ancient origin that the name of the saint to whom it was dedicated has been forgotten, but buried in the churchyard is one whose name will not easily be forgotten by historians and Northumbrians; this is the Reverend John Hodgson, vicar of Hartburn, whose work and research did so much to preserve for all time the history of Northumberland. It was this John Hodgson who began the monumental series of the history of the county. Dying in his sixties, John Hodgson left his tremendous undertaking unfinished. In 1890 Thomas Hodgkin formed a committee with the object of carrying on John Hodgsons' work. Under the presidency of the then Duke of Northumberland and other prominent men, an appeal was made for funds, and with material made available by Hodgson's grandson the scheme was put into operation. There are now fifteen volumes of *The County History*, written by various authorities, which are of inestimable value to those who wish to make a scholarly study of the rich and varied history of Northumberland.

One of the most famous of Northumberland's legends is associated with Meldon, a few miles from Hartburn. Meldon Hall was originally a seat of the Heron's, passing as so many estates did from one great family to another; Fenwicks and Radcliffes have in their turn been the owners of Meldon, until with the sequestration of the Derwentwater estates it became the property of the Greenwich Hospital who sold it to the present owners, the Cooksons. The hall, which is modern, has a most attractive setting in parkland—land where, tradition says, Cromwell rested his troops in 1651 on his return from Scotland. Meg of Meldon's ghost is surely one of the most restless in the county and a great deal of her tribulations she appears to have brought upon her-

Simonside from Rothbury, the capital of Coquetdale

self by her mean and grasping disposition. Born a Selby, Meg married Sir William Fenwick of Wallington. Hated by the tenants on the Meldon estate, Meg had the reputation of being a witch. Having no trust or faith in anyone when it came to money, apparently not even her husband, Meg, rather like a squirrel, was in the habit of hiding her money and treasures and then forgetting where the hiding-place was. When death at last overtook Meg, her ghost haunted the Meldon lands for seven years searching for the treasure. Then, the legend does not explain why, Meg was allowed seven years' rest before starting the search again. Several times her ghost was reported to have been seen; sometimes this versatile lady assumed the shape of a black dog, at others that of a lovely woman, and then, after taking a rest in a stone coffin at Newminster Abbey, she would be seen crossing the bridge at Meldon, which is known by the name of Meg's Bridge. In an old house at Meldon, once used as a village school, the ceiling is said to have collapsed and pieces of gold fallen upon the heads of the astonished children. At one time a picture of Meg was in existence, in which she was portrayed as a witch. Whether or not Meg has found peace is not known, but she is still remembered in the Morpeth country; one of the point-to-point winners a short time ago was named "Meg's Bridge". How pleased Meg would have been to know that her name was associated with money!

Close to Meldon at Pole Hill is held the Morpeth Hunt Point-to-Point. Life has changed little in this part of the county. Where the Scots once drove the lifted cattle through the Gap is a busy auction mart for live-stock. The foursquare stone-built farm houses of Northumberland, though now with all the modern comforts within, are still scattered over the landscape. No industry has penetrated into this pleasant land, and if the ghost of Meg still wanders she will recognize with ease the land she knew in life.

A Victorian writer in 1885 described Whalton as a village of "tastefully ornamented gardens enclosed with elegant palisades"; this description of Whalton is still applicable today. On either side of the wide village street are the attractive stone-built houses within their "palisades", and a row of typical Northumbrian cottages, many of which have been modernized and are used as country homes by people from the busy industrial area of Tyneside which, it is difficult to believe, is only about twenty miles away. Whalton has an atmosphere of peace, with only grim reminders of the stormy past in some of the place names, such as Gallow Hill which tells its own story.

The village pub is "The Beresford Arms"; the name commemorating a family who were connected by marriage with the Gay Delavals. Whalton is one of the few places in England which still observes the ancient custom of a Bale or Baal Fire. On the 4th of July (Old Midsummer's Eve) a bonfire blazes on the village green. In days gone by

10

The mother of Darnley was born at Harbottle

the Whalton people used to leap through the flames, now they celebrate this survival of paganism in a more restrained manner.

At nearby Bolam is an artificial lake, designed in the last century
by the well-known north country architect, Dobson, who planned so
many of the streets of Newcastle.

Close to Bolam and Whalton are the remains of ancient British
camps, set in some of the most pastoral scenery in the county. Here in
the heart of the Morpeth Hunt country, the people are employed in
agriculture or in working on many of the big estates which still survive.
Some of the few remaining blacksmiths' shops carry on their craft
in this sporting district.

Of the many great houses which are within easy reach of Morpeth,
Wallington is the most famous. Now National Trust property, this
estate is the largest Trust property in England. Ten miles from Morpeth, and only a mile from the busy Newcastle to Carter Bar road,
is the "new" house of Wallington. In the year of The Glorious Revolution, 1688, Sir William Blackett became the owner of this land, which
for generations had been the home of the Fenwick family. The last
of the Fenwick line was Sir John, who was beheaded for his part in
the conspiracy to assassinate William of Orange. The old house of the
Fenwicks, and the even older part which had been built in the fourteenth century, were demolished by Sir William, and the huge sum
of £35,000 was spent to build the great house which today attracts
visitors from far and near. From April to September Wallington is
open to the public, on Saturdays, Sundays, Wednesdays and Bank
Holidays. Close to the River Wansbeck, which inspired the Northumbrian poet Swinburne to write

> The Wansbeck sings with all her springs,
> The bents and braes give ear;
> But the wood that rings with the song she sings
> I may not see or hear;
> For far and far the blythe burns are,
> And strange is a' things here,

are the gardens and parklands of Wallington which are sheer delight.
One of the most famous landscape gardeners of his age, Capability
Brown, who went to school in the adjoining village of Cambo, may
have been responsible for laying out some of the Wallington gardens.
This boy from Northumberland was in later years to gain fame as the
designer of some of the most famous gardens in the south of England,
including those of Blenheim Palace.

Not only were the gardens of the then home of the Blacketts made
beautiful, but in the eighteenth century the land was enclosed; roads
were made to take the place of the rough tracks, new farm houses

were built and old ones restored; the whole scene was changed to such an extent that when the celebrated agriculturist Arthur Young came to Wallington he was deeply impressed by the improvements carried out by the Blackett family. This family's connection with Wallington ended when, through the failure of the male line, a Blackett heiress married a Trevelyan from Cornwall.

In 1936, Sir Charles Trevelyan handed over his property to the National Trust, on the condition that members of his family remain as tenants. One of the show pieces of the house is a piece of needlework done by Mary, Lady Trevelyan, the widow of Sir Charles. The work incorporates the coats of arms of the various owners of Wallington, together with a picture of a legendary Trevelyan landing on the Cornish coast. To Northumbrians, perhaps the most interesting of the many treasures are the huge coloured murals in the Central Hall. The work of a Newcastle artist, William Bell Scott, they portray some of the most outstanding episodes in Northumbrian history, while above the murals are portraits of some of the county's most famous sons. Though not by any means great works of art, the figures are alive and vividly bring the past to life. Like Lady Waterford's murals at Ford, many of the local people posed as characters for the artist.

The most famous Trevelyan of his generation was G. M., the historian, who died not long ago. G. M. Trevelyan's *Social History of England* is one of the best of its kind ever written. Another historian connected with this family was Macaulay who wrote his *History of England* in the nineteenth century.

The road from Wallington leads north to Cambo village, with its church perched on a steep eminence. After Cambo, the lush wooded country is left behind and the road climbs north to fall and rise again at Rothley Crags, a wild tract of country which was once Sir William Blackett's deer-park. With the mania our ancestors had for ruins, and surely there were enough in Northumberland already without building them, Sir William had some most realistic castellated ruins built on the top of the crags! The little Rothley lake breaks the bareness of the scenery. The road from Rothley "switchbacks" its way to Rothbury and the valley of the Coquet.

The Morpeth country provides the greatest contrasts in all the county, sharply divided as it is into the urban and the rural. As the old rhyme says,

> Harnham was headless, Bradford breadless,
> Shafto picked at the craw,
> Capheaton was a bonny wee place,
> But Wallington banged them a'.

Wallington certainly has the most beautiful house, but little Harnham a few miles away can boast of having been the home of a most beautiful lady. This lady, whose first husband was a Fenwick, had her portrait included in The Book of Beauty of her day, which was in the later part of the seventeenth century. Marrying for a second time, the Governor of Berwick, a Major Babington, this beauty's career was one of disputes with the established Church. So bitter were the feelings between Madam, as she was known, and the local vicar, that when she died he refused to bury her in consecrated ground. She was buried in a vault hewn out of the rock, but this tomb was afterwards desecrated and the bones of the once famous beauty scattered. Now at Harnham, which is a farm house, can be seen the remains of her vault, in what was once known as "The Tomb Garden".

The charm of the Morpeth country is its variety. As in so many parts of Northumberland, the traveller passes so quickly from one type of scenery to another that there is no monotony in these by-roads. Roads that lead to a great house such as Nunnykirk Hall on the River Font, or to the isolated village of Wingates from which there are panoramic views.

Could Leland return now to a more civilized Northumberland, he would regard "the XII long miles" to Morpeth as well worth while. Morpeth country is not for those visitors who are doing a whistle-stop tour. There is so much to be seen and explored at leisure. In the spring when the point-to-point is held, the "two" Morpeths merge. Squire and miner, townsman and countryman are united in their love of sport. There is no better place to study a cross section of Northumbrian life than at these local hunt meetings, where social differences and varying political beliefs cease to exist—for the Morpeth division, although largely agricultural, takes in much of the densely populated coalfield, which at one time assured the return of a Labour candidate to Westminster.

XII

COQUETDALE AND THE VALE OF WHITTINGHAM

Coquetdale The Coquet for ever,
The Coquet for aye;
The Coquet, the king
Of the bank and the brae.

Anon.

Rising at Coquethead in the wild Border country that is Thirlmoor, the Coquet is the most famous trout river in Northumberland. Thought by many people to be the loveliest river in the county, Coquet, from its source to where it empties its peaty waters into the North Sea, spans Northumberland from west to east. Winding its way by loops and bends, the country people say that the river forms the letters of its name.

Covering an area of 286,762 acres, Coquetdale includes the beautiful Vale of Whittingham, through which the River Aln flows. Rising in the north of Coquetdale near the little village of Alnham, the Aln flows by way of Alnwick to end its course at Alnmouth. Coquetdale is a "green" land with its conical grass-covered hills and rich pastures or "haughs" which fringe its banks. Joined at Alwinton by the River Alwin, which is formed by the many burns which mingle their waters at Kidlandlee, the country of the wild goats, Coquet has many claims to be "the king of the bank and the brae".

Wild and solitary is the country of upper Coquetdale. It is a land inhabited by sheep which graze the green hills; for Coquetdale, like all Northumberland beyond the boundaries of the industrial belt, is purely agricultural. With the "outbye" farms of the hill country and the "inbye" farms of its lower reaches, Coquetdale is a great stock-raising district. In the hill country live the shepherds who tend the scores of Blackfaced and Cheviots and the "half breds" of Northumberland which are a strain of Cheviot and Border Leicester. Remote and lonely are the cottages in which the shepherds and their families live. The little school at the appropriately named Windyhaugh, which many of these shepherds' children attend, must be one of the most isolated schools in the country.

At Alwinton in October is held the most famous Shepherds' Show in all Northumberland. In this setting of hills and green valley, when the bracken is a blaze of gold and the rowan trees are heavy with red berries, Alwinton Show is held in the most beautiful surroundings imaginable. From their lonely homes in the hills the shepherds and their families come to this gathering of the clans. Not only do the sheep and lambs compete for prizes; there are classes for the sheep dogs, the "collies" which play such an important part in the life of a shepherd, and for working terriers, the biggest class in this section being the hardy Border breed. There is wrestling, Cumberland and Westmorland style, which attracts entrants from many parts of the Border country, and, of course, a hound trail of which the spectators have a wonderful view. Hand-dressed (hand-carved) sticks are exhibited and in the marquee trestle tables are laden with home-baked cakes and scones, jams and preserves, made by the shepherds' wives. Long after the Show is officially over, the celebrations go on and the inn and the beer tent do a roaring trade!

There is, however, a darker side to the life of a hill shepherd than celebrations such as Alwinton Show. In November of 1962, the winter of the Great Storm, tragedy came to upper Coquetdale when two shepherds, Jock Scott and Bill Middlemiss, lost their lives. It was on Saturday, the 17th of November, a day that will be long remembered in the valley, that the two men, who had been at Rothbury Mart, set off for home. The blizzard had begun when they reached the farmhouse at Alnham where their master lived. Bad though the storm was by then, they decided to make for their home at Ewartley Shank. How long they struggled and when they actually died will never be known. When they had not reached home by nightfall Scott's wife assumed that they had decided to spend the night at Alnham and was not unduly alarmed. With no telephone and only a rough track from the cottage to Alnham, Ewartley Shank was cut off from the outside world. It was Monday before someone managed to reach the house and Mrs. Scott asked where the menfolk were. Realizing then that something untoward had happened, the alarm was raised and search parties set out into the snow-covered countryside. The bodies were found in a snow drift close to a hayshed which, if only the unfortunate men could have reached it, would have provided them with shelter.

Typical of Northumberland, the sympathy shown to the families of the Cheviot shepherds was practical. At every auction mart in the county "Free Gift" sales were held. The stock provided by the farmers was bid up to prices far exceeding its value and the proceeds given to the relatives of Bill and Jock. Those of Middlemiss, who was a bachelor, handed over their share to Mrs. Scott and her children, and the Duke of Northumberland gave the widow a house at Lesbury. Now a road has been made to Ewartley and a telephone installed so that, in future, there will be some means of sending for help should there ever be another winter as severe as that of the Great Storm.

The church at Alwinton is of Norman foundation. Dedicated to St. Michael, it stands on a steep slope above the river. Extensively restored in the nineteenth century, it has the unusual feature of the nave being separated from the chancel by ten steps. Buried in the chancel are many of the ancient family of Selby, whose home was at Biddlestone Hall. The Selbys, as lay-rectors, exercised their right to this privilege of a resting place in the chancel. Biddlestone Hall claims to be the Osbaldistone Hall of Scott's novel *Rob Roy*. The outlawed chief of the McGregor clan is said to have found refuge in a cave near Dove Crag Burn not very far from Holystone.

The wild hill country which lies between Alwinton and Alnham is watered by countless burns and through this country runs the old road of Clennel Street. Nearby is the ruined Tower of Clennel now forming part of the comparatively modern house where, at one time, lived the ancient family of that name which, by whose marriages with the equally ancient family of Fenwick, became the Fenwicke-Clennells.

Upper Coquetdale has numerous remains of Roman forts and camps as well as those of prehistoric man. The most famous of the Roman camps are those at Makendon, south-west of Windyhaugh, 1,436 feet above the level of the sea. These camps appear to have covered an extensive area and were garrisoned by the Ninth Legion. Situated close to where Watling Street crosses the Border, these camps were of strategic importance. Stone pillars with the delightful names of Outer Golden Pot and Middle Golden Pot are thought to have marked the distances on Watling Street. Traces of Roman roads can be seen in many parts of Coquetdale, roads which are clearly marked on the Ordnance Maps. How wild and remote the men of the Legions must have found this outpost of their empire and how unruly the inhabitants, for, sad to say, the men of Coquetdale had a reputation as bad as any in the county. To have once been the Cradle of Christianity, it is remarkable that after the conversion of so many Northumbrians they should have lapsed so badly into the old ways. In Roman times utterly uncivilized, then, after the legions departed, embracing the new Faith and apparently becoming reformed characters for a short time, the inhabitants of Coquetdale, in common with the men of Tyne and Rede, were, from the time of the Unification of the Kingdom until the Union, the most lawless of the king's subjects.

It would be a refreshing change to be able to record that Coquetdale's history is a peaceful one, but it is in fact as lurid as any in Northumberland.

Under the shadow of Cushat Law are the ruins of the little chapel of Memmerkirk, where it is said that a priest had so little to do that he employed his time in making bee skeps! The Northumbrians were too busy reiving and raiding to have much time to attend to their devotions.

Tomlinson in his *Northumberland in the Sixteenth Century* presents a sorry picture of the state of the county's many lovely churches.

The names of the hills and pastures of Coquetdale tell their own story. The Bloody Moss, Angryhaugh at Alwinton, The Beacon and The Thieves Road, which in the eighteenth century became the Salters Road, are self explanatory. Some of the burns and the houses have enchanting names: Grasslees Burn flows close by the strangely named farmhouse of Midgy Ha'; and Linn Shiels which, according to a survey of the Border made in 1542, derives its name from the fact that "about the beginning of April the Borderers were accustomed to take their cattle into the high waste grounds towards the Borders and build themselves frail huts which they call scheals and depasture their cattle in the valleys and hopes as well as on the high ground till August, and this they call summering or 'schealing'." At Uswayford not far away, where there is a shepherd's cottage, many of these cattle "summered" at Linn Shiels would be driven through the ford in the "raiding season".

Of all the villages of the upper reaches of Coquet, Holystone is one of the most historic and pleasing. Here is St. Ninian's Well or, as it is more usually known, the Lady's Well. Within a circular enclosure surrounded by trees and now owned by the National Trust is the spring of pure water where Paulinus baptized the heathen Northumbrians. The National Trust sign which has been erected has an inscription which reads: "This holy well was once a watering place beside the Roman Road from Bremenium in Redesdale to the coast. It was walled round and given its proper shape either in Roman or medieval times. St. Ninian, the fifth century apostle of the Border, is associated with the site and with other wells beside the Roman roads in Northumberland. The name Lady's Well came into use after the first half of the twelfth century when Holystone became the home of a Priory of Augustinian canonesses dedicated to St. Mary the Virgin. The well was repaired and adorned with a cross and the statue was brought from Alnwick in the eighteenth and nineteenth centuries."

The stone statue of St. Paulinus which stands in the centre of the well bears an inscription which affirms that on Easter Day DCXXVII the saint baptized three thousand Northumbrians. It seems to be an incredibly large number to have baptized in one day and, according to some historians, Paulinus was at York at the time when he is alleged to have been so busily engaged at Holystone! At the east end of the pool is a stone table or altar, the origin of which is obscure. Whether or not the baptisms were ever carried out is doubtful and, if they were, they had no lasting effect on the Northumbrians.

The village of Holystone is supplied with drinking water from the Lady's Well and the tests carried out monthly by the Water Company are entirely satisfactory. Though there are scanty remains left of

Holystone Priory and the thatched cottages have gone, today, nestling as it does among craggy hills, Holystone, with its church and its pleasant inn, "The Salmon", ranks with Hepple and Harbottle as one of the most attractive villages in Coquetdale.

Lying on the south side of Coquet is the ancient village of Harbottle, the name being a corruption of the Saxon *here botl*, the station or abode of the army. Little remains of the once mighty castle which from its elevated position on a steep hill was a barrier against the invading Scots. Battered and besieged like all Northumbrian fortresses, the castle was built in the reign of Henry II on what was then Umfraville property. Built on the site of much older fortifications used by the Saxons on what appears to have been a mote hill, Harbottle had fallen into ruin by 1543 and its condition was so bad that the garrison was unable to occupy it. In the grim dungeons of Harbottle were imprisoned the outlaws who were captured in the liberty of Ridsdale. Seldom would these dungeons be empty. In fact they were more likely overcrowded by the numbers of wild men from Ridsdale.

Harbottle's greatest claim to fame is that here in 1515 was born the baby who grew up to become the mother of Darnley, Lady Margaret Douglas who married the Earl of Lennox. This baby's mother was the Tudor Princess Margaret, who shot the buck at Alnwick on her way to Scotland to marry James IV and become Queen of Scotland and who, after King Jamie's death on Flodden Field, married the Earl of Angus. It was Princess Margaret's brother, Henry VIII, who assigned to her the castle of Harbottle which was the headquarters of the warden of the Middle March. Forty-eight hours after her arrival, the Countess of Angus gave birth to her baby and it is recorded that only a short time after the birth the Tudor princess made her attendants hold up her rich gowns for her inspection to relieve the boredom of her stay at Harbottle for, as soon as she was able to travel, the royal mother with her baby journeyed to Morpeth where some time was spent in the castle above the Wansbeck.

The Coquet which encircles the castle then takes one of its many bends, this one known as the Devil's Elbow, and from the river a path leads to Harbottle Hill crowned by the 27-foot high Drake or Draag Stone. Composed of a great block of reddish-grey stone, this is said to be a relic of the Druids and here were carried out their strange forms of worship. At one time sick children were passed over the stone in the belief that the process had healing powers. Beyond the stone are the lonely waters of Harbottle Lough shut in by bare crags.

At Hepple are the ruins of a Pele tower, one of the many which formed a chain of defence which stretched across Coquetdale to the coast at Warkworth. In the reign of Henry III Hepple was the property of "Joo Taylleboys" who is said to have traced his descent from Charlemagne. Assuming the name of Hepple, the family estates passed by marriage into the hands of the Ogles, while today Hepple is the property of the Buchanan Riddells. Close to Hepple on Kirkhill there at one time was a chapel, destroyed in the raiding days, whose stones were used to build a farm house. In the chancel was discovered a tombstone so defaced that it was impossible to decipher some of the curious rhyme with which it was engraved or to whom the inscription referred. What was deciphered is most unusual.

> Here lies ... Countess of ... who died ... her age ...
> I loved my lord, obeyed my king,
> And kept my conscience clear;
> Which Death disarmeth of his sting
> And Christians all endear.
> My puissant posterity
> Still the forlorn befriend:
> Peace, pleasure and prosperity
> My tenantry attend.
> There lay my head to Long Acres,
> Where shearers sweetly sing,
> And feet toward the Key-heugh scares
> Which foxhounds cause to ring.
> Farewell survivors in the gross!
> When you behold my bust,
> Lament your late liege lady's loss,
> Then blending with the dust.

Who was this "liege lady" and did she compose her own epitaph? The reference to foxhounds is significant as there has been foxhunting in Coquetdale from very early times. Hunted now by the West Percy, which was given this name in 1919, the Coquetdale hunt had many different names, while its list of masters includes many names familiar in the annals of the county. Selbys, Greys and Fenwicke-Clennells have at times hunted hounds in Coquetdale.

Between Hepple and Holystone is Harehaugh Hill, one of the many Celtic strongholds which are so numerous in this part of Northumberland. It was close to Harehaugh, at Woodhouses, that a celebrated player on the Northumbrian pipes, one James Allan, was born; a man who, like many of the Coquetdale men of those days, came to a bad end. Condemned to death for horse stealing, he was reprieved and imprisoned for life. Although there are still pipers in Northumberland (with very different characters from that of James Allan) their numbers are diminishing. The most celebrated of the pipers of today is Jack Armstrong, official piper to the Duke of Northumberland. Varying in many ways from the better-known Highland pipes, the Northumbrian pipes are sweet sounding and have their origin in the mists of time. They are operated by an arm bellow and designed mainly for indoor use. It will be sad indeed if they become museum pieces.

At Hepple where the valley begins to broaden, the Coquet twists and winds its way by Caistron and Flotterton to Thropton, a village divided by the river and from where the roads branch off to the north to Alnham and to Callaly in the Vale of Whittingham. The scenery is now dominated by the Simonside Hills which guard the valley on its southern side. Rising to a height of 1,409 feet, Simonside gives its name to the whole range and from its summit there is a magnificent view of the far away coast of Northumberland. Composed of sandstone, these hills are a landmark which can be seen from practically all over Northumberland. Covered with purple heather in August when the fertile lower reaches of Coquetdale are golden with the ripening corn and the river is looping its way towards the capital of the valley, the town of Rothbury, Simonside is indeed delightful country. Little sheets of water at Chartners and Fallowleas add to the charm of the scenery and on these lonely lakes the blackheaded gulls breed. Tosson, the highest point of the Simonside ridge, overshadows the little hamlet of Great Tosson with its ruined Pele tower which is surrounded by ash and sycamore trees.

This district was once part of the great Rothbury Forest wherein was the Celtic camp called Lordenshaw, of which there are extensive remains.

The name of Rothbury, according to Tomlinson, means a clearing in the forest. Rothbury is one of the most delightful of the Northumbrian towns with its magnificent hill and river scenery. It is a typical Border town with sturdy-looking stone-built houses which line each side of its steep main street. The verges are planted with trees, and from the west end of the town where the ground rises sharply there is a pleasant view of the winding river in the haughs below. In 1205 King John granted the manor of Rothbury to Robert Fitzroger, Baron of Warkworth. The street known now as Rotten Row is said to owe its name to the fact that King John when he visited the town (which he seems to have treated more leniently than he did other parts of the county) travelled by this route, the "route de roi". Reverting to the Crown in the reign of Edward III, the manor was bestowed upon a member of the Percy family in whose possession it still remains.

The greatest attraction of Rothbury today for the visitor is the grounds of Cragside, the home of Lord Armstrong. Standing high above the river at the east end of the town, this house built on a plateau was begun in 1863 and is a peculiar combination of what the architects of those days regarded as romantic. However unusual the house may be, the grounds are deservedly famous. A mass of rhododendrons and azaleas in their season, with beautifully laid-out rock gardens and artificial lakes, Cragside grounds are open to the public every day from Easter to September.

Approached by the various lodge gates on the main road, the ground rises steeply above the Debdon Burn. Cragside claims to have been one of the first houses in England to have had electricity installed, use having been made of one of the many burns to work the generating engine. As the Armstrongs were famous inventors this nineteenth-century enterprise is not surprising.

In the old lawless days there was an illicit whisky still above the Debdon Burn: this, however, was long before the Armstrongs came to Cragside.

Many distinguished guests have stayed at Lord Armstrong's home, among them the Prince and Princess of Wales in 1884.

Below Cragside the Coquet passes through spectacular scenery where the water forces its way through a narrow chasm known as the Thrum. At one time the more foolhardy people of Rothbury amused themselves by leaping across the boiling torrent, often with disastrous results. Here the banks are thickly wooded and the river, after its escape from the Thrum, wends its course through soft and pleasant country by Pauperhaugh to Weldon Bridge and that haunt of fishermen, the "Anglers' Arms".

There is a delightful description of Rothbury as it was in 1811, by an unknown writer, who says: "Rothbury is much frequented in the summer season by valetudinarians in order to drink goat's whey and enjoy the salubrious air of the place, which has often wonderful effects in bracing the relaxed tone of the nervous system. Here nature may be viewed at one glance, in all her native wildness and also decked in her best attire. The adjoining hills afford pleasant and dry walks, while the vale is equally favourable for contemplation or amusement. The water is remarkably pure and the inhabitants civil and attentive to strangers."

It is pleasant to hear that the inhabitants were "civil and attentive to strangers" as, in common with the rest of Northumberland in the past, the Coquetdale men had a notorious reputation. At the time of the Reformation they were described as such adepts in the art of thieving that they "could twist a cow's horn or mark a horse so that its owners could not know it".

Bernard Gilpin, The Apostle of the North, who was rector of Houghton-le-Spring in the county of Durham, ventured into this wild country to preach the gospel and there is a graphic description of Gilpin settling a feud in Rothbury church in Mackenzie's history of the county. This episode is the subject of one of W. B. Scott's pictures at Wallington Hall. Rothbury church was practically rebuilt in 1850 and very little of the thirteenth-century building remains. The font is interesting as its pedestal is part of an old Saxon cross. Even the rectors of Rothbury in the old days were involved in many of the lawless pursuits in which the Coquetdale men were expert. One rector was heavily fined for a breach of the Forest Laws. Fighting, drinking, gaming and "lifting" occupied most of the time in this now peaceful valley. Cock-fighting was one of the most popular "sports" in all the villages and it is still possible to trace the sites of some of the cockpits. Netherton village, once one of the "ten towns of Coquetdale", was famous for greyhound coursing, cockfights and merry nights.

For more than two hundred years there has been racing at Rothbury but, unhappily, the one-day meeting, held in April under National Hunt Rules, is one of those abolished by the stewards of the National Hunt Committee. Deep resentment was felt not only in Coquetdale but all over the county and strong protests were made to have the meeting saved, but without success. Rothbury Races were a tradition and as long ago as 1762 a meeting was held. An old race bill tells us that:

ROTHBURY RACES
To be run on Rothbury Haugh on Wednesday, the 28th day
of April 1762, Thursday, the 29th and Friday, the 30th.
A Purse of GOLD, by horses etc. rising four years old.
Heats: two miles. Each to carry nine stones.

This was a three-day meeting and the bill ends with the information that "There will be a Main of Cocks each day". One can only hope that the National Hunt Committee Stewards will allow the people of Coquetdale to enjoy their racing for many years to come.*

Past and present mingle in the valley of the Coquet; close to the river where it makes one of its many loops, not far from Pauperhaugh, are the picturesque ruins of Brinkburn Priory, now managed by the Ministry of Works. Said to have been founded in the reign of Henry I, a community of Black Canons was established here and the remains of their priory are considerable. The church of St. Peter and St. Paul was partly restored in 1858. Little is known of the history of these canons or whether their example had much effect on the wild inhabitants of the valley.

Another of Coquetdale's ruins is Cartington Castle, about two miles to the north-west of Rothbury on the road which runs from Thropton, by way of Lorbottle, to Callaly. Cartington is one of the places visited by the Countess of Angus on her journey from Harbottle to Morpeth. Built by the Cartington family, the castle passed by marriage to the Radcliffes and then by the marriage of a Radcliffe to a Widdrington, one of whom supported Charles I in the Civil Wars and, by the orders of Cromwell, the castle was razed to the ground. Rebuilt by a Widdrington in the reign of Charles II, it became the property of the Talbot

*See pp. 196-8

family, passing out of their possession after the Rebellion of the '15 in which the owner of Cartington had taken part. The history of this Border stronghold has been a chequered one. Restored by Lord Armstrong in 1887, it is difficult to picture what the original castle must have been like.

Coquetdale is indeed a lovely land, with its ever-changing scenery, its many picturesque villages, its hamlets with their quaint names, as at Snitter and Flotterton, and it is a happy hunting ground for the sportsman and the historian. So lovely are some of the parts of the valley that one can believe that there were once fairies at Brinkburn, where tradition says that there was a fairies burial ground! At every season of the year Coquetdale is enchanting and, as the old rhyme says:

> At Weldon Bridge there's wale o' wine,
> If ye hae coin in pocket;
> If ye can thraw a heckle fine,
> There's wale o' trout in Coquet.

The Vale of Whittingham Are you going to Whittingham Fair?
> Parsley, sage, rosemary and thyme.
> Remember me to one who lives there,
> For once she was a true love of mine.

Although within the confines of Coquetdale ward, the Vale of Whittingham, through which the River Aln flows, is separated from the Coquet Valley by a range of hills composed mainly of Callaly and Thrunton Crags. In this lovely vale are two of the most historic and interesting houses in all the county: Callaly Castle and Eslington Park.

Included in the list of Border fortresses in 1416, Callaly has one of the most interesting legends of the many which are so frequent in this Border country. The story goes that a lord of Callaly and his lady had a dispute as to where the castle should be built. The lord was determined that it should be built on a height and his lady was equally determined that it should be built on the level ground below. Disguising one of her attendants as a boar, as fast as her lord raised the towers of Callaly on the height, the "boar" pulled it down and the country people regarded this as a supernatural manifestation, reporting to the lord of Callaly that the boar had pronounced that:

> Callaly Castle built on the height,
> Up in the day and down in the night;
> Builded down in the shepherd's shaw,
> It shall stand for aye and never fa'.

The lady had her own way and the castle, which is still inhabited today, was "builded down in the shepherd's shaw". Owned by the Clavering family for generations, Callaly Castle is now the home of Major A. S. C. Browne, whose ancestors bought the estate in 1877. In Callaly Crags, a sandstone ridge, is a priest's cave, hewn out of the sandstone by a chaplain of Callaly Castle.

Eslington Park, or Tower, as it was known in the old days, is famous as the home of George Collingwood who rode out in the '15 and who in Surtees' Ballad is referred to by Derwentwater as:

> Fare thee well, George Collingwood!
> Since Fate has put us down;
> If thou and I have lost our lives,
> Our king has lost his crown.

This George Collingwood paid the extreme penalty for his loyalty to the House of Stuart.

The present house at Eslington was built on the site of the old home of the Collingwoods in 1720 by the Liddell family from Durham, the head of which is Lord Ravensworth.

In the Vale of Whittingham are some of the most attractive and historic villages in Northumberland: Eglingham and Edlingham both pronounced with the Northumbrian "jum", are two of the many delightful villages of this outpost of Coquetdale. At Eglingham Hall there is a room where Cromwell is alleged to have spent a night on his return from ravaging Scotland. This visit is commemorated in a poem by a local poet, James Hall, in which he tells us that:

> T'was Cromwell's self in furious mood,
> That now in Ogle's mansion stood,
> And vented thus his spleen;
> And though two centuries have rolled
> That noted chamber, quaint and old,
> Is perfect to be seen.

Eglingham Hall was in the possession of the Ogle family for generations and in the church are memorials to this ancient family.

Edlingham church dates from Saxon times though little of the Saxon building remains. Rebuilt in the twelfth century, the church possesses a wonderful Norman doorway, while the nave and chancel are also splendid examples of Norman architecture. There is evidence that the ancient tower, which has narrow slit windows, was used as a prison in the raiding days; while close to the church are the ruins of the castle, once a twelfth-century Pele tower.

Edlingham is noteworthy as being the birthplace of a witch who was credited with the supernatural powers these unfortunate women were supposed to possess. Although the usual evidence was given against the Edlingham witch she escaped the horrible fate which befell so many witches in those far-off days. A long account of her "goings on" is given in Mackenzie's *History of Northumberland*.

In 1746 the lord of the manor at Ellingham, another "jum", a Haggerston, whose sympathies were with the Stuart cause, was forced to send his coach to convey the notorious Duke of Cumberland, the "Butcher" as he was so rightly called, from Belford to Berwick. The lord of the manor gave instructions that the coach was to be overturned on the way!

Whittingham is the capital of the vale which bears its name and a more charming place it would be difficult to find. According to Tomlinson the name is derived from "the dwelling in the white meadow". There is an ancient church and at one time a vicarage, which was part of a Pele tower. The fortified house, once the property of the Herons, now bears the inscription: "By the munificence and piety of Lady Ravensworth, this ancient tower, which was formerly used by the villagers as a place of refuge in times of rapine and insecurity, was repaired and otherwise embellished for the use of the deserving poor. A.D. 1845." Intersected by the River Aln, Whittingham is one of the most attractive of Northumberland's many delightful villages. With its Castle Inn and statue to one of the Liddell family, Whittingham rivals Blanchland as the "perfect village". In days gone by Whittingham was famous for its fair, which the song commemorates.

On the ridge north of Whittingham is Glanton which commands fine views of the Aln and Breamish. As in many parts of Coquetdale, there are extensive remains of Early British camps in the country surrounding Glanton, while in modern times a bird sanctuary has been established in the village. Close to Whittingham, at Swarland, are the only signs of industry in all Coquetdale, the Swarland Brickworks.

In 1895 a book by David Dippie Dixon was published, entitled *Whittingham Vale, Northumberland: Its History, Traditions and Folklore*. Although now out of print, this book is a fascinating account of this lovely vale and is an invaluable guide for those who wish to explore it. Between Whittingham and Glanton is the Roman Catholic church of St. Mary's. From the twelfth century until 1877 there had been a priest at Callaly. The estate then passed into a non-Catholic family and the present church was erected.

Whittingham Fair was held on the 29th of August and was a gathering place for the people of the vale. From the Castle Inn a cavalcade of horsemen rode out, led by the bailiff and the fiddlers and, to quote from Dippie Dixon's book, there were "publicans' refreshment tents from Alnwick, Eglingham, Rothbury, Snitter, Thropton, Netherton,

Whittingham

Harbottle, Alwinton, Longframlington and Glanton, numerous hucksters' stalls from Alnwick, on which 'Shanter Jack', 'Ailee Canair', 'Dutch Billy' and many others offered for sale nuts and oranges, apples and claggum, gingerbread, sherbet and gooseberries. There were hardware and cutlery stalls from Kelso; hats, caps and sickles from Rothbury; boots and shoes from Alnwick; and 'cow cheese' by the score from the hilly districts of the Breamish and the Aln."

The many Irish labourers who came over from their own country for the hay-time and harvest used to beat up Whittingham Fair and on one occasion they got so out of hand that for many years afterwards this event was remembered as "the year the Irish took the fair". But the fair is best remembered by the ballad:

> When he has done and finished his work,
> Parsley, sage, rosemary and thyme;
> O, tell him to come and he'll have his shirt,
> For once he was a true love of mine.

Whittingham Fair as such is no more, but for a hundred and eight years "Games" have been held on the Saturday in August nearest to the date of St. Bartholomew's Day, which is the 24th. Held in a field beside the Castle Inn, the Games attract competitors from as far away as Westmorland, who take part in the wrestling matches and the various running heats, which are a feature of Whittingham Games, while sheepdogs demonstrate their skill in trials. Unfortunately there were no Games in 1964, owing to the illness of the Secretary, but this important event was revived in 1965.

The song "Whittingham Fair" is part of the folk-lore of Northumberland and, though the fair is now history, the song is evergreen:

> Tell him to find me an acre of land,
> Parsley, sage, rosemary and thyme;
> And sow it all over with one peppercorn,
> For once he was a true love of mine.

11

Eslington, once the home of George Collingwood

XIII

COWGATE TO CARTER BAR

Hae ye ever crossed the Border.
Ower the Carter Fell.
An' thowt o' the ghosts o' the raiders.
Or o' Parcy Reed hord tell?
Gan doon the road to Ridsdale.
Wheor the Otterburn ran red,
Wheor Hotspur fought the Douglas,
An' the heather was thor bed.
If ye've nivor hord o' Elsdon,
A'll tell ye noo beware,
For its curlew's eggs and heather broth
Ye'll get for supper there.

Nancy Ridley, WOR OWN NORTHUMBERLAND

At Cowgate on the edge of Newcastle's Town Moor the Carter Bar road leaves the city behind and for some fifty miles, until it crosses the Border on Carter Fell, 1,600 feet above sea level, it passes through scenery which produces a variety of landscape as great as any in this county of contrasts.

Until the road reaches the little village of Kirkwhelpington, perched high above the Wansbeck, the country is lush and green with well-wooded parklands, then dramatically the scene changes to the wild treeless heights of the Ottercops.

The road to the Border descends steeply from the heights of the Ottercops, passing through Otterburn, the scene of the battle immortalized in Chevy Chase. Along this route the armies of Percy and Douglas marched to fight the famous battle in the moonlight.

Now, six hundred years afterwards, when the traveller to the Border leaves the industrial area behind him at Kenton Bar, even though the housing estates and urbanization are all too obvious, the view from here can have changed very little throughout the centuries. Spread out like a map, Northumberland rolls on towards the Border hills.

At Ponteland, "the island on the Pont", is one of the oldest inns in the county, "The Blackbird". Partly Pele tower, partly a Jacobean house built by the Erringtons, "The Blackbird" has been expertly restored without losing its character. Would that the same could be said for Ponteland itself! The village atmosphere has disappeared and what was once an attractive Northumbrian village is now, with its many housing estates, a dormitory for Newcastle.

The parish church of St. Mary was built in Norman times, and though extensively altered is still a very lovely church. Although Ponteland has lost its rural atmosphere, the many small villages which lie off the main road are unspoilt. Ogle with its castle, once the seat of that important family who settled in Northumberland before the Conquest, lies between Ponteland and Whalton, and in the triangle which lies south of Ponteland, between the road to the Carter and The Military Road, are some of the pleasantest of Northumbrian villages.

Ingoe, standing on its crags; Ryal on the switchback road that joins Watling Street at the Five Lane Ends; Kirkheaton with its Pele tower and Stamfordham with its village green are some of the many in this little-known part of the county.

Stamfordham has a long history and a proud record today of being one of the best-kept villages in the county. Some of Stamfordham's delightful old houses, in danger of demolition, have been modernized, not always with the happiest results.

Just before the village of Belsay is reached is The Highlander Inn, the last inn for twenty miles. Belsay is quite different from any other village in the county, the village street being built in the form of an arcade, which is oddly out of keeping with the scenery. Belsay can boast of having both a castle and a hall, both built by the ancient family of Middleton who, like the Ogles, are one of the few pre-Conquest families. Although the present head of the family, Sir Stephen, no longer lives in the hall, he has made his home near Belsay. Surrounded by trees, this seat of the Middleton family has a most attractive setting, the scenery enriched by the lake in the grounds.

In 1472 a John Middleton was high sheriff of the county. Like many of the old families, the Middletons have had many vicissitudes in their long history. In the reign of Edward II, Sir Gilbert de Middleton was a menace to the countryside. Not content with rebelling against his king, Sir Gilbert ransacked his own county, only the castles of Alnwick, Norham and Bamburgh holding out against him. Not content with the havoc he had wrought, this rebellious knight kidnapped the bishop-elect of Durham and held him to ransom at Morpeth and Mitford. This sort of behaviour was going rather far even for those days, and it is not surprising that Sir Gilbert lost his head. A later member of the family regained his estates through his marriage to the heiress of Sir John Striveling, to whom the forfeited lands of the Middletons had been granted.

Not far from Belsay is one of the most attractive of Northumberland's smaller houses, West Bitchfield, which has a delightful walled garden, which on occasions is open to the public.

Some little distance beyond Belsay where the Devil's Causeway crosses the main road, the scenery begins to change. The line of Shafto Crags stands out prominently to the north. On the heights of the Crags are extensive remains of camps and earthworks. Capheaton, with its hall, the property of the Browne-Swinburnes, evokes memories of Lord Derwentwater and the '15, as does Little Harle Tower near Kirkharle. Here was born Capability Brown, one of the greatest landscape gardeners of his age. It was far from his native Northumberland that the boy, Lancelot Brown from Kirkharle, climbed to the top of his profession, to become head gardener at Windsor and High Sheriff of Huntingdon and Cambridge. Born in the year that Derwentwater was executed "Capability" began as a gardener with Sir William Loraine of Kirkharle.

From Kirkharle a road makes its way through the wild and lovely scenery that is bounded on the north by Watling Street. Earthworks and settlements of prehistoric man abound among these hills. Near Hallington reservoir is a *tumulus* or barrow, where the earliest inhabitants of Northumbria were buried. From Moot Law, close to Watling Street, there is a wonderful view. Here fires were lighted long ago as a warning of approaching danger. Thockrington church which stands so prominently on a spur of the Great Whin-Sill is one of the oldest churches in the county.

Here are buried several members of the ancient family of Shafto, the earliest mention of whom is in 1240. The Shaftos lived at Bavington until the eighteenth century when, as a result of their support of the Jacobite cause in 1715, their estates were confiscated by the Crown, and ultimately sold to a Delaval. The Shaftos had connections with the county of Durham and lived on their Durham estates until 1953, when Mr. R. D. Shafto returned to Bavington Hall.

At Knowesgate the road to the Carter begins its ascent of the Otter-cops. Inhabited only by sheep and game, this stark scenery has a peculiar attraction of its own. In the "backend" when the hills are purple and the bees have been brought to the heather, the Ottercop scenery is at its grandest. North of the Ottercops the road drops down into Ridsdale, once one of the most lawless valleys in Northumberland. Raiding and reiving were the chief occupations of the Ridsdale men until the Union of the Crown brought peace to the Border country.

One of the most notorious of Ridsdale's villages was Elsdon, now a peaceful place whose houses are built in a hollow square which borders the village green. Surrounded by the wild uplands, the Mote Hills which are one of Elsdon's attractions, are two mounds which stand on the east side of the Elsdon Burn. There are many theories regarding the origin and purpose of these mounds. They may have been Roman, Celtic, or fortifications to protect the inhabitants of the village, and not, as their name implies, heights from which justice was dispensed. At one time the property of the Umfravilles, the notorious Robin-Mend-the-Market, who indulged in lifting habits, died in 1436 in the Pele tower or Elsdon Castle as it was then known. This fortified dwelling was the vicarage until recent times. Close to the fortified vicarage is Elsdon's church which claims to have been a resting place for St. Cuthbert's body and is one of the many dedicated to his memory. Of much historical interest, it is also larger than many Northumbrian churches. In the nineteenth century when alterations were taking place, a large number of skeletons were discovered which appeared to have been buried in a communal grave, an indication that the bodies had been buried at Elsdon after the Battle of Otterburn.

Elsdon has a grim reminder of the past in the gibbet that rears its gaunt outline on the hill known as Steng Cross. Strangely enough this gallows has no connection with the Border raiders, many of whom met their death "high on the gallows tree". The present gibbet stands on the site of one from which the body of William Winter was suspended in chains after he had been hanged at The Westgate in Newcastle. Today this grisly relic is called Winter's Gibbet.

In 1791, a very nasty murder took place of an old woman, Margaret Crozier. It is impossible to resist quoting from Tomlinson's *Guide to Northumberland*, to show the enjoyment which the old writers took in recounting horrors in all their bloodthirsty detail! Tomlinson says: "Believing her to be rich, one William Winter, a desperate character, but recently returned from transportation, at the instigation, and with the assistance of two female faws [vendors of crockery and tinwork] named Jane and Eleanor Clark, who in their wanderings had experienced the kindness of Margaret Crozier, broke into the lonely Pele on the night of 29th August 1791, and cruelly murdered the poor old woman, loading the ass they had brought with her goods.

"The day before they had rested and dined in a sheep fold on Whiskershield Common, which overlooked the Raw, and it was from a description given of them by a shepherd boy, who had seen them and taken particular notice of the number and character of the nails in Winter's shoes, and also the peculiar gully, or butcher's knife with which he divided the food that brought them to justice." The shepherd lad must have had very good eyesight to count the number of nails in Winter's shoes!

A well-known local poem, written by a man named Chatt, paints a very unflattering picture of Elsdon, a picture which bears no resemblance to the village or its inhabitants today. The poet tells us:

Yen neet aw cam tiv Elsdon,
Sae tired after dark;
Aw'ed travelled many a leynsom meyle
Wet through the varra sark.
Ma' legs were warkin' fit to brik,
An' empty was ma kite
But nowther luve nor money could
Get nowther bed nor bite . . .

Continuing in the same uncomplimentary strain, Chatt goes on to say:

For a hungry hole like Elsdon,
Aw never yet did see;
An' if aw gan back tiv Elsdon,
The de'il may carry me.

These sentiments are in keeping with Dr. Johnson's remarks about Ridsdale, who "was repelled by the wide expanse of hopeless sterility". Why Johnson was such an inveterate traveller is something of a mystery, as he rarely appears to have been impressed by anything he saw.

Northwards, the road from Elsdon climbs the steep heights of Bilsmoor, which is the pass to Coquetdale. From the top of Bilsmoor there is a magnificent panorama of the Cheviots and the Simonside Hills.

Close to where the Otter joins the Rede is the village of Otterburn, the name forever associated with those of Percy and Douglas. Today Otterburn is a pleasant village, with a long main street, the new houses which have been built standing behind it. Encircled by the hills which divide Ridsdale from North Tyne and Coquetdale, an old ballad truly describes the Border village as

The Otterburn's a bonnie burn
Tis pleasant there to be.

There is some doubt as to the exact site of the battle which made Otterburn so famous, and the Percy Cross was moved from its original position to make way for the "new" road. On the Ordnance map, the site of the battlefield is shown as being about a couple of miles north-west of the village, immediately behind where the Percy Cross stands today, and in front of the modern hall.

This deed was done at Otterbourne,
About the breaking of the day;
Earl Douglas was buried at the bracken bush,
And the Percy led captive away.

All that remains of the Pele tower at the east end of the village has been incorporated into a modern house known as Otterburn Tower. On their way to battle the Scots made an attack on this Pele tower, but its defences were strong enough to withstand the assault. Owned at one time by the Umfravilles who held the manor of Ridsdale, the house passed into the possession of the Hall family. It was here that "Mad Jack Ha'" lived, who was hanged at Tyburn for his part in the Rebellion of the '15. Otterburn Tower is now an hotel, one of the two which are in the village; the other, "The Percy Arms", is a long whitewashed building at the opposite end. Visitors who stay at this very pleasant inn have the privilege of fishing in the Rede and in the waters of Sweethope Lough.

Famous though the battle has made Otterburn, it has a more modern fame in the tweeds and woollen goods woven in the mill beside the Rede. This mill has been owned by the Waddell family for generations, and the quality of the goods which bear the "Otterburn" label is not only nationally, but world famous. Lengths of tweed, blankets, rugs and scarves are exported to many parts of the world. Otterburn, with its well-kept gardens and old stone houses is indeed "a pleasant place to be".

North-west of Otterburn and close to Catcleugh Reservoir is the hamlet of Byrness, which stands by the road-side. The tiny church possesses a stained-glass window which must be unique. It is to the memory of the workmen who lost their lives in accidents during the building of the reservoir. Instead of the conventional biblical pictures, the figures are those of working men, in the clothes worn at the beginning of the century; one most appealing figure is that of a small boy, carrying his "bait" (lunch) in a red spotted handkerchief.

In Redesdale Forest (the Forestry Commission use this form of spelling) a new village, also called Byrness, has been built to house the forestry workers. Most of the men who work in the forests are from other parts of the country and are not natives of Ridsdale. In some cases these "incomers" have found it difficult, especially the women, to adapt themselves to an entirely new way of life. Many of them townsfolk, the isolation and remoteness of the villages have in some cases proved too much for them to bear, while others have settled down happily in their new world. Practically every village has a general store, and mobile shops tour the district. No doubt the Ridsdale folk who have spent all their lives in such surroundings would find it just as difficult to settle down in an urban area.

Until a few years ago "The Redesdale Arms" at Horsley claimed to be the last public house in England; now there is a hotel at Byrness, to which a licence has been granted. In this house once lived Mr. Jacob Robson, the master and joint master of the Border Hunt for fifty-four years. This pack hunts both sides of the Border, and has the distinction of having had as masters, from the beginning of the nineteenth century until 1954, a member either of the Robson or Dodd family. It is now hunted by a committee. The acting master is one of the Hedleys, a name familiar in Ridsdale for generations.

The vast plantations of the Forestry Commission have changed the character of the upper reaches of the valley, and the hunting country is now very much restricted. Many of the hill farms have gone to make way for the forests. In these forests deer are increasing rapidly, and there have been rumours that wild cats have been seen. At one time wild cats abounded at Catcleugh, where the reservoir is today.

The Romans came to Ridsdale by way of Watling Street which joins the road to the Border at Elishaw Bridge just north of Otterburn. Remains of Roman camps are scattered over the district, that at High Rochester being the largest. The Early Britons too have left extensive remains of hill forts. Now a great tract of Ridsdale is the property of the War Department with a permanent camp and artillery range which is a prohibited area when the red flags are hoisted. The range extends into Coquetdale and as far as the Border.

From the little village of Byrness the road climbs steeply towards the Border line. Wild and bare is the scenery and the snow fences remind the traveller of the hazards of this road in the winter. Here at Carter Bar is the Border where England and Scotland meet, and where in 1575 was fought the last battle between the "auld enemies" before the Union brought an end to the strife. Sir Walter Scott, in *The Minstrelsy of the Scottish Border*, gives a vivid description of the fray, "The Raid of the Redeswire". On the lonely waste of the Redeswire the River Rede rises, the river that in its course to join the North Tyne at Redesmouth flows through wild Ridsdale. Rich in history and legend is this valley, whose evil reputation is now buried as deeply as the hatred that once existed between the Borderers.

Most of the history of Ridsdale is connected with bloodshed and dark deeds. At one time the behaviour of its inhabitants was so outrageous that we are told "the King's writ runneth not", and when William the Conqueror came to this most northerly part of his kingdom, he had to defend himself not only from his rebellious subjects, but also from the wolves which added to the terrors of the countryside: a mass of rock between Elsdon and Woodburn is named Wolf Crag.

In 1421 Parliament ordered drastic measures to be taken against the Ridsdale men, as had already been taken against their neighbours in Tynedale and Hexham Shire. These measures do not seem to have had much effect, even though "Jethart" Justice was enforced, that is to say, a reiver was hanged first and then tried! The wardens of the Marches often failed to keep order, and "The Raid of the Redeswire" is an instance of how often the wardens themselves were involved in the feuds and quarrels.

On a June day in 1575, the English and Scottish wardens, with their followers, met on Carter Fell to discuss ways and means of settling the disputes.

> Yet was our meeting meek enough
> Begun wi' merriment and mowes,
> And at the brae above the heugh,
> The clerk sat down to call the rowes [rolls].
> And some for kyne and some for ewes
> Call'd in from Dandrie, Hob and Jock—
> We saw come marching ower the knowes
> Five hundred Fenwicks in a flock.

This gathering, optimistically arranged to settle disputes, resulted in the Raid, so graphically described by Scott. The two wardens, the Northumbrian Sir John Forster, and the Scottish Sir John Carmichael, keeper of Liddisdale, became involved in a heated argument as to the justice meted out to an English reiver by the name of Farnstein. The "keepers of the peace" began to insult one another, making uncomplimentary remarks about one another's families. The Ridsdale and Tynedale men, always ready for a row, drew their bows against the Scots. With cries of "a Tynedale", "a Jedworth", the fight was on. The Scots, as at Otterburn, were victorious, and the Northumbrians were chased for three miles over the Border. The keeper of Ridsdale was killed, Sir John Forster taken prisoner, and three hundred head of cattle were driven home by the triumphant Scots. The ballad tells us that:

> Proud Wallington was wounded sair,
> Albeit but he a Fenwick fierce.

Such was the last "official" Border fray, although even after James of Scotland's accession to the English throne, the Borderers still went in for a bit of "lifting".

Lawless and rebellious though the Northumbrians undoubtedly were in days gone by there are very few records of treachery; of the few instances there are "The Death of Parcy Reed" is the blackest. In the lonely glen of Batinghope, overshadowed by Carter Fell, Parcy Reed was brutally murdered by some Halls of Girsonfield and a band of mosstroopers named Crozier. This dark deed gained for the Halls, once one of the most important of the Ridsdale clans, the designation of false.

> To the hunting ho! cried Parcy Reed;
> And to the hunting he has gane,
> And the three fause Ha's o' Girsonfield
> Alang wi' him he has them ta'en.

The Reeds, one of the many old Northumbrian families, have long been in Ridsdale. In 1542, they are mentioned as being second in importance to the Halls. Although not deserving his horrible death, Parcy's own reputation was not above reproach, and as keeper of the Rede he made many enemies. It is recorded that on one occasion, when for some reason he was angry with the Vicar of Elsdon, he seized the poor man by his beard! When summoned by the outraged vicar to do penance in Elsdon church, Parcy sent his wife to make excuses for his behaviour.

The Halls of Girsonfield acted as decoys to lure their enemy to his fate. Pretending friendship, they invited Parcy to join them in a day's hunting, having arranged with their Crozier accomplices where and when they were to carry out the murder.

> They hunted high, they hunted low,
> They made the echoes ring amain.
> Wi' music sweet o' horn and hound,
> They merry made fair Redesdale glen.

Then as the sun was setting over the Cheviots, the Halls and Parcy, their day's sport over, were resting in Batinghope Glen, when the doomed man fell asleep. The Croziers, who had been lying in wait, fell upon their victim and stabbed him to death, while the False Halls rode off for home, abandoning the keeper of the Rede. Such was the outcry against the treachery of the Hall brothers, that they fled from the district.

Parcy's ghost is said to haunt the scene of his murder, wearing his green hunting dress, carrying his horn and his gun; the colourful spectre was said to have been seen on many occasions. At times Parcy is credited with appearing in the form of a dove, a most inappropriate guise for a Ridsdale man of his time. Long after the death of Parcy Reed the Ridsdale men still took the law into their own hands, driving the lifted cattle and sheep from the Scottish side—some of the drove roads can still be traced—and they were not above going in for some illicit distilling.

The names of the hills and crags, and those of the farmhouses recall how wild this part of Northumberland was. Ravenscleugh, Todholes (*tod* is the Border word for a fox), Birdhope Crag, where there is a

Presbyterian church, and Corby Pike, another local word used for carrion crows, are some of the unusual names heard in Ridsdale.

The reservoir at Catcleugh breaks the monotony of the bare scenery, with trees growing at its northern end, and is the haunt of fishermen. Owned by The Newcastle and Gateshead Water Company, Catcleugh is of course private property, and permission has to be obtained to fish its waters. The reservoir was completed in 1906, and is linked with a chain of others, at Colt Crag, Hallington and Whittle Dene, until the piped supply reaches the congested area of Tyneside. How far off Tyneside seems from this thinly populated country, yet it is only about forty miles away.

Wild life is abundant in the hills and forests; the red squirrel is appearing in the plantations of spruce, the badger and the otter are increasing in number and the hill foxes are multiplying, as a result of less hunting, where the forests flourish. The unmistakable cry of the grouse is heard in the upper reaches of the valley, and on the many burns which tumble down from the hills, the dippers and wagtails have their haunts. On the Glorious Twelfth, the guns are heard on the grouse moors, while in the lower reaches of the rivers and more fertile parts of the county, it is the partridge and pheasants in their season which are the targets of the "shutters", as the countrymen persist in calling them.

The Northumbrian speech varies from valley to valley; many of the dialect words used are shared with Lowland Scotland, but the Northumbrian r is heard almost all over the county. Although "English" is spoken, many of the words and expressions used by the Border raiders are still heard today. A real Northumbrian man refers to his braces as "gallises"; has this any connection with the many Borderers who were suspended from the gallows?

Birds and beasts have their own peculiar district names; the thrush is a "mavis", as in Scotland; the mole a "mowdie"; the owl a "houlet"; a ewe a "yowe"; a ram is a "tup" and a yellowhammer becomes a "yeller-yowlie"! A "burn" is of course a stream, while a "knowe" (as at Knowesgate) is a small rounded hill; a "moss" is peat bog, such as The Muckle Moss in the Roman Wall country; a ditch becomes a "dyke" and a "rig" the ridge of a hill or old plough ridges as in head rigs. Heslop's *Dictionary of Northumberland Words* list more than six hundred which are peculiar to Northumberland.

The journey from Cowgate to Carter Bar is over, the long road that leads to the Border. This is a land of legend and romance, of Otterburn and Parcy Reed and the Raid of the Redeswire, commemorated every year when the Jedburgh men ride to The Carter Bar, where long ago they had the Northumbrians on the run. Loved by its people is Ridsdale, and a fitting finale is a verse of Wilfrid Gibson's poem:

Cloud shadows swept o'er Kielder Head,
And over Carter Fell;
And when at last we rose to go,
There seemed no more to tell.

XIV

THE ALLENDALES

O, the oak and the ash and the bonnie ivy tree,
Do flourish at home in my North Country.

Trad.

Far away from the River Aln of north Northumberland, on the south-west edge of the county and south of the River Tyne, is that great tract of country watered by the East and West Allens, which forms the district known as Allendale. Like all Northumberland's rivers, the East and West Allens are fed by the many burns which rush down from the hills, peaty burns which froth and foam when they are in spate.

With a history less bloodthirsty than the rest of Northumberland, in Allendale is some of the most spectacular scenery.

Allendale is rich in mineral wealth and at one time hundreds of men were employed in the lead-mines, which were the property of the Beaumont family. It was these lead-miners who demonstrated in Hexham Market Place in 1761 against the recruiting regulations for raising the Militia. The Beaumont family took their title from the Dale, and the present Viscount Allendale, whose principal seat is at Bywell on the River Tyne, has a shooting box at Allenheads.

There are still many evidences of the days of the lead-mining in the tall chimneys scattered over the district. One reason why there are so many small farms in Allendale is that in the years when lead was mined and smelted, many of the miners had small holdings to augment their pay, rather in the style of the Scottish crofters.

The principal land owners are Viscount Allendale, on whose estates are some of the best grouse moors in Northumberland, and Mr. J. C. Blackett-Ord of Whitfield Hall. This estate is one of the best managed in the county, and gained The Bledisloe Award at The Royal Agricultural Society of England's Show for its excellence.

The prosperity of the lead mines began to decline in 1861, and now there is no more lead mined in Allendale, which is a land of hill farms, another of the many stock raising districts of this great farming county.

Allendale Common which covers an area of approximately 32,000 acres is divided into "stints", and each farm bounded by the Common

Land is given so many of these stints, each of which is worth five sheep. The Farmers' Union points out that Northumberland employs only about a quarter of the farm workers which it is usual to do in a county of its size. The Northumbrian farm worker is still hired from year to year, from the various term days. Most of the workers on the land live in "tied" cottages, many of which have recently been modernized. In days gone by, a hind's wife was hired with him, and known as a bondager. This custom survived in the Berwick area until the thirties, the women wearing a distinctive costume.

At the Royal Show held at Newcastle in 1962, the Women's Institutes of the three Northern counties staged an exhibition which was called "Come Due North". Here were exhibited some most beautifully dressed dolls in the costume of the Berwick Bondagers.

The speech of the Allendale people is different from that of the rest of the county; being so close to the borders of Durham and Cumberland, the dialect words are of infinite variety, and the Allendale tongue cannot cope with the guttural Northumbrian *r* of Harry Hotspur.

The two rivers, the East and West Allen, rise on the very border of the county at Allenheads and Coalclough and go their separate ways to where they join, near the Cupola Bridge, in glorious surroundings. Capital of the dale is Allendale Town, now a most attractive and well-kept village, popular with holiday-makers from all over the country. How refreshing it would be to read that some of the older writers enjoyed their visits—so many of them, in the manner of Dr. Johnson, can find nothing good to say about a place.

One nineteenth-century writer dismisses Allendale, or Allenton as he calls it, as "a straggling dreary looking place, situated 1400 feet above sea level". One sometimes wonders if these writers had really visited the places they condemn so recklessly, or were they simply quoting from some old and garbled story. Certainly the Allendale of today is no straggling dreary place. The scenery where the river flows past the mill and through the grounds of "The Riding", now a hotel, is some of the most picturesque in the county. The town itself is composed of pleasant stone houses with well-kept gardens and hotels and boarding-houses, to which the same people come back year after year.

In Allendale Town on New Year's Eve is held a celebration, which has its origin in pagan times. Most of these celebrations are associated with fire-worship, and at Allendale a huge bonfire blazes in the square, round which dance the Guisers, with their blackened faces. This custom may have originated with the Norsemen, as in far-away Lerwick in the Shetlands the Chief Guiser is chosen to celebrate their New Year, which they keep according to the old calendar. At Allendale, the town band plays, barrels of tar are thrown on the bonfire, and the celebrations go on all night, as no true Northumbrian would ever go to bed until he has seen the New Year in.

The custom of first-footing is still kept up in this Border county. That is, as soon as twelve o'clock has struck, the first foot, who to bring good luck for the coming year must be a dark man, knocks at the door and is welcomed inside with refreshments, largely liquid! With him the dark man must bring salt, coal and money, although these offerings vary in different parts of the county. No one does anything but essential work in Northumberland on New Year's Day for obvious reasons.

So famous is the Allendale event that people attend it from as far away as Newcastle, and it is said that on one occasion there were four thousand cars parked in the approaches to the town, although this may be a slight exaggeration. It is rather strange that this pagan custom should have survived in a district which is a Nonconformist stronghold, for the Allendonians are mainly "chapel". There are also a considerable number of The Society of Friends in the Allendales, with their own meeting place and burial ground.

The most notorious Vicar of Allendale was the Renegade Patten, who was chaplain to General Tom Forster in the '15 Rebellion. This man who turned king's evidence to save his life at the expense of his friends', afterwards wrote his *History of the Rebellion*. The church of St. Cuthbert, of seventeenth century origin, has been extensively restored.

A poet, Robert Anderson, wrote a sentimental ballad about an Allendale girl who, true to type, went into a decline; her death so much affected her "betrothed", as the old books describe him, that he made matters worse by dying too. The lover's lament is as follows:

> Say have you seen the blushing rosé,
> The blooming pink or lily pale?
> Fairer than any flower that blows
> Was Lucy Gray of Allendale.
> Pensive at eve down by the burn
> Where oft the maid they used to hail,
> The shepherds now are heard to mourn
> For Lucy Gray of Allendale.
> With her to join the sportive dance
> Far have I strayed o'er hill and vale;
> Then pleased, each rustic stole a glance
> At Lucy Gray of Allendale.
> I sighing view the hawthorn shade,
> Where first I told a lover's tale;
> For low now lies the matchless maid,
> Sweet Lucy Gray of Allendale.

I cannot toil, and seldom weep;
My parents wonder what I ail;
While others rest, I wake and weep,
For Lucy Gray of Allendale.
A load of grief preys on my heart,
In cottage or in darken'd vale—
Come welcome death, O let me rest
Near Lucy Gray of Allendale.

Who this unfortunate couple were or where they lived we are unaware, even after six heart-rending verses!

At the head of the East Allen valley is Allenheads, where at one time the Allenhead lead mines produced a seventh of all the lead mined in the kingdom. It is even said the lead was discovered by the Romans. Allenheads is also written off by the old guide books as being "a place which has taken to decent ways"! This is rather hard as the Allendale people in the past had a much better reputation than their neighbours in Tynedale.

Once part of the regality of Hexham, the Allendale country was used as a hunting ground where the game was preserved. Spared the ravages of the Border raiders, and with few great houses or castles, Allendale is less rich in history than many parts of Northumberland. It is Allendale's spectacular scenery which is the great attraction for the visitor. From the lonely country of Kilhope Law, which is 2,000 feet above sea level, the East Allen winds its way by little hamlets and isolated farmsteads to Allendale Town. Wild and bleak is the country in the upper reaches of the river while, after Allendale Town is left behind, the country has a softer appearance with the river banks well wooded.

West Allen, too, in its early stages passes through wild country, past farms with names like "Farney Shield" and "Far Pasture" until it reaches the little village of Ninebanks. In this village are the remains of one of the few Pele towers to be found in Allendale, although at the Farm of Old Town, close to where the rivers Allen meet there are fragmentary remains of fortified dwellings.

From Ninebanks, where the valley is overshadowed on the west by the great mass of Whitfield Fell, the river's course is now through most beautiful scenery where the wooded slopes of the Monk Wood tower high above the valley. To commemorate the coronation of King George VI, different trees were planted in the Monk Wood in the form G.R. VI—a delightful idea, which was repeated at the time of the accession of King George's daughter on another plantation on the Blackett-Ord estate on the west side of the river; this time the trees form the letters and numbers E.R. II.

Part of the Blackbird Inn at Ponteland is a Pele tower

Whitfield, set amid trees by the banks of the West Allen, is undoubtedly the most attractive village in Allendale. The Hall is the home of the Blackett-Ord family, with a history deep in the roots of the county. Originally the property of the Whitfields, Whitfield and its Hall were in earlier days granted by William the Lion, King of Scots, to the Canons of Hexham. After passing into the possession of the Blackett-Ords, the Hall was practically rebuilt, and very little remains of the old house of the Whitfields.

Whitfield has two churches known as the "Old" and the "New". The old church is tucked away off the main road, while the new church, built at the expense of a Mrs. Blackett-Ord, in memory of her uncle, was erected in 1860, and is dedicated to the Holy Trinity.

The river is spanned at Whitfield by the Blueback Bridge, from which the road makes a sharp ascent on its long climb to Allendale Town. At the east end of the bridge is a memorial to a cyclist who, at the beginning of the century, lost his life when his machine got out of control on the steep hill.

At one time there was a Temperance Hotel at Whitfield, but now there is no place of refreshment as there are no public houses on the Blackett-Ord estate. The nearest public house is "The Green Tree", locally called "The Cartsbog", which is on the high ground over which the road to Haydon Bridge passes.

Where there was once a blacksmith's shop, a gated road climbs over the hills by way of isolated farmsteads, till the road drops down into South Tynedale over Plenmeller Common. Strange as are many of the place names in Northumberland, few are stranger than those to be found near Whitfield: Tarry Back and Gingle Pot are two of the most unusual.

The road from Whitfield to the Cupola Bridge is lined with trees; "the oak and the ash and the bonnie ivy tree" are seen at their best in this truly enchanting corner of Northumberland where the sister rivers unite at the meeting of the waters. Great cliffs of rock tower above the road which climbs by many hair-pin bends up The Grindstone Elbow, at the summit of which is the wonderful view of the deep ravine at Staward, through which the united Allens run by banks thick with trees, and perched on an eminence the ruins of Staward Pele are outlined. In the First World War most of these woods were felled to supply the demands of the War Effort, but were replanted during the years of uneasy peace, only to suffer, though not quite so drastically, in the Second World War. Now the trees are maturing again, and in autumn when the leaves are changing colour Staward is indescribably lovely.

The scanty remains of the Pele tower at Staward stand in a strategic position above where the Allen is joined by the Harsondale Burn. With a natural defence on three sides, it is built on a promontory where

12

The banks of Allen Water near Staward
Bywell Castle: "bonnier shine the braes of Tyne"

the ground drops steeply away. The early history of Staward-le-Pele, as it was called by the old people, is rather obscure, and the first mention is in 1386, when it was given by the Duke of York to the friars of Hexham, to be held by an annual payment of five marks. At the Dissolution of the Monasteries, in the reign of Henry VIII, the grant reverted to the Crown, subsequently becoming the property of the Bacon-Gray family.

In more modern times Staward-le-Pele was famous as the scene of picnics which were held on the wide expanse of turf. In the latter half of the nineteenth century this was one of the most popular events in Allendale. The writer can remember her maternal grandmother, who was an Allendale woman, describing how brake-loads of young people gathered at this picnic, of which as an old lady she still had vivid memories. Unfortunately it has proved impossible to discover why and when this event was held. But it is no trouble to trace the many stories of the Allendale Wolf, which caused such consternation in the dale, and then rather prosaically turned out to be a dog, meeting its death on a railway line in Cumberland.

A path from the ruined Pele tower leads down to the river below, a steep and rocky scramble enclosed by thick trees. When at last the descent is accomplished at the risk of life and limb, the path ends above a deep pool in the river known as Cypher's Linn. In such romantic surroundings it would be strange if there was no legend, and that of Cypher's Linn is the oft-repeated one of buried treasure. It is possible, of course, that when the friars were in residence, they may have had warning of a raid and sunk some of their gold in the reputedly bottom-less pool. Many years afterwards someone anxious to prove the truth of the legend went through the usual procedure of gathering together horses and oxen, and yoking them to the box of gold. How this was accomplished the legend does not say, nor if the pool is bottomless how the rope could reach the box. There was the usual disastrous result; in this case everything, man and beast, fell into the Linn and was drowned. An imaginative fisherman in the last century claimed that when the water was low the horns of an ox could be seen below the surface.

From Cypher's Linn it is possible to follow a rough footpath by the riverside to Plankey Mill, and of all the stretches of Allen Water this is the loveliest.

> Flow on lovely Allen, through groves of rude grandeur,
> Flow on, in thy serpentine course to the Tyne;
> My heart throbs with rapture as onward I wander,
> And fancy leaps back to the days of lang syne.

I've roamed thro' the woods where the birds are resorting,
And mused 'neath the shade of the sweet birchen tree,
And strayed down the glen where the lambkins were sporting,
On banks of rich verdure so blythesome and free.

These two verses by no means exaggerate the beauty of this lovely
glen, where the great forest of trees which is the Kingswood clothes
the steep heights on the west bank of the river. Long after the Union,
there was a "gentleman" known as Dickie of Kingswood, who spent
most of his time emulating his ancestors and going in for a little private
"lifting". Sometimes Dickie left his home in the Kingswood and made
his home in the ruins of Staward Pele. Dickie travelled as far as Newcastle on his forays, and the most famous episode in Dickie's misspent
life was how he lifted a pair of oxen from a field near Denton Burn on
the city boundary. The enterprising eighteenth-century freebooter
drove the cattle to Lanercost in Cumberland where he sold them to
an unsuspecting farmer. Not content with this deal, Dickie helped
himself to a mare of which the owner had said he would not exchange
for any other and, riding off during the night, Dickie made for home.
Next morning when crossing Haltwhistle Fell, Dickie met a man
who asked him if had seen a yoke of oxen in his travels. Directing the
man to Lanercost, Dickie then offered to sell the owner of the stolen
oxen the mare which he had lifted in Cumberland! When the rider
and mare arrived at Lanercost where the man from Denton Burn
recognized his oxen in a field, it is difficult to imagine who would be
the more enraged, the owner of the mare or the owner of the oxen.
By this time Dickie was safe in his stronghold above the Allen and for
many a year to come he carried on his lawless way of life.

Plankey Mill lies in the narrow glen formed by the heights which
rise so steeply from the river. Here where the zig-zag path climbs up
to Briarwood Farm grow the most luscious brambles, as blackberries
are called in Northumberland. In the autumn the hazel trees are heavy
with nuts, and on the springy turf the wild pansies grow. Here the
river is crossed by a suspension bridge and Plankey Mill is a favourite
picnic spot.

As the river goes on towards the Tyne, it flows under the Raven's
Crag, which overhangs a deep pool. Here the National Trust Property
begins which was bequeathed to the nation by the Honourable Francis
Bowes-Lyon, who was an uncle of Queen Elizabeth the Queen Mother.

Ridley Woods are a mass of bluebells in spring time, when the herons
build their nests in the tall trees which fringe the little lake. Winding
paths lead through the woods and rustic bridges cross the river. At one
time there were two summer houses in the wood, The Swiss Cottage
and one where sheeps' bones had been used to secure the roof. King-
fishers can sometimes be seen flashing their way along the water and

from the heather-clad heights of Morley Banks there is a magnificent view of the valley of the South Tyne.

Ridley Hall, as its name implies, was once a home of that unruly South Tyne clan. When the Ridleys lost their lands Ridley Hall became the home of the Lowes family, one of whom was the keeper of Tynedale referred to in the ballad which describes him as "the flower o' them a' ". After the days of the Ridleys and the Lowes, Ridley Hall had many owners and was drastically rebuilt in a rather unfortunate style of architecture. Now a teachers' training college, it is the setting of the house which is so attractive. Allen Water is now nearing the end of its course from the wild hill country where it rises to join the waters of the South Tyne.

In the uplands, Allendale is stone-wall country, the fields enclosed by the dry stone walls so typical of this hill country. In the Great Storm of 1962–3, the stone walls of Allendale suffered more from the efforts of the snow ploughs than from the heavy falls of snow. Miles of these walls were laid low and it is only now that the powers that be have decided on the amount of recompense payable to the landowners and farmers.

The rate-payers' money was used in a most astonishing way in 1885, and a negligible amount appears to have been spent on education. The amount of the county rate was twopence and one-eighth of a penny in the pound! The poor of Allendale received the sum of £10 from a charity founded by one John Shield in 1617. Allendale Grammar School as it was then received £62 5s., the source of this bequest being described simply as "W. Hutchinson and C. Wilkinson (rent) 1692". Now a new county school has been built at Allendale; its equipment would no doubt surprise W. Hutchinson and C. Wilkinson. The rateable value of Allendale parish was then £20,884!

Allendale holds a one-day Agricultural Show annually; this part of Northumberland has never been so horse-minded as other parts of the county—it is the cattle and sheep which predominate at Allendale Show.

In an old directory of the county there are nine boot, shoe and clog makers listed. The cloggers have disappeared and this form of footwear is rarely worn now, although in some of the more remote parts of the Allen valleys they are occasionally seen.

Allendale's scenery and villages present many contrasts, from lonely little hamlets like Carrshield, and Limestone Brae, to the "metropolis" of the town itself, charming Whitfield and the grandeur of Staward (where at the nearby Hall, Lord Derwentwater is said to have found refuge when he was hiding from the Hanoverians). These combine to make this south-western division of Northumberland one of the most attractive in the county; a land of sheep and grouse moors, sparsely populated and utterly unspoilt, as is so much of Northumberland. Long may Allendale be spared from the so-called march of progress, and "The Banks of Allen Water" inspire poets and writers in the centuries to come as they have done in the past.

XV

THE TYNE VALLEY TO THE SEA

O lordly flow the Loire and Seine
And loud the dark Durance,
But bonnier shine the braes of Tyne
Than a' the fields of France.

A. C. Swinburne, A JACOBITE'S EXILE

The above lines from Algernon Charles Swinburne's poem, written in the nineteenth century by a member of the ancient family who have lived at Capheaton for generations, express the love and pride which those Northumbrians whose roots are in this part of the county have for the Tyne valley. United at Warden Rocks, the Tyne, which flows through the wide valley past Hexham, is not industrialized until a little way below Wylam when it becomes:

The Tyne, the Tyne, the coaly Tyne,
The Queen of all the rivers.

This river, which has made Northumberland world famous, runs in its course from Warden to Wylam through fertile farm land, its banks bordered by trees, marred only at Prudhoe by the ugliness left by the I.C.I. works. The Tyne valley is a land of castles and great houses; of historic and attractive villages and some of the oldest churches in the county. To the north the land rises steeply towards the line of the Roman Wall and The Military Road while to the south, east of Hex-hamshire, the rolling countryside sweeps on to march with the Durham border.

The largest and most important village in the valley is Corbridge. On the north side of the river, which is crossed by the grey stone bridge, there has been erected a sign which gives the visitor a list of the most important events and historic buildings in and near Corbridge. This enterprise is one that could well be emulated in other places as it enables the visitor, who may only be passing through, to decide which of the many interesting places to see, without consulting a guide book. The information recorded reads as follows:

CORBRIDGE
The Scene of Stormy Events in the Past

In 796 A.D.   Ethelred, King of Northumbria, was slain here.

In 918   King Ragnal, the Dane, defeated the English and
               Scots Armies here.

In 1138   King David I (Scotland) occupied the town.

In 1201   It was searched by King John and three times burnt
               —in 1296 by Wallace: in 1312 by Robert Bruce; and
               in 1346 by David II of Scotland.

The present bridge—built in 1674—was the only Tyne bridge to
survive the floods in 1771.

A Saxon and Roman Town

Later in medieval days a town of importance, sending two bur-
gesses to the first English Parliaments in the 13th century.
Corstopitum (Corchester) Roman town. About 80–400. A.D.
Extensive remains. Agricola's Road. York to the North-east.
Dere St.
St. Andrews: Surviving church of the original four: 7th cen-
tury. Saxon Tower. Roman Arch.

Pele Towers

Dilston and Aydon Castles and the Roman Wall of Hadrian
are nearby.

Corbridge has indeed had a stormy history. Today, with its many
historical remains, it has managed very successfully to combine the
old with the new. Although many new houses have been built within
recent years, there are some very beautiful old houses in the village
and the Angel Inn is one of the oldest in Northumberland. It is said
that the king's commissioners, on their way to suppress the monastery
at Hexham, stayed here. The inn was then known as "The Head Inn".
In coaching days the "Angel" was a famous posting inn and today,
although some of the structure has been rebuilt, it still has a genuine
old world atmosphere. Above the main doorway is a sundial bearing
the inscription: "E.W.A. 1726. for Edward Winship and his wife
Anne." The church of St. Andrew, which is a Saxon foundation, is the
only surviving church of the four which at one time existed in Corbridge. Nothing now remains of St. Helen's, St. Mary's and Holy
Trinity and little is known of their history. St. Andrew's is, next to
Hexham, the most important Saxon foundation in the county. In 771
there was a monastery on the site of where the church now stands and
it is mentioned by Prior Richard of Hexham as being the scene of the
consecration of a Bishop of Lichfield in 786. The church of St. Andrew

suffered badly on the many occasions on which the town was sacked and traces of fire can still be seen on some of the stonework. In the churchyard is a Pele tower, once the fortified vicarage.

At one time Corbridge had a weekly market but after the Civil Wars the importance of the town appears to have declined and a most unflattering account is given, not only of the village, but of its inhabitants, both by Hutchinson, who visited it in 1755–6, and Hodgson in 1830. Any writer making the same remarks today would be drummed out of the county!

During the Middle Ages the inhabitants of Corbridge were almost wiped out by the plague and the streets were grass-grown.

The Roman Dere Street (Watling Street, as the Northumbrians persist in calling it even though it is described on the village sign as Dere Street) runs through the centre of Corbridge on its way to the north.

Beyond The Military Road, which Watling Street crosses at Stagshaw Bank, are the pretty little villages of the Woodburns where the road drops down into Ridsdale.

Standing as it does high above the Tyne, Corbridge, with its well-kept gardens, is very different from the gloomy picture that Hutchinson and Hodgson so unkindly described. Gone are the days when people died in their hundreds from the ravages of the plague. Now Corbridge has two hospitals, The Charlotte Straker Memorial Hospital, erected by the Straker family who at one time lived at Howden Dene, and The Bridge End Maternity Hospital where so many young Northumbrians come into the world.

On a site beside the Cor Burn and overlooking the Tyne is the once important Roman town of Corstopitum. This fort covered an area of forty acres and there are extensive remains today. When the river is low the foundations of the Roman bridge can be traced. Much excavation has been done at Corstopitum and there is an interesting museum. The view from this outpost of the Roman Empire is one of the loveliest in the Tyne valley and, even if the visitor has no interest in Roman remains, Corstopitum is worth a visit for the view itself.

Those who are deeply interested in the Romans must read Dr. Collingwood Bruce's *Handbook*, revised by the late Sir Ian Richmond, LL.D., M.A., F.S.A., when studying this or any other Roman remains in Northumberland. Much valuable work has also been done by Professor Eric Birley of Durham University.

Close to the camp is a well-known boys' preparatory school with the appropriate name of Corchester. The scenery on both sides of the Tyne here is delightful. On the northern slopes the castle of Beaufront, Stagshaw House and Sandhoe command glorious views of the hilly country to the south and hidden away from the main roads are the ancient strongholds of Aydon and Halton. Situated between the Roman road and a road that joins the "Military" at Wallhouses, these fortified houses are two of the finest in the county.

Aydon, standing above the Cor Burn, is still in a wonderful state of preservation after more than seven hundred years. In its early days the castle and manor were in the possession of the family from whom it takes its name. Aydon has had many different owners through the centuries. Licence to crenellate the castle was granted in 1305 but there was probably some building done before that date. Legend says that two Scots who had been captured by Sir Robert Clavering were condemned to die, the horrible manner of their death to be by hurling them from the roof into the stream below. One of the Scotsmen escaped his awful end by a superhuman leap across the burn and this deed is commemorated in the name "Jock's Leap". Not far from this romantically placed castle, until recently a farm house, is a pleasant country house with the date 1684 above the door. This is Aydon White House, the home of Colonel Neil Speke.

Halton Castle is Blackett property. The Blacketts are a family long associated with Northumberland. Halton is really three "houses", the old Pele tower, a manor house and one of the few Jacobean houses in Northumberland. Like so many of the early castles, Halton takes its name from its original owners who are said to have been settled in Northumberland in Saxon times. Long though the pedigree of the Haltons was, they were not above a bit of "lifting" for, in 1276, Sir John (who, to make matters worse, was Sheriff of Northumberland) was found guilty of carrying off some cattle, the property of Thomas Fairbairn of Wark, in North Tynedale, and driving them to his manor of Sewingshields. However, being sheriff had its compensations and, instead of hanging from the gallows as many a Tynedale man was to do in the years to come, Sir John bought himself off and paid "ten marks in silver" to Thomas Fairbairn.

After the Haltons, the Carnabys became lords of the manor of Halton and their history is not above reproach either; in fact one, Sir Reginald, who had the power of life and death over any mosstroopers he managed to capture, seems to have been even more ruthless than many in those savage times. He was a bitter enemy of the Herons of Chipchase; legend has it that at last a Heron captured Sir Reginald and threw him into his dungeons at Chipchase where he died of starvation.

The Blacketts who succeeded the bloodthirsty Carnabys have a very different reputation as landowners and sportsmen and a most lovely garden has been made at Halton with views across the Tyne valley to the Pennines. Close to the castle is a little chapel, of Norman origin, which was rebuilt in the seventeenth century.

To the Tyne valley in the eighteenth century came the Methodist missionaries John and Charles Wesley. A most informative little book entitled *A Look Backward. In the Steps of the Reverend John and Charles Wesley at Horsley and Nafferton Farm. 1742–1791* was published for private circulation recently. Written by Joseph Tait it gives a detailed account of the many visits paid to Northumberland by the brothers; John, who founded the Methodist Church, and Charles, who wrote many of the rousing Methodist hymns.

Standing to the north of the Newcastle–Carlisle road, "the Low Road", Nafferton, where the Wesley brothers stayed, is now an experimental farm attached to the Agricultural Department of the University of Newcastle upon Tyne.

A little to the east of Nafferton is the straggling village of Horsley. The house where John Wesley stayed is at the west end of the village beside the present-day garage. Mr. Tait tells us that, as John and Charles rode through the wild countryside of the eighteenth century, converting and preaching in villages, by the road side and where anyone gathered to listen to them, they visited Horsley nine times, Nafferton four, Alnwick twenty-four, Morpeth and Berwick twenty-four each and Allendale three.

The Allendale people, who had the least number of visits, must have been ready for "conversion" as it is one of the strongholds of Methodism today. Alnwick, Morpeth and Berwick must have been tougher propositions.

Horsley has been very much spoilt in the last few years by opencast coal-mining and the view across the valley unfortunately looks onto I.C.I. at Prudhoe. Nevertheless Horsley has an old and attractive inn, "The Lion and Lamb", which dates from 1718. Though the view from Horsley has been spoilt, the scenery below Corbridge is enchanting. Here the Tyne is wide and deep as it flows past Styford Hall, set in the midst of parkland. River and railway run parallel and the country through which the Newcastle to Carlisle railway passes is some of the most delightful and varied, not only in Northumberland, but in the British Isles. From Wylam to the Cumberland border at Gilsland it is practically unspoilt.

Set above the banks of Tyne, Riding Mill is a village which is growing rapidly. On the outskirts of the village are some charming country houses and there is a very old inn, "The Wellington". Here in 1673 was held a trial for witchcraft which created a great deal of excitement. It is the usual nonsensical tale of some silly old woman but, in those days of superstition, it was implicitly believed. Built in 1660 by an Errington, "The Wellington", or "The Riding House" as it was then called, was new when the witch trial was held. The roads which run south from Riding Mill travel through upland scenery of infinite variety.

Divided from the county of Durham by the River Derwent, this country is hunted by a pack with the delightful name of "The Braes of Derwent".

Two "Big" houses in this part of Northumberland are Healey Hall and Minsteracres. The road which leads to Healey, the home of Major Warde-Aldam, is flanked by magnificent beech hedges which, in the spring when the leaves are fresh and green or in autumn when they are changing colour, make this one of the most charming by-ways in the county. The church at Healey is eighteenth century and is dedicated to St. John. Not far from Healey, at Minsteracres, is a monastery occupied by the Passionists. This estate belonged to the Roman Catholic family of Silvertop, who have now left the district. The house was originally eighteenth century but has had many additions.

At Shepherds Dene, near Riding Mill, there is another religious house, a retreat for Anglican clergy and laymen.

In this district, where there are so many thriving communities of religious life, there is none more interesting or set in such rich and glorious scenery than the "twin" churches of Bywell St. Peter and St. Andrew. On the north bank of the Tyne, within a stone's throw of each other, stand these churches around which so much legend has gathered. Bywell is indescribably lovely. There is everything here to delight the eye.

The river makes a wide bend below the overhanging banks; the old grey walls of the fifteenth-century castle, the mansion house of Viscount Allendale and the wide expense of parkland, make Bywell, with its handful of houses, a gem.

Yet in days gone by this quiet retreat was one of the busiest places in the Tyne valley. In 1570 the Royal Commissioners reported that "The town of Bywell is builded in length all of one street upon the river or water of Tyne, on the north and west part of the same; and it is divided into several parishes, and inhabited with handicraftsmen, whose trade is all in iron work for the horsemen and Borderers of that country, as in making bits, stirrups, buckles and such others, wherein they are very expert and cunning; and are subject to the incursions of the thieves of Tynedale, and compelled winter and summer to bring all their cattle and sheep into the street in the night time, and watch both ends of the street; and when the enemy approacheth to raise hue and cry, whereupon all the town prepareth for rescue of their goods; which is very populous, by reason of their trade, and stout and hardy by continual practice against the enemy."

Such was Bywell in the sixteenth century; while in 1676, when the judges travelled from Newcastle to Carlisle, so unruly and dangerous were the Tynedale men that the lords of the manor called out their retainers to guard the no doubt rather nervous travellers as they passed through the manor of Bywell. In Saxon times a church was erected at Bywell by St. Wilfrid. After the coming of the Normans, the barony was given to Guy de Balliol, but, as was so common in those days, this de Balliol plotted against the Crown and lost his estates.

In the reign of Elizabeth I the castle of Bywell was in the possession of the Earls of Westmorland, one of whom, the last of his line, lost not only his estates but his head, through his participation with the Earl of Northumberland in "The Rising of the North", the abortive attempt to release Mary, Queen of Scots. There is at Bywell Hall a kerchief embroidered by Scotland's unfortunate queen.

A modern house has been built close to what remains of the castle which after the Earl of Westmorland's execution was sold by the Crown to the Fenwick family. It is now the property of Viscount Allendale. It is this Viscount Allendale whose Aberdeen-Angus herd is world famous, and who is also a steward of the Jockey Club.

There is no foundation in the many times repeated story that the "twin" churches were built by two sisters to outdo one another but it has been told so often that many people believe in its veracity. St. Andrew's has a wonderful Saxon tower while St. Peter's is of Norman origin. Sometimes called the "Black and White" churches, they were at one time served by the Benedictines, or "Black" monks, and the Premonstratensian, or "White" canons.

It is difficult to believe that, not very far below the Bywell bridge which spans the wide river, the industrial belt begins, when the water of Tyne changes its clear colour to that of smoke and grime, but in the three or four miles before the river becomes tidal there is pleasant country; villages and churches, full of history.

On the south side of the Tyne from Bywell and east of Stocksfield at Cherryburn was born one of Tyneside's most famous sons, Thomas Bewick, the engraver. Much of Bewick's work is in the Hancock Museum in Newcastle. The illustrations in *The History of British Birds* are exquisite examples of his art. The eldest of eight children, Thomas Bewick was born in 1753 and received his early education at Mickley school. As a child Bewick spent most of his time sketching on his slate and, when no other materials were available, he drew pictures in chalk on the gravestones in Ovingham churchyard. Birds and animals were his favourite subjects and his vast knowledge of the wild life of his native valley, which he sketched so delicately, brought him fame in later life. After serving his apprenticeship with Ralph Beilby, a copper-plate engraver in Newcastle, Thomas Bewick remained with Beilby for a short time—and was paid a guinea a week for his work!

Spending about a year in London, Bewick returned to his beloved north country and set up his own workshop near St. Nicholas's church, now Newcastle cathedral. A small memorial and inscription commemorate the site of the workshop which was demolished when Milburn House was built.

The name of Thomas Bewick became famous throughout the land and his work was brought to the notice of George III who at first refused to believe that the engravings had been transferred from wood until he was shown the blocks. Famous and prosperous though he became, Thomas Bewick never forgot his birthplace in the Tyne valley and every weekend he walked the twelve miles to Cherryburn to visit his family. When at last the celebrated engraver retired to live across the river in Gateshead, his son, Robert, carried on the business in the workshop which his father had founded. In November of 1828 Thomas Bewick died and is buried with other members of his family in the churchyard at Ovingham. In this ancient church, which dates from the eleventh century and is noteworthy for its Saxon tower, are memorial tablets to the Bewicks. The Bewick Collection, as it is called, is in the Newcastle Central Library.

In Ovingham village, which is connected with Prudhoe by a bridge, are some interesting old houses but it is to Thomas Bewick that this Tyneside village owes its fame. Bewick tells us in his autobiography: "As soon as I filled all the blank pages in my books, I had recourse at all spare times to the gravestones and the floor of the church porch with a bit of chalk to give vent to this propensity of mind of figuring whatever I had seen. At that time I had never heard of the word drawing, nor did I know of any other paintings besides the king's arms in the church and the signs in Ovingham of The Black Bull, The White Horse, The Salmon and The Hounds and Hare. I always thought I could make a far better hunting scene than the latter; the others were beyond my hand." In the years to come there was nothing "beyond the hand" of this Tyneside genius.

Prudhoe Castle, perched on a promontory overlooking the valley to the north, is now almost engulfed by the site of the I.C.I. works. Once a stronghold of the Umfravilles, Prudhoe passed by marriage to the Percys in whose possession it still remains. A comparatively modern house has been built within the ruins of the castle, a house which is occupied today.

On this south side of the river Northumberland and Durham are divided by the Stanley burn and from thence to the sea the Tyne forms the boundary between the two counties. The last rural village on the Tyne is Wylam, or, rather, the two Wylams, North and South, which stand on either bank of the river. The Wylams, like Riding Mill and Stocksfield, are popular with the many people who travel into the city of Newcastle daily.

On the north side of the Tyne and close to the railway is the house where George Stephenson, "The Father of Railways", as he has been called, was born in 1781. This brilliant engineer who educated himself, learning to read at the age of nineteen, was the inventor of the first successful locomotive, "The Rocket". At the time of his birth George Stephenson's father, who was a miner, was earning the sum of nine shillings a week on which he had to support his wife and family.

George's first job at the age of twelve was herding cows on Throckley Fell for which he was paid twopence a day. When, at the age of sixty-seven, George Stephenson died, he was not only famous but a man of means. At the end of his life this boy, born of humble parentage, was living the life of a country gentleman at Tapton House, near Chesterfield. George Stephenson had to work hard and for many years before his design for "The Rocket" was recognized, he was an engine man at Killingworth Colliery. The achievement of his career was when the Darlington and Stockton Railway was opened in 1825 with a train of eleven wagons, the engine driven by Stephenson himself.

It is ironical that the Beeching Axe is to fall most heavily on Darlington which was known in the past as "The Railway Town". Foreign governments called on George Stephenson for advice and there is a plaque on the portico of Turin railway station to the effect that the Italian Government asked advice of this man from the valley of the Tyne. In 1948 the red-tiled cottage where Stephenson was born was given to the National Trust by the North-East Coast Institution of Engineers and Shipbuilders. Above the cottage door is a metal plaque, with "The Rocket" in relief, which was unveiled by the lord mayor of Newcastle in 1929.

The famous engine, "Locomotion No. 1", stands in Darlington station today, Stephenson's greatest memorial; while in the city of Newcastle in Neville Street stands a monument to this famous Tynesider. This monument is the work of the Newcastle sculptor, Lough, who was born at Black Hedley on the borders of Northumberland and Durham.

Not very far from where George Stephenson was born is the mansion of Close House, now owned by the University of Newcastle upon Tyne. Originally the home of the Bewicke family, which has no connection with that of the engraver, Close House was for a time the home of Sir James Knott, the Tyneside shipowner who amassed a fortune and made so many bequests to charities. The church of St. James and St. Basil, in Fenham, was erected by Sir James to the memory of his two sons who were killed in the First World War.

Standing on the hillside between the now disused railway station of Heddon and the village of Heddon on the Wall, is Heddon Hall once the home of C. J. Bates, the historian, who restored Langley Castle in South Tynedale.

The Tyne now leaves rural Northumberland behind and, until it enters the North Sea, is within the great industrial belt of Tyneside. Newburn, Lemington, Scotswood and Elswick may all be described as part of Greater Tyneside.

It was in Newburn Church that George Stephenson was married to his first wife in 1802, and after her death he married for the second time, again in Newburn church. It is said that his second wife was his first love. These entries are preserved in the Parish Register.

A delightful custom dating from as recently as 1955 is the presentation of a red rose to the Duke of Northumberland or his representative every August as a token rent for a piece of land near the church, given by His Grace and used by the council as an open space. This is a much more attractive acknowledgement than the more usual peppercorn.

On two occasions Scottish armies were encamped at Newburn and forded the river here. In the Civil Wars the Scots occupied the tower of the church, their artillery breaching the defences of the English army on the opposite side of the river.

Scotswood, as its name implies, was where there was on some occasion a Scottish encampment. Elswick is famous the world over for the engineering works of Vickers Armstrong and Scotswood Road which is immortalized in the Tyneside National Anthem "Blaydon Races". Those who were "gannin' alang the Scotswood Road" in 1862 to see the Blaydon Races would fail to recognize it now. Practically all the old houses and numerous pubs have gone and in their place are multiple blocks of flats.

Now within the city boundary of Newcastle is the land of the Geordies, as Tynesiders are known throughout the world. Much controversy and many theories have been expounded as to the origin of this designation, with few if any substantial explanations. One theory is that in the days of the early Georges, when there were so many keelmen called George employed on the Tyne, they were called the "Geordies". Whatever the origin it has stuck and, to those unfamiliar with the county, is erroneously applied to all Northumbrians. The Geordie and the Northumbrian are different races: the language is different; the Geordie is a townsman, the Northumbrian a countryman. The writer's theory is that to be true Geordie one must be born on the banks of the industrial Tyne.

The keelmen, who manned the shallow boats in which the coal was transported to the colliers, inspired the well-known song: "The Keel Row".

> O whe is like me Johnny?
> Se leish, se blyth and bonnie,
> He's foremost mang the monny
> Keel lads o' coaly Tyne.
>
> As I cam through Sandgate,
> Through Sandgate, through Sandgate,
> As I cam through Sandgate
> I heard a lassie sing.

The keelmen wore a distinctive dress consisting of a short blue jacket, slate-coloured trousers and a yellow waistcoat. Their shoes were tied with ribbons; they wore black silk hats with flat brims and lived chiefly in the Sandgate mentioned in the song. The keelmen are mentioned as long ago as the reign of Henry VIII.

The city and county of Newcastle upon Tyne is the capital of the North-East with a population of 244,880. Built upon the site of the Roman station of Pons Aelii, it has been a place of importance since Roman times. Today Newcastle is a city of bridges. The most important are the railway bridge, opened by King Edward VII and named after him; the Swing Bridge; the Redheugh; the High Level and the Tyne Bridge. The High Level is built in two tiers and carries both road and rail traffic. It was designed by Robert Stephenson, son of the famous George, and was completed in 1849. The Tyne Bridge is a single arch and was built by Dorman Long's of Middlesbrough who also built the Sydney Harbour Bridge. This bridge too was declared open by royalty: in 1928 King George V came to Tyneside, accompanied by Queen Mary, and officially opened the bridge to traffic.

The writer has no intention of describing the history of Newcastle in detail. This has been done on so many occasions, and in 1950 Mr. S. Middlebrook, M.A., at one time senior history master at the Royal Grammar School, published his *History of Newcastle upon Tyne: Its Growth and Achievement*. Only just in time did Mr. Middlebrook write his book, as the ruthless "planners" of the new city are destroying much that is worthy of preservation and, in place of buildings of historic and architectural beauty, are erecting horrors such as the new Town Hall, which "they" insist must be called "The Civic Centre". Future generations owe a debt to Mr. Middlebrook for his admirable descriptions of Newcastle, not only in the distant past, but as it was at the time when he wrote his book.

The Newcastle of the celebrated local architect, Dobson, and Grainger, the builder, is fast disappearing to make way for progress. Eldon Square in the heart of the city is under a demolition threat. The Royal Arcade has gone to make way for the new Ring Road. The Liberal Club where Dickens stayed stands empty and by the time this book is published many more of the city's landmarks may have been demolished. The Victorians were regarded as vandals; it will be interesting to see what history's verdict is on modern architecture. Once a walled city, most of the old walls have disappeared. Mercifully those near where the West Gate stood have been preserved; and the once mighty castle, built in the reign of William Rufus, and the Black Gate are protected by the Society of Antiquaries.

The cathedral is famous for its Lantern Tower where a light burns every evening after dusk. The two oldest churches in the city are St. Andrew's and St. John's, both dating from Norman times. In the

Halton Castle, Tynedale

City Road is the Holy Jesus Hospital, deserted and in a shocking state of repair. By far the most impressive street in the city, and comparing favourably with the curve of London's Regent Street, is Grey Street, designed by Dobson. Here are the Theatre Royal and the Bank of England while at the junction of Grey Street with Blackett Street stands the tall monument to Grey of the Reform Bill.

Newcastle now has a university of its own, the chancellor of which is the Duke of Northumberland. At one time part of the University of Durham, the Newcastle branch was known as Armstrong, and subsequently King's College. Naval Architecture and Engineering have always been outstanding subjects, which is not surprising in a city so dependent on the shipbuilding and ship-repairing industries.

The Laing Art Gallery and the Hancock Museum, in front of which stands a statue of the first Lord Armstrong, are well worth a visit. Newcastle has many parks and open spaces. The many "moors", the Town Moor, Hunters', Nuns', Duke's and the "Little" Moor are all breathing spaces for the city dwellers, while the grounds of Jesmond Dene, with its trees and flower beds, is one of the most delightful natural beauty spots, although a cleansing of the Ouse Burn which flows through the Dene would be most desirable. On either side of the Great North Road are the Exhibition and Brandling Parks, while the verges of the road are planted with flowers which, strange to say in these days of vandalism, are rarely touched.

The Quayside, once bustling with activity when the coal trade was booming, is now a little-visited part of the city, yet here are the oldest houses in the city. The "Chares", as the entries between the buildings are called, still remains, as does The Side, Sandhill, the historic Trinity House and Newcastle's Guildhall. This was designed in 1658 by a local architect and, although the exterior was changed in 1796, the interior remains much as it was in the seventeenth century. Here in these beautiful surroundings the ceremony of "Calling the Guilde" is still held.

Parts of the Quayside used to be approached by flights of steps, some of which still remain: Dog Leap Stairs, where the cloggers used to work, and those which lead from the precincts of the cathedral into Dean Street are still in existence. Newcastle is primarily an industrial city but it has many attractions. The Old Assembly Rooms in Westgate Road are Georgian and the crystal chandeliers sparkled brilliantly when balls were held, as they were for nearly two hundred years in these delightful "Rooms". Now it's fate hangs in the balance. The Royal Grammar School was founded in the reign of Henry VIII and Dame Allan's is also a school with a very old foundation.

Today Newcastle is an active and up-to-date city with excellent shops and restaurants, a very different Newcastle from the general impression of a dour, grey city. From the city to the sea the river banks

13

Esso Northumbria *leaves the Tyne, February* 1970

are lined with factories and shipyards. Here in these Tyneside yards great ships have been built and launched into the grimy waters of the Tyne. In 1906 the old *Mauretania* was launched from Swan, Hunters; this ship which wrested the Blue Riband of the Atlantic from the Germans and was to be known in her old age as "The Grand Old Lady". In 1935 when the *Mauretania* made her last voyage on her way to the breakers' yard, all Tyneside turned out as they had long ago when she sailed in all her glory on her maiden voyage. Among those who watched the old ship head north for Rosyth was Sir George Hunter, then ninety years of age, and one of the founders of the firm which is so enterprising and prominent today.

King George VI visited Tyneside in 1939 to launch from the Naval Yard the ship which was named after the late King George V—the ship known as "K.G.V.". This was the end of the Great Slump from which Tyneside suffered so severely, and the order was placed with a Tyneside yard to alleviate the unemployment. *K.G.V.* was the first battleship to be built on the Tyne since H.M.S. *Nelson* in 1922. *K.G.V.* figured prominently in the last war and ended her days in the Gareloch before going to the breakers. The days of the great battleships are over and it is tankers which are largely built in the Tyne yards today, although in 1961 Queen Elizabeth the Queen Mother came to the Naval Yard to name the *Northern Star*, a passenger liner of the most up-to-date type.

The river makes many twists and bends on its way to the sea as it nears the end of its course. The river which is the combination of the clear waters of the North and South Tynes is almost unrecognizable now, so polluted are its waters. Very, very few salmon come up the Tyne now, as they did long ago when salmon was so cheap that the apprentices complained because it was served so often! Some method must be found to cleanse the water of Tyne. A great river and a proud river should not be subjected to such degradation.

At North Shields, famous for its fish quay, the trawlers go out, some as far as Iceland, to bring home their catches for the busy fish market. No cobles sail from Cullercoats now, and only five from North Shields, some of which are manned by Cullercoats men. It is the same sad story of big business against which the little man cannot compete. Cullercoats and North Shields have long been famous for inshore fishing and the "fishing" families are some of the oldest in the county. No more do the Cullercoats fishwives wear their picturesque costume or travel with their creels all over Northumberland as they used to do. When the Duchess of Northumberland named the new Cullercoats lifeboat, *Sir James Knott*, in May 1964 there was only one representative of the fishwives, wearing her traditional costume, and that was only brought out for the occasion.

North Shields is very proud of its "Wooden Dolly", a figure designed by Miss May Spence to represent a Cullercoats fishwife. At one time this figure stood at the end of a passage leading down to the Quay, but with the passing of time the "Dolly" became rather weatherbeaten and a new life-size figure has been made and placed in Northumberland Square in North Shields.

"The Cliffs of Old Tynemouth" stand high above the sea; Admiral Collingwood keeps guard over the entrance to the Tyne; the tugs wait to bring the ships up the river and the gulls sweep overhead. The Water of Tyne has mingled with the North Sea and the sun has set. When dawn breaks over the coast of Northumberland and the busy day begins, when fishermen and farmers, shepherds and stockmen go about their duties, they are carrying on the tradition of their fore-fathers who have made Northumberland the historic and glorious county it is today.

THE COUNTY IN 1970

As plans and protests gather momentum and the wind of change reaches gale-force, it is necessary to add an appendix to this new edition of *Portrait of Northumberland*.

Suspended over the whole country, not only Northumberland, is the sword of Damocles, in the form of the Redcliffe-Maud Report with its sweeping recommendations for changes in the structure of local government. Should these recommendations be implemented to the full, a great part of the county of Northumberland will be swallowed up in the vast conurbation of Tyneside. That certain reforms are necessary no one doubts, but one cannot help feeling that so many changes are now made simply for the sake of change, and not for the good of either people or places. The very word, "planning", has acquired a sinister connotation. One can only hope that after the dust of controversy has settled, commonsense will prevail.

In the five years that have elapsed since this book was first published many changes have already taken place, and many more are threatened. The hitherto unspoiled and beautiful valley of the North Tyne is possibly to be the site of a reservoir to supply water for Yorkshire. Should this plan be carried out the whole character of the upper reaches of the North Tyne will change, and no longer will the river rush in spate towards the meeting of the waters, but will have what is euphemistically described as an "even flow". Many people in the Falstone district will lose their homes, and the peace which is North Tynedale's greatest charm will be destroyed. That horrible word development has already reared its ugly head, and I have read that the reservoir could be a tourist attraction with "facilities for sport and amusement". One shudders at the thought.

A committee has already been formed by those lovers of rural England who wish to preserve their valley. A prime mover in this newly formed "protest" movement is Major F. J. Charlton of Hesleyside, and the Chairman Sir Rupert Speir, who was for so many years the member of Parliament for the Hexham Division. (It was by Sir Rupert's efforts that the Haltwhistle to Alston railway line was reprieved.) It seems ironical in 1970, Conservation Year, that more and more of the country-side is to be sacrificed for the greedy maw of the industrial areas. The people who are opposing the reservoir plan are not sickly sentimentalists, but men and women who have the welfare of their district at heart.

The Tyne Valley, too, is threatened by perhaps an even worse fate than that which hangs over North Tynedale, and that is the possibility that a Pulp Mill may be built at Prudhoe. An eminent Northumbrian who visited one of the Scandinavian countries to find out exactly what effect industry such as this has on the surrounding district, reported on his return that a "smell like over-cooked vegetables" pervaded the atmosphere. The waste products would poison the river, and add to the pollution which already has done such havoc to the "Queen of all the rivers" in its lower reaches. As in North Tynedale, the residents of Prudhoe and the surrounding districts have formed their protest committee, collectively named the Tyne Valley Action Group. Leaflets have been circulated throughout the area for the signatures of those either opposed or in favour of this project. I may say that my signature is for the opposition. My village of Wylam is only one mile from the proposed site, although the effects would be felt as far away as Hexham in the west, Belsay to the north and in part of County Durham, south of the Tyne. Prudhoe has done much in recent years to improve its image, and the ancient castle perched on a rock overlooking the valley has been restored and a caretaker installed; all this would be work in vain should this monstrous project ever materialise.

Northumbrians are not the type of people who demonstrate their views by means of protest marches and sit-down strikes, they are on the whole a law-abiding race, but when aroused they are "bonnie fighters".

One of the most far-reaching changes which has already taken place is the disbandment of the Territorial Army as such, and the disappearance, by amalgamation with others, of many county regiments. Northumberland has suffered greatly from this purge, and what I wrote about our regiments in my chapter "Alnwick and the House of Percy" is now obsolete. The Royal Northumberland Fusiliers have lost their identity and The Hussars disbanded, although what is called a cadre has been maintained, and who knows one day the "Noodles" may arise again like a Phoenix from the ashes of Government destruction. On Saturday 15th March 1969 the Freedom of the City of Newcastle was conferred upon the regiment when it paraded in public for the last time. The history of The Northumberland Hussars has been told by Henry Tegner in his *Story of A Regiment*.

One of the hopes I expressed when I wrote this book in 1965 has not been fulfilled, and that was for the revival of Rothbury Races, abolished by The National Hunt Committee. The Coquetdale people put up a brave fight, but their efforts were of no avail against the edicts of men, who, as His Grace, The Duke of Northumberland said in a letter to the press, had never to his knowledge ever raced at Rothbury!

I heard sometime ago that due to lack of support, the County Show, held for many years in Hulne Park at Alnwick, may have to be abandoned and join the ever-increasing list of what "used to be". These agricultural Shows are having a struggle to survive, the once flourishing Tyneside Show, which has its venue at Corbridge is in a precarious financial position. The change of date, due to the abolition of August Bank Holiday had an adverse effect on the gate, and in 1969, that summer of otherwise glorious memory, the rain "teemed" down all day and nearly washed "The Tyneside" into the river. In the hope that the event may regain its popularity the 1970 Show is to be held on "old" August Bank Holiday.

There are certain aspects of people and places which the planners cannot change, and one is the ability of Tynesiders to build great ships. The biggest ship ever built in Britain, the *Esso Northumbria*, was launched by H.R.H. Princess Anne on Friday 2nd May 1969 from the Wallsend Yard of Swan Hunter Shipbuilders Limited. Thousands of people watched the truly royal event as the giant tanker left the ways and nosed her way into the river. It was from this same yard, then designated Swan, Hunter and Wigham Richardson's, that the "old" *Mauretania* was launched in 1906; built for The Cunard White Star Line, the *Mauretania's* tonnage was 31,938, that of *Esso Northumbria* was 253,000!

On a cold winter's day in February 1970 *Esso Northumbria* sailed from the Tyne watched by even greater crowds than saw the launch. The great ship left the river of her birth from which so many famous ships have sailed before her: R.M.S. *Mauretania;* the battleship *King George V;* the "K.G.V." which was launched by Princess Anne's grand-father, King George VI; and the destroyer H.M.S. *Kelly* of undying memory, commanded by Her Royal Highness's great-uncle Admiral Earl Mountbatten of Burma; these are some of the Tyne-built ships which have made history.

It is on this note of pride that this appendix ends, and should the occasion ever arise for me to write another, may my address still be Wylam in the County of Northumberland.

INDEX